POLITICAL IDEAS IN THE MODERN WORLD

By the same author

ORDER AND REBELLION: A HISTORY OF EUROPE
    IN THE EIGHTEENTH CENTURY (Harrap)
THE COLD WAR (O.U.P.)
(*Editor*) THE TEACHING OF POLITICS (Methuen Educational)
(*With* G. M. OWEN) WORLD AFFAIRS
    (Harrap "New Generation" series)

Political Ideas in the Modern World

by

D. B. HEATER

PRINCIPAL LECTURER AND HEAD OF THE
HISTORY DEPARTMENT BRIGHTON COLLEGE OF EDUCATION

FOURTH EDITION REVISED

First published in Great Britain 1960
by GEORGE G. HARRAP & Co. LTD
182–184 High Holborn, London WC1V 7AX

Second Edition, revised and enlarged, 1964

Third Edition, revised, 1967

Fourth Edition, revised, 1971

© *D. B. Heater* 1960, 1964, 1967, 1971

Published in the U.S.A. 1972 by:
HARPER & ROW PUBLISHERS, INC.
BARNES & NOBLE IMPORT DIVISION

ISBN 06-492782-2

Made in Great Britain

PREFACE TO THE THIRD EDITION

This book was first written in 1959-60 as an aid to the teaching of Current Affairs. Two assumptions were made. Firstly, that a wider understanding of modern political ideas and their weaknesses has an intrinsic educational value. Secondly, that a study of the practical working out of these ideas could give coherence to what might otherwise be a rather amorphous course in Current Affairs.

Since the book was conceived rapid developments have occurred both in our teaching of this kind of material and also in the operation of the ideas the book describes. In the past few years the study of contemporary history has become increasingly popular both for examination purposes and as part of a General or Liberal Studies syllabus in sixth forms and Colleges of Further Education. In the wider world, patterns have shifted, and, particularly in the fields of Nationalism and Communism, have become much less clearly defined than seemed to be the case in 1960.

Demand for the book has continued, and the preparation of new editions has given the opportunity to make adjustments which changes in the world have made vitally necessary.

In approaching the preparation of this third edition it became clear that two kinds of adjustment were needed. In the first place, quite simply, the text had to be brought up to date chronologically to take account of most recent events. But more difficult was the need to adjust the perspective of some of the more general statements to take into account our changing attitudes to and the changing nature of, for example, Communism and African nationalism. In order to avoid too much alteration in the structure of the book no attempt has been made to bring the bulk of the text chronologically up to date. Instead, the Epilogue chapter which appeared in the second edition has been rewritten to deal with the major events of the years 1960-66. Within the body of the text, however, many changes have been made to allow for changing perspectives, so that general statements and illustrative examples are more apposite. In particular, some sections on Nationalism and Communism have been rewritten. The Selected Book List and Chronological Table have also been brought up to date.

Finally, I should like to record my thanks to my wife for help with the preparation of the typescript.

D. B. H.

PREFACE TO THE FOURTH EDITION

In this new edition a major revision has been undertaken of Chapter 7. Not only has the content been brought chronologically up-to-date, but a new section on racialism has been introduced—an "ism" that is, unfortunately, not a new ideology, but which has become particularly virulent in the form of the clash between colours in recent years. It has not been possible to devote a completely separate chapter to this topic; nevertheless it is hoped that the new material in the Epilogue chapter will meet students' needs more satisfactorily than the brief, scattered, and passing references that appeared in the Third Edition. Some detailed up-dating has also been made throughout the general body of the text.

D. B. H.

ACKNOWLEDGMENTS

The author's thanks are due to the following for permission to quote copyright material: George Allen and Unwin, Ltd (C. W. Hostler, *Turkism and the Soviets*, and H. J. Laski, *Communist Manifesto: A Socialist Landmark*); Ampersand, Ltd (John Bowle, *The Nationalist Idea*); A. and C. Black (H. Pelling, *The British Communist Party*); Cambridge University Press (Bertrand de Jouvenal, *Sovereignty*, and A. Victor Murray, *The State and the Church in a Free Society*); Doubleday and Co., Ltd, and Pall Mall Press, Ltd (Massimo Salvadori, *Liberal Democracy*); Hamish Hamilton, Ltd (D. W. Brogan, *The Price of Revolution*); George G. Harrap and Co., Ltd (George H. Sabine, *A History of Political Theory*); Michael Joseph, Ltd (Edward Crankshaw, *Russia without Stalin*); Longmans, Green and Co., Ltd (A. F. Pollard, *The Evolution of Parliament*); Stanley Mayes (*Forces and Pressures in South-East Asia*—B.B.C. talk); Oxford University Press (F. M. Cornford, *The Republic of Plato* and *Nationalism*—for the Royal Institute of International Affairs); Penguin Books, Ltd (Alfred Cobban, *A History of Modern France*, vol. i; Lord Hailsham, *The Case for Conservatism*; Thucydides, *The Peloponnesian War*—trans. Rex Warner); Phoenix House, Ltd (John Bowle, *Adapt or Perish*); Prentice-Hall, Inc. (Crane Brinton, *Ideas and Men: The Story of Western Thought*); Presses Universitaires de France (Georges Lefebvre, *Napoléon*); G. P. Putnam and Sons (Count Coudenhove-Kalergi, *Crusade for Pan-Europe*); Routledge and Kegan Paul, Ltd (M. P. Fogarty, *Christian Democracy in Western Europe*, and W. Z. Laqueur, *Communism and Nationalism in the Middle East*); Secker and Warburg (J. L. Talmon, *The Origins of Totalitarian Democracy*); Thames and Hudson, Ltd (Milovan Djilas, *The New Class*).

Some parts of this book originally appeared as articles in *Air Power*, the Air Forces quarterly, though certain adjustments have been made to the original text. The author would like, therefore, to thank Gale and Polden, Ltd, for their permission to reprint the articles which originally appeared in *Air Power* for autumn 1958, winter 1958-59, summer 1959, autumn 1959.

CONTENTS

Chapter	Page
1. INTRODUCTION	11

The importance of ideas—The development of political ideas.

2. NATIONALISM … 29

Definitions—Origins—The nineteenth century—Totalitarian nationalism—The expansion of the nationalist idea—Asia—The Middle East—Africa—Conclusions.

3. COMMUNISM … 72

The bases of Communism—Marx and Engels—Lenin—Stalin—Khrushchev—The expansion of Communism—National Communism—China—Conclusions.

4. DEMOCRACY … 116

Introduction—Classical Greece—The English, American, and French Revolutions—Utilitarianism and Liberalism—Democratic Socialism—The basic elements—The myth of 'totalitarian democracy'—Conditions for democracy—Conclusions.

5. RELIGION … 159

Introduction — Nationalism — Communism — Democracy — The Papacy.

6. CONCLUSIONS … 179

The theoretical basis of the modern political crisis—The possibility of solutions.

7. EPILOGUE … 188

Introduction—Racialism—The Main Events—Conclusions.

APPENDIX A. References … 210

APPENDIX B. Selected Book List … 217

APPENDIX C. Chronological Table … 219

APPENDIX D. Essay Questions … 224

INDEX … 225

CHAPTER ONE

INTRODUCTION

THE ARGUMENT

The Importance of Ideas. The ideological basis of political action—ideas and the common man—the question of rigidity or flexibility—the danger of ideas—conclusions.

The Development of Political Ideas. The nature of political theory—the Western tradition—the Greeks—the theories of cosmopolitanism—the origins of the modern state—the Whig and Liberal traditions—the organic theories of the eighteenth and nineteenth centuries—modern sterility.

THE IMPORTANCE OF IDEAS

In an age of specialization, when every branch of knowledge and human activity tends to develop in isolation from the others, there is a tendency to overlook the validity of the Aristotelean concept of the essential oneness of life. The assumed dichotomy between theory and practice is perhaps the most serious fallacy of this nature. Political theory, it is declared by those who hold this view, is an intricate web of philosophical propositions spun by dons cooped up in ivory towers. Such theories, it is asserted, for all the dogmatism of their expression, have no relation to the rough-and-tumble of practical political activity. Man is guided in his political action merely by his primitive acquisitive instincts, not by the striving of his mind and soul for higher things.

It is necessary to state at the beginning that there underlies this book a belief that such a view of politics is quite wrong. Little political action of importance, it is suggested, is undertaken without formulating the proposed action into a plan, which in turn reflects some basic assumption of what the aim of politics should be. And once an idea or theory has been formulated, faith in that idea can move, if not mountains, at least Governments. The lives of all of us living to-day, certainly in Great Britain, have been and still are affected by the clash of political ideas—of totalitarianism, nationalism, Communism, and democracy. Such is the power of the 'unpractical' theorist!

But, to be fair, it must be admitted that the other point of view—of the theory of economic motivation—is not without validity. For men are not entirely unconscious of their standard of living when they are asked to make a political decision. According to this argument people will risk their lives in violent demonstrations or revolutions only when their standard of living is so low that they have nothing to lose in their struggle against authority. Men are driven to desperate measures, in fact, only to free themselves from a desperate economic situation and when there are reasonable odds of their achieving a tangible—*i.e.*, material—gain. This reasoning was the basis for Karl Marx's optimistic outburst: "Let the ruling classes tremble at a communist revolution. The proletarians have nothing to lose but their chains. They have a world to win."[1] The negative side of this argument is that men do not risk their lives voluntarily for vague slogans such as "Sovereignty of the People," "The Rights of Man," and so forth, which they do not understand.

Are political ideals, then, sheer hypocrisy? Professor Crane Brinton at least denies this most firmly: "We know," he writes,

> that men in groups fight men in other groups with most determination and success when they feel they are right and their enemy wrong, that they are saints and their enemies sinners.... It is men's ideas and ideals, or if you still must be hard-boiled, men's appetites sublimated into something not limited by our poor bodies—that drive on to the magnificent, the impossible, the Napoleonic. The heart and the head are not tied to a caloric intake.[2]

Throughout history, indeed, men have persecuted, tortured, and killed in the belief that their enemies or victims were not only wrong but bad. The Inquisition, the Jacobin agents of the Terror, the Gestapo, the Ogpu, all killed and tortured basically in the belief that Catholicism, the Revolution, Nazism, and Communism respectively were 'right' and ought to be defended, whatever the cost in human suffering. If one views the political tensions in the contemporary world in the light of this argument it can be seen that, although they are magnified by the unequal distribution of wealth, they are essentially the result of conflicts of ideas: between totalitarian Communism and liberal democracy; between colonialism and nationalism.

Moreover, there is an interesting paradox here to illustrate the importance of ideas: the 'materialist' Marxism is one of the great ideologies struggling for predominance in the world to-day!

It is suggested, then, that political ideas are of fundamental importance in determining man's reaction to any situation. But, it may well be asked, are not ideas poor weapons against the tanks and machine-guns of the modern authoritarian state? The savage suppression of the Hungarian revolution in the autumn of 1956 seemed to prove conclusively that even the strength of modern nationalism when armed with little more than 'Molotov cocktails' is insufficient against a large well-equipped army. This is perfectly true in a military context, but the moral opprobrium heaped upon the Soviet Union for her action in this crisis was sufficient to make the operation a Pyrrhic victory for international Communism, at least. For, inasmuch as the contest between East and West to-day is a conflict of propaganda, any proof that one side or the other is relying on force to control any part of its sphere of influence is automatically a point in favour of the other side. In the context of the Hungarian revolution the ideal of national independence was not strong enough to achieve success, but it was strong enough to discredit the Communist system in the eyes of many hitherto 'fellow-travellers.' Moreover, negative tactics of suppression can never be successfully adopted as a permanent policy; for a policy of repression implies a static state of society, whereas intellectual and political change and development are the natural conditions of human life in society. And no Government can ignore these conditions entirely.

One of the most potent political forces in the world for the past century and a half has been nationalism—a force whose strength derives from its essentially ideological and popular bases. When a people are convinced of their right to exist as a free and undivided community it is very difficult to oppose their will. The resistance movements against the Hitlerian occupation, especially in Western Europe, and the restlessness of the East European satellites in protest against Soviet domination have been adequate proof in recent years of the strength of national idealism still in Europe. Unfortunately the force of nationalism can be used for evil as well as good, depending on the ideal towards which the nation is striving. Nazism was as much an expression of nationalism as was the Maquis.

The potentiality of uniting the mass of the people with a cogent idea was first made evident in the modern world by the French Revolution, when the crack armies of Prussia and Austria were rolled back by the ill-trained mobs drafted into service by such comparative amateurs as Danton and Carnot. If the French nation of the seventeen-nineties could be whipped into a frenzy, how much easier is it to-day to weld a nation into a motive force? Present-day Governments have at their disposal all the paraphernalia of mass propaganda. Indeed, much of life in modern society is geared to the dissemination and reception of ideas. This state of affairs has been noted by Walter Lippmann, who has written: "In the familiar daylight world we cannot act as if ideas had no consequence. The whole vast labour and passion of public life would be nonsense if we did not believe that it makes a difference what is done by parties, newspapers, books, broadcasts, schools and churches."[3] And when these means of distributing ideas are controlled by a totalitarian propaganda machine they can mould the entire political thinking of the ordinary citizen once the basic beliefs of a community have been shattered. The success of Dr Goebbels was evidence enough of the plasticity of the popular mind in such circumstances. Furthermore, in our present era the 'radio war,' fought out by great barrages from Radio Moscow, Cairo Radio, and Voice of America, has been an important factor exacerbating world political tensions. He who controls the dissemination of ideas can indeed wield great power. And the power is flexible and widespread. "Man is a rational animal, and doctrine and slogan provide at different intellectual levels the inoculation which gives immunity from more active or more restless thinking, and keeps the citizen or the party-member confident, purposive, and responsive."[4]

Unfortunately, there is no adequate antidote to this power over the popular mind if the propagandists are determined to abuse it. The attitude of the Government is naturally of great importance: it is the totalitarian form of Government that has the opportunity and inclination to make extravagant use of propaganda. The extension of popular education is no solution to this problem of the vulnerability of the popular mind to propaganda; rather does it aid the propagandist. In the first place, the educational system of a country is usually controlled by the state, and thus propaganda can be instilled at the most receptive age. Secondly, an increase in literacy expands the Press-reading public, but education to a standard sufficient to penetrate the fallacies of a well-laid propaganda would require a subtlety of mind far beyond the capacity of the majority of the people even of the most advanced nations. Even counter-propaganda has an almost negligible effect once a system of ideas has been firmly implanted in a people's mind.

From the above remarks it would appear that totalitarian regimes can produce more closely knit, and therefore stronger, communities, for they have a greater control over the public mind. But is this in fact true? Let us compare the situations in a totalitarian and a democratic society.

An authoritarian society has the advantage not only of being able to mould the popular mind, but also of being based on a positive political ideal. In other words, the Government of such a society has a definite body of ideas with which to feed the people's minds. And the mass of people find cut-and-dried slogans more acceptable than the less dogmatic propositions which form the bases of freer societies. In a totalitarian state, then, the people's political thinking is done for them, and with this central direction a semblance of political unity is achieved.

Yet this rigidity of theory is also a disadvantage. Complete unanimity is impossible, and if ideas in opposition to the established doctrine are not allowed their natural expression they may become unnaturally explosive. For, as has already been stated, a static society is an unnatural society; and an unnatural society is a potentially unstable one too. In so far as Mr Khrushchev relaxed the intellectual rigidity of the Stalinist regime he revealed an active appreciation of this truth. A society which allows a multitude of ideas to flourish has thus the advantage of natural, intellectual flexibility.

Given this flexibility in political opinion, a free society can hope for peaceful evolution rather than revolution in its political and social development. In normal times, and given the civilizing influence of tolerance, such lack of ideological unity is on the whole to be recommended. Unfortunately, in a world racked by the tensions of conflicting doctrines, flexibility may lead to a lack of direction and therefore to uncertainty.

Our generation has witnessed the intensification of the conflict between liberal democracy and totalitarian Communism. Many in the West know that they dislike Communism. But that is a negative attitude; rather must we have a positive conception of what we are defending. Yet this is precisely where we meet the difficulty; for the greater the flexibility in political ideology the more nebulous it becomes and the more difficult it is to define, and the more rigid our ideas the less acceptable are they to a free society.

The strength of movements based on potent ideas has already been noticed, but that strength at times mounts to fanaticism. A strong following for a beneficent idea is, naturally, to be encouraged, but fanaticism is always to be deplored. And herein lies the greatest danger of ideas, for so often does a fanatical adherence to a doctrine lead to the persecution of non-adherents either to convert or eliminate them. Fanatical belief in the French Revolution led to the Terror; fanatical belief in Nazism led to the horrors of Auschwitz and Belsen. The individual counts for nothing when balanced against the movement, the revolution, the party, or whatever embodies the idea.

If so many political ideas contain the seeds of so much evil, it may well be asked, why do they receive such widespread support? Is man by nature so disposed to political sin? Surely not. The Terrorist or Secret Police mentality is the exception rather than the rule. The masses are drawn to support a particular programme usually by the plausibility of the ideas; they are fed on slogans which, although purporting to explain the doctrine, rather more frequently distort it. And so the populace is drawn to support the ideas which promise Utopia. There is no desire here to condemn this gullibility; indeed, it is almost inevitable in a world of complex political philosophies and 'double talk.' It is very difficult for the man in the street to distinguish political truth when different political systems in the world all claim to represent true democracy and provide true liberty and equality.

If the masses are guiltless in their support of pernicious doctrines, in whom lies the blame? The root of the problem is to be discovered in the handful of leaders who, consciously or unconsciously, are infected by dangerous political ideas and whose aims are to put these theories into practice irrespective of the cost in terms of human suffering. The masses certainly did not understand Rousseau, but Robespierre did; the masses did not understand Marx, but Lenin was his disciple. And it is such men as Robespierre and Lenin who wield the power, based on popular support, to impose the ideas of the theorists on their countries.

The world is sick. During the past century and a half or more the world, and especially Europe, has suffered the miseries of three major wars. Each of these wars was followed by schemes to retain the hard-won, precarious peace, and yet to-day our peace is still in the balance. If this sad condition is viewed in the light of the above discussion the explanation should be reasonably clear. The machinery of a Concert of Europe, a League of Nations, or a United Nations Organization is powerless if the mind of man is poisoned by intolerant political ideologies, for "reform is not to be found in the establishment of new institutions to be run in the old spirit, but in a change of spirit."[5] *The Leviathan, Du Contrat Social, Das Kapital*, and their like may seem academic works divorced from the practical problems of everyday politics; nevertheless it is such works that have lasting influence. For even the simplest soul requires a philosophy of life, an ideal, or, at its lowliest, a dream of a better life to come. Man cannot live in a spiritual vacuum; and so, when one system of beliefs has been destroyed or has collapsed through sheer old age, another must inevitably take its place. But our world will continue to be unsettled all the while our political thinking is muddled, tinged with emotion, or divorced from humanity.

It is in the belief that political ideas have a vital effect on world politics and that this effect to-day is, on the whole, a harmful one, due to the maladjustment of our ideas, that this book has been written. The vast mass of politically conscious people in the world to-day are affected in their political thinking by one or more of the four great influences—namely, nationalism, Communism, democracy, and the political implications of the great religions. But before we deal with each of these major influences it is intended to provide a very brief survey of the Western tradition of political theory.

The Development of Political Ideas

The task of providing for man's spiritual needs in the political sphere has exercised the minds of philosophers for two and a half millennia; and these needs have been satisfied by the theorists' development of acceptable answers, suited to the conditions of the time, to such questions as: How can the authority of the state be justified? What are the proper limits of the state's authority? How can the authority of the state be made compatible with liberty? What is the true relationship between the state and the individual?

There are almost as many philosophies of politics as there have been political theorists, and no single thinker has divined the absolute truth. Similarly, no classification of their approximations to truth gives a completely correct picture; nevertheless an attempt to group the various theories does shed light on this vast subject. Some political theorists, for example, have assumed that the state is a natural entity and that man is something less than human if he is not a member of such a political society. True liberty even, on this premiss, is impossible without living in accordance with the laws of society. The individual is therefore of less importance than the state, and his relation to it is analogous to that of a cell to the whole body; for this, indeed, is known as the organic theory of the state. It is a mystical theory, and, although it is still influential in the twentieth century, it lost much of its appeal during the rationalistic eighteenth century, which upheld the newly developed mechanistic theory interpreting the state as the contrivance and therefore the tool of man.

The organic theory of the state tends to assume that there can be a naturally perfect state and that any given society must be judged in accordance with this model. The mechanistic theory, on the other hand, is pragmatic in its analysis of states and allows for human adjustments to changing conditions.

The history of political thought is a long and ample story; it is the story of ideas, how those ideas have affected the lives of men, and how men have in turn shaped ideas. Men of varying professions, callings, and turns of mind have contributed to our structure of political wisdom, and each age bears the characteristic stamp of the dominant influences at work at the time. The political thinkers of Periclean Athens were philosophers who considered it the very nature of man to live in political society, while the meagre contribution of Rome was made by lawyers who viewed the relationship between man and society as a purely legal one. Medieval thought was, in its turn, dominated by the theologians, who naturally emphasized the Divine Image in man. Modern Europe, on the other hand, has seen the successive influences of philosophy, science, and history, with man raised to the heights of dignified individuality and depressed to the depths of slave of the state. Finally, in our own day, the wheel has come full circle and the logical positivism which is the most potent influence in philosophy has been carried by its exponents into the realm of political thinking also, and political thinking has become a complicated philosophical tool for correcting fallacies in our thought.

Political theory is partially a reflection of political form, though the question of priority is very often a hen-and-egg problem. Just as each age, then, has its own distinctive political ideas, so does each age have its own distinctive political organization. The ancient Greeks lived in a world of city-states—smallish towns surrounded by their supporting agricultural lands. Rome started as just such a city-state, but, from about 200 B.C., expanded at so rapid a rate that the old republican constitution had to be replaced by the Empire. Medieval Europe was based on the myth of the Holy Roman Empire and the reality of feudalism—that hierarchical form of society and state whose connecting links stretched from king to peasant. The increase in royal power which characterized the close of the Middle Ages was the occasion for the closer integration of the state, now identified with the nation. The nation-state is, indeed, the typical political unit of the modern world—an institution strengthened and made more widespread by the nationalist movements of the nineteenth and twentieth centuries. Nevertheless, there are signs that the jealous retention of national sovereignty is on the wane, at least in Europe, in the second half of the present century. Supra-national groupings are becoming more common as political units.

If we look back to the Greeks for inspiration in the arts—to Homer for epic poetry, to Sophocles for tragic drama, to Phidias for sculpture—no less do we look to the Greeks for the masters of political thought. The great works of Plato and Aristotle, *The Republic* and *The Politics* respectively, remain among the most important studies in political literature.

Plato himself sat at the feet of Socrates and, indeed, *The Republic* is written in the form of a dialogue between the author's master and several of his pupils, the fallacies of whose ideas on the nature of justice, the subject in hand, are steadily but surely revealed by typical Socratic logic. The main ideas are, first, that each citizen should perform the task in the state to which his abilities best suit him. Only in this way will a perfectly balanced, just state be achieved. Plato assumes that there are, in fact, three kinds of men—those in whom brains, courage, and strength predominate respectively. Only those with the most outstanding ability and the most thorough training should formulate policy. These are the 'philosopher-kings,' suited for their most difficult task by both knowledge and virtue. They are drawn from the aristocratic 'Guardian' class, the rest of whom carry out the day-to-day functions of government and, as their name suggests, perform the necessary military duties. The mass of the people are engaged only in manual tasks, especially the production of food. The second interesting point is the communal way of life which is laid down for the Guardians—"a kind of military monasticism," as it has been called.[6] No separate family life is allowed for them, they are to live a common life in barracks, and private property is forbidden. Although this austere and rigid political system was in certain respects a reflection of contemporary Spartan life, Plato admits that such an organization represents the ideal and is hardly attainable with far from ideal human nature. Philosophers cannot be induced to become kings, nor kings be made philosophers. Moreover, in a state that does not attain perfection, the element of change must be taken into consideration. In his declining years, in fact, Plato turned to a consideration of the practical in *The Laws*, in which a certain democratic element is introduced and the ideal of the philosopher-king is replaced by a just code of law and a mixed constitution incorporating the freedom of democracy and the wisdom of monarchy.

Plato was not only a writer; he was also a teacher. The most brilliant and prolific of his pupils was Aristotle. *The Politics* is a more exhaustive and scientific work than *The Republic*; it is also less of a work of art. The differences are due to a difference of origin and purpose. *The Politics* is a collection of essays or lectures and must inevitably be disjointed; it is also an attempt at practical analysis and practical advice on typical problems which were being faced by Greek politicians in the late fourth century B.C. Aristotle discusses such diverse questions as slavery, property, the classification of different types of constitutions, the causes of revolutions, the methods of stabilizing Governments, and methods of education. He also, incidentally, criticizes *The Republic* for being too impracticable and *The Laws* for propounding a constitution too oligarchical in structure. In general Aristotle believes in the golden mean—the avoidance of excessive measures and territorial size, and the mixture of all elements of society in the constitution. Weight of numbers in the masses must be balanced by the wisdom of the few; but the tendency of the few to oppress the masses must be counterbalanced by providing the people at large with the necessary safeguards.

Underlying all Greek political thinking there are two interconnected ideas—namely, that life in a political society is the natural mode of existence for man and, second, that this political society should be a city-state. When the Greek world became engulfed in the Macedonian empire of Philip and Alexander this rather parochial attitude was shattered. Most of the new thinkers denied the essential connexion between man and politics entirely. Consideration for the individual and not the community was the common teaching of Cynic, Sceptic, Stoic, and Epicurean alike. From the point of view of political theory the Hellenistic age marks the end of the great period of activity and the opening of the comparatively sterile Roman era. Political thought now becomes legalistic and cosmopolitan, and the one important idea which does emerge from the Hellenistic period is the Stoic postulation of a natural law. This was the idea that there exists an eternal code of right and wrong capable of being discerned by all men through the exercise of reason. In various guises the idea of natural law has had a long and active life well into the modern age.

The Romans were not in general given to philosophical speculation, and the only important contributions made by them are to be found in the works of Cicero and Seneca. Cicero's importance lies in his work of popularization rather than in invention, for "he gave the Stoic doctrine of natural law a statement in which it was universally known throughout Western Europe from his own day down to the nineteenth century."[7] Cicero deduced from the existence of an eternal and universal law of nature the further idea of the essential equality of men. The century which elapsed between Cicero and Seneca saw the decline of the Roman Republic, the establishment of the Empire, and the foundation of Christianity. By postulating the equality of mankind Cicero had started to undermine the classical Greek distinction between the civilized citizen and the barbarian. Seneca completed this process by a total denial of the moral qualities of the state. Indeed, he pictures the state as an imperfect attempt to deal with the natural wickedness of man. There is, in short, a religious flavour to Seneca's thought and one which connects him to the early Christian thinkers.

The Christian Fathers explained the coercive nature of the state as a necessary, if unpleasant, result of the Fall of man: it was, in fact, one of God's methods of punishing man's sin. Furthermore, of course, the divine origin of government requires absolute obedience to constituted authority.

It was Christianity in large measure which gave the Stoic and Roman idea of cosmopolitanism a much more real expression. In theory, at least, medieval Europe was a unit bound together by the common faith of the Christian Church, under the common secular authority of the Emperor and spiritual authority of the Pope. The essentially religious basis of civil society is fundamental to the ideas of all the great medieval thinkers from St Augustine's *City of God* to the works of Aquinas and Dante. Augustine's book was compiled between the years 413 and 426, during the time of the barbarian invasions, and sets out to answer the question, why God had allowed the Roman Empire to fall. In discussing the problem the Bishop of Hippo came to two main political conclusions. In the first place, the state is less important than justice, a quality that is only really perceived in the whole body of the faithful—the so-called "City of God." Secondly, since God is omnipotent and wills all actions on this earth, and since life on this earth is but a pilgrimage on the way to heaven, then resistance to authority by a Christian is neither righteous nor expedient. Submission now became the accepted Christian political attitude. Although the Christian tradition of Augustine remained the strongest influence, the rediscovery of Aristotle in the thirteenth century made the fusion of the theological and philosophical traditions an urgent need. It was this task that St Thomas Aquinas performed. But his study of the nature of law led him to adjust Augustine's conclusion that rebellion is never justified. Aquinas was writing in the mid-thirteenth century. His support of the authority of the Church in the *Summa Theologica* was challenged half a century later by another Italian, Dante, in his *De Monarchia*—a defence of an idealized empire. Nevertheless, the argument is still theological, for Dante supports an imperial power independent of Papal control by claiming direct divine authority for the Emperor.

But Christianity was not the only element in the political theory of the Middle Ages. For the states of Europe had crystallized into their feudal patterns out of the barbarian invasions which had destroyed the Roman Empire. Moreover, feudal society was based on a complex of rights and duties in which no man had absolute authority. The king was merely *primus inter pares* and had responsibilities to his nobles as well as rights over them. If the king broke the contract of customary rights and duties he could be forcibly reminded that there were bounds to his power. Magna Carta for example, was just such a reminder. It was the law which was supreme. Thus was the tradition of the legal structure of the state revived—a tradition which had to a certain extent been obscured by the Christian emphasis on the religious purpose of the state.

The unity, and therefore the essence, of medieval Europe was shattered early in the sixteenth century by two not unrelated events: the Reformation and the rise of the nation-state. The unity of Christendom, which, if one ignores the Orthodox Churches, was a reality in the Middle Ages, was now destroyed by the movement unleashed by Luther; the authority of the Emperor, never much more than a myth, could not be upheld even in theory now that states were becoming so integrated and differentiated[8] and their princes acquiring so much power. Such changes were bound to bring about a flood of philosophical speculation.

The concentration of power in the hands of the national monarch was achieved, from a theoretical standpoint, in three ways: from religious, pragmatic, and philosophical points of view. In the first place, although Luther's doctrine of the priesthood of every Christian and the emphasis on the authority of the Bible eventually led to a greater sense of individual independence, such a political attitude was a misinterpretation of his true aim. After the shock of the Peasants' Revolt of 1525 Luther came out strongly in favour of the constituted authority of the prince, whose power he claimed was directly delegated by God. Rebellion, therefore, is not only wrong, it is sinful. The purely religious authority of the prince was further emphasized by the Peace of Augsburg of 1555, when the new principle *cuius regio eius religio* gave the prince the right to determine the accepted religion of his land. From the religious conflicts of the sixteenth century, indeed, there arose in France and later in England the theory of the Divine Right of Kings. According to this theory power is derived from God, but only a monarch can acquire divine authority. Once one has accepted that the office of kingship has divine sanction it is only a short step to claiming divine authority for the king himself and therefore insistence on the divine right of succession or the inheritance of divine authority. The king was thus given a mystical position apart from his subjects. The principle was an important one in consolidating royal power, because not only could it be used against the king's subjects, however mighty, as in the wars of religion in France and the civil conflicts in seventeenth-century England; but it was also a powerful weapon against the Church, and especially the Papacy, in the hands of such people as Luther and Elizabeth I, for the monarch's power was now based on the same source as the authority claimed by the Church.

But if the theorists of the Reformation destroyed the restraints of the Church on state sovereignty, Machiavelli destroyed the restraints of morality, and his name has suffered the taint ever since, especially in the pejorative term of "Old Nick." Niccolo Machiavelli was a Florentine statesman. He deplored the chaos and immorality of Renaissance Italy, but realized, albeit with a heavy heart, the necessity of ignoring moral considerations in the interests of establishing peace. In a small handbook for politicians, called *The Prince*, Machiavelli argued that a ruler is judged by his success, that success in prevailing conditions meant the establishment of a strong Government, and that any means were justifiable for the attainment of this end. The dichotomy between politics and ethics is thus inaugurated. "A prince," states Machiavelli, "who desires to maintain himself must learn to be not always good, but to be so or not as necessity may require.... Nor need he care about incurring censure for such vices, without which the preservation of his state may be difficult."[9]

In the sixteenth century, then, the removal of all restraints paved the way for the emergence of absolute sovereignty. The first important political theorist to proclaim such a concept was the Frenchman Jean Bodin, who basically took Machiavelli's practical considerations and put them in theoretical terms. Perhaps the central point of Bodin's argument is his assertion that the sovereign has complete authority to alter and create law; there remains then little restriction on his power. Bodin wrote his *Republic* during the French religious wars of the sixteenth century, and his aim was to strengthen the central authority so seriously weakened by these wars.

Nearly a century after Bodin civil war rent England, and the disorganization thus engendered produced a book similar in scope to Bodin's, though greater in stature. This was Thomas Hobbes's *The Leviathan*, published in 1651. *The Leviathan* is one of the most important works of English political philosophy. Its theory of the absolute state certainly had a great impact on future thought. The work is inspired by two fundamental ideas—namely, that extensive legalized authority must be placed in the king's hands, and the conviction that man is motivated by self-interest. In the view of Hobbes sovereignty or political authority resided originally with man in general. But because, in this original condition or state of nature, authority was completely lacking, "every man is Enemy to every man," and there is "continuall feare, and danger of violent death; And the life of man, solitary, poore, nasty, brutish and short."[10] Men, therefore, came together out of regard for nothing but their own self-preservation, and agreed to surrender their sovereignty to some civil authority. Thereafter, following the conclusion of this social contract, the individual had no rights over and against the Government except the natural right of self-preservation. The use of force to coerce the people is justified by the terms of the contract and in the interests of maintaining peace; furthermore, it is effective, as man is motivated by fear and will, therefore, respond to the exercise of force. Absolute monarchy was thus theoretically justified.

The idea of the social contract was used by Hobbes to justify the concentration of political power into the hands of an absolute monarch. This was, in fact, an unusual twist to a relatively common idea. For most of the contract school of theorists used the device to justify a restriction on the powers of the monarch—a more natural conclusion. Such a conclusion was based on the argument that a contract would be made to defend the natural rights of man and that no laws or actions by the Government thus constituted can justly infringe these rights. An attempt by the monarch, for example, to act in this way is *ipso facto* a breach of the contract, and the people have no obligation to obey him. Thus Locke justified the dethronement of James II. Locke put forward his ideas in his treatises *Of Civil Government* published in 1689. Civil society, he argued was established because of the inconvenience of the state of nature, not because of the violence depicted by Hobbes. It is an impartial judge that is needed, not an instrument of coercion. But the impartial judge, or king, who is established holds his position on trust: he has only limited authority, and in particular must not violate the natural laws of life, health, liberty, and property. Locke's theory of the social contract had a great impact on the early eighteenth century, which was in fact a period of digestion rather than invention. America and France were particularly receptive. It was a Frenchman, Montesquieu, who gave the classic formulation to another Lockean idea, that of the separation of powers. Both these ideas are fundamental to political freedom—the right to rebel in defence of one's natural rights and the dilution of power by its distribution among the various parts of the constitution.

But, apart from the idea that the state exists to defend man's natural rights, the Lockean standpoint became rather a negative attitude. During the second half of the eighteenth century it was being added to by the more positive idea of the pursuit of happiness, and in the nineteenth by the pursuit of freedom as a good in itself. Voltaire and the French Encyclopedists, Bentham, John Stuart Mill, and the English Utilitarians upheld this tradition and gave it roots of sufficient strength to withstand the hostile organic theory of the state which was revived by Rousseau and the German theorists at much the same time. The ideas of the Utilitarians will be considered in the chapter on democracy. Before we go on to deal with Rousseau's ideas, however, it is necessary to take a brief glance at the contribution to political thought of one further English thinker—Edmund Burke. Burke was one of the most eloquent Members of Parliament in an age noted for its rhetoric, and he had plenty of opportunity to express his philosophy on the floor of the House. His greatest work, however, was his *Reflections on the Revolution in France*, published in 1790. In this book and elsewhere Burke provides the classic case for Conservatism. He rebelled against the rationalism of the Enlightenment in the belief that the human mind cannot satisfactorily replace institutions that have the support of tradition behind them. He believed that society can develop only by organic growth; any attempt to create a brand-new constitution, for example, without reference to the country's constitutional background would be doomed to failure. It is for this reason that he crusaded so fervently against the French Revolution.

Jean-Jacques Rousseau defies categorization as a political thinker. Although he started out as an exponent of the individualist Contract school (his great political treatise is called *The Social Contract*), he unwittingly inspired a school of state-worship reducing the individual to a non-entity. As C. E. Vaughan wrote, "A stern asserter of the State on the one hand, a fiery champion of the individual on the other, he could never bring himself wholly to sacrifice the one ideal to the other."[11] Although Rousseau lived much of his life in France, he was born (in 1712) in Geneva. The fact of his birthplace is of significance, as many of his ideas are more relevant to the conditions of a city-state than to the large monarchical states of eighteenth-century Europe. The central theme of *The Social Contract* is as follows. Man is faced with a paradoxical situation: he cannot attain moral maturity, which to Rousseau is synonymous with true freedom, unless he enters a civil society; yet when he does he is open to the corrupting influences of human society. The only way of retaining the moral advantages of the communal life and avoiding its tendency to corrupt is by adherence to the General Will. Rousseau's concept of the General Will is his most individual contribution to political theory, and is the technique whereby he hoped to resolve the opposition of the individual and the state. The General Will is binding on the whole community, but, by very definition, is exercised only when the decision arrived at is for the good of the community. A decision arrived at by a majority, even unanimously, is not an expression of the General Will if it is not in accordance with the true interests of the community. Conversely, the opinion of a minority or even a single individual can be the true expression of the General Will. Here, of course, is the basis for authoritarianism. If a dictator asserts that he is the embodiment of the General Will, any opposition to him, even by the vast majority of the people, is merely proof of their continued moral enslavement, and the dictator is perfectly justified in continuing with his policy in order to "force the people to be free."

The strength of Rousseau's ideas lies not so much in the logical development of his argument as in his emotional appeal. The General Will is in the nature of an emotional unity of society. Similarly, the opening sentence of the first chapter of *The Social Contract*—"Man is born free, and everywhere he is in chains"—has been one of the great political slogans of modern times. It is this emotional and mystical atmosphere, especially when combined with the theory of the General Will, that inspired other political theorists of the organic school who followed him. The debt of the Communist brand of 'totalitarian democracy' to the fundamental ideas of Rousseau will be dealt with in a later chapter.

It will also be necessary to refer to the ideas of Hegel in other chapters, for modern nationalism and Communism owe much to his work. Nevertheless, it will be useful to provide a brief account of his contribution to political thought here, in its historical context. Hegel was born in Württemberg in 1770, eight years after the publication of Rousseau's *Social Contract*, and eventually became President of Berlin University. It was at Berlin that he produced his most influential works—his book *Philosophy of Right* and his lectures *Philosophy of History*. With Hegel the mystical unity of society as expressed by Rousseau's General Will becomes the nation-state—"The Divine Idea as it exists on Earth."[12] The Divine Idea or Spirit is the ultimate reality or truth. In such an exalted position the state can, therefore, allow no opposition to its purpose either from the individual or from another state or, indeed, from morality. The state is supreme. Although subordinate to the state, the individual, as in Plato's scheme, can never be a mature social being without this subordination. Yet it must not be thought that Hegel's philosophy is a static one. It does, indeed, postulate the continual striving to attain the perfection of the Idea. The method of progress is the dialectic—progress by the clash of opposites and the emergence of an improved situation.

Hegel has had a widespread influence. In England the necessary adjustments to the extreme individualism of the Victorian Liberals, especially by T. H. Green, were undertaken under the inspiration of Hegel. Mussolini's Fascism was also to a certain extent justified by an appeal to Hegelianism. But it was in Germany, not unnaturally, that the influence of Hegel was most strongly felt. Marx, as a young student, came under the influence of Hegelian philosophy and adapted the dialectic to his own needs. The organic nation-state, ignoring any principles of international morality, was the basis of Bismarckian and Nazi practice as it was of Hegelian theory.

The ideas of the social contract and natural law, of the general will and the dialectic, the ideas with which we have concluded our brief historical survey of the Western tradition in political thought, are ideas of past ages. They were useful interpretations of the eighteenth and nineteenth centuries, but the necessary adaptation of our basic thoughts to the conditions of the modern, twentieth-century world has not taken place. Political thinking has become sterile. Russian Communists repeat, like cracked records, the nineteenth-century ideas of Karl Marx; English logical positivists write esoteric chapters on the meaning of political vocabulary. But when the more enlightened political theorists, urged on by the sense of crisis in the modern world, produce some original lines of thought they seem incapable of creating new masterpieces themselves or of inspiring such works from the pens of others. The reasons for and significance of this failing must evidently be discussed; but discussion can more profitably be left until the ideas which are currently used have been analysed.

CHAPTER TWO

NATIONALISM

The Argument

Definitions. Nation—nationalism.
Origins. The nation-state—Rousseau and the French Revolution—Napoleon and the German theorists.
The Nineteenth Century. The Vienna Settlement—the twin themes—the Versailles Settlement.
Totalitarian Nationalism. Fascism—Nazism.
The Expansion of the Nationalist Idea. Introduction—the general pattern of development.
Asia. Introduction—India, Pakistan, and Ceylon—Russia, China, and Japan—South-east Asia.
The Middle East. Origins to 1945—Israel—the Maghreb—the Levant and Iraq—Egypt and Pan-Arabism.
Africa. Introduction—West Africa—East and Central Africa—Southern Africa.
Conclusions. The values of nationalism—problems and dangers—contradictions and essence—the present position.

Definitions

Nationalism has been truly described as "the strongest single factor in the existing network of interests, sentiments and ideas binding men into territorially based political groups."[1] Originating in Europe, it has spread with other European ideas throughout the world, building here, destroying there, as is its nature. Yet, for all its widespread expression, it is an idea that many people have failed to understand or truly appreciate. Such terms as 'nation,' 'nationality,' 'nation-state,' and 'nationalism' are bandied about frequently with only a vague understanding of their true meaning.

Before analysing the ways in which nationalism grew up and the present-day expressions of the idea we must therefore define our terms. Firstly, the word 'nation.' It is unfortunate that the word has two distinct meanings in English: it can denote either a political unit (a state) or an ethnological unit (a race). These two meanings may or may not be synonymous in practice. For example, many Welsh people who are content to be part of the English political state still consider themselves a separate ethnological people. They are part of the English nation politically, though not ethnically. A nation in the political sense is quite easy to define in most cases. It is a sovereign state, a country with its own Government, and it is in this sense that the word is used in the term United Nations Organization, for example.

A neat, workable definition of a nation in the ethnological sense, however, is impossible. Evidently a nation in this sense is a unit generally identifiable by a common race and common language, common religion and common cultural tradition, and a specific geographical location. France is a nation because it consists mainly of the Gallic race, speaking the French language, adhering to the Roman Catholic form of the Christian religion, and enjoying a rich cultural tradition based on centuries of living together in one state clearly defined by natural boundaries of sea, mountain, and river. But the Bretons of the West and the Germans of Alsace are different races with different languages and cultural traditions. Furthermore, there are strong elements of Calvinism and atheism to dilute the Catholic tradition. And finally the northern and eastern frontiers, for lack of obvious natural boundaries, have been in a constant state of flux. How far, then, is a German-speaking Protestant from Alsace a true member of the French nation? Further examples can be given of this problem of definition. The identification of a nation and a race is falsified by a glance at the ethnic structure of Britain. Even if we admit that Irish, Scots, and Welsh are different nations, the English are a mixture of the Celtic, Roman, Anglo-Saxon, Danish, Norwegian, and Norman-French races, planted in England by successive invasions and welded into a national unity by generations of intermarriage. Secondly, although the test of language is the most important and least fallible in seeking a nation, the existence of the multi-lingual Swiss nation is striking proof that it does not always hold good, for Switzerland is a country where four different tongues —French, Italian, German, and Romansh—are in common use. The question of language was, indeed, taken as the basic test of nationality by the statesmen at Versailles in 1919, but an appeal to the people themselves in areas of mixed tongues gave some surprising answers. As Alfred Cobban has pointed out, "The results of some of the plebiscites did in fact suggest that language was not invariably a guide to nationality."[2] Again, although religious divisions seemed likely to sunder nations at the time of the Reformation, Lutherans, Calvinists, and Catholics were forged by Bismarck into a German nation, for example, even if it did take over two centuries to overcome the bitterness and chaos of the Thirty Years War. A common cultural tradition is perhaps more important—though, of course, there can be great differences in the inheritance of the various classes that make up a nation. There was little in common in the cultural backgrounds of the factory workers of Industrial Revolution England, for example, and the aristocracy that ruled them. Yet they all fought as a closely knit nation against the threat of Napoleon. Finally, there existed surely a conscious Jewish nation before the creation of Israel as a specifically geographically located state.

When so many tests for a nation can be so easily destroyed by exceptions, we can say little more than that a nation is a group of people who think of themselves as a nation. As Professor Renier has said, "Outside men's minds there can be no nationality, because nationality is a manner of looking at oneself—not an entity 'an sich.' "[3] The same point has been made by John Bowle: "It is a manifestation, not of environmental compulsion, but of mind. A people are a nation, not through the chances of geography and descent, but when they think they are."[4]

If the word 'nation' presents difficulties, the term 'nationalism' has caused even more confusion. It has been used to describe a whole range of sentiments from the proud patriotism of Gaunt, "This blessed plot, this earth, this realm, this England,"[5] to the fanatical racialism of Hitler, "Ein Reich, ein Volk, ein Fuehrer." If this semantic confusion is allowed to pass unnoticed we are in danger of confusing the general, restrained 'national sentiment' or 'patriotism' with the essentially different modern and highly emotional 'nationalism.' For the former does not reject the possibility of other loyalties; the latter in effect does—it is a "mental disease which places a nation's interests, real or alleged, above material, spiritual, religious and ethical values."[6] What are these "interests" of the nation? First and foremost nationalism demands independence: the sentiment is most easily roused when a people is subjected to the rule of another, as is evidenced by the strength of the movement in India before 1947. Secondly, nationalism seeks unity in one state for those who consider themselves members of the nation. Nationalist-minded Germans and Italians in post-Napoleonic Europe were discontented because they were dispersed among thirty-nine and eight separate states respectively. Conversely, there must be a certain uniformity, frequently in language in particular, among the people who make up an already constituted nation-state. The weakness in this respect of the old 'ramshackle' empire of the Habsburgs in a nationalist-minded world is evident when one views its linguistic patchwork of German, Slav, Magyar, and Rumanian-speaking peoples. Finally, nationalism seeks to satisfy the pride of the nation by increasing its strength, usually in a military context, the self-conscious military movements of Fascism and Nazism in post-1918 Italy and Germany being, perhaps, the obvious examples of this development. And this self-assertive aspect of the idea leads away from the liberal demand for independence to totalitarianism and expansion. The two traditions are, in fact, so different that some political thinkers would restrict the use of the word 'nationalism' to the aggressive brand of the phenomenon. Frederick Hertz, for example, has made a plea for confining the term to "a specific form of national consciousness centred on superiority, prestige, power and domination."[7]

Such, then, is the force which it is our purpose to discuss in this chapter. Nationalism properly defined, as opposed to patriotism, was the twin product with democracy of the Western world of the later years of the eighteenth century. It burst forth on a startled Europe in the French Revolution; it spread throughout the Continent during the nineteenth century; it festered into totalitarian Fascism in the twentieth; and, in our own day, it has overflowed into Asia, the Middle East, and on into tropical Africa.

Origins

Medieval political society was pyramidal in structure: barons owed allegiance to dukes, dukes to kings, and kings to the Emperor—at any rate, in theory. The political units were fiefs, duchies, and kingdoms, and it was only in the fifteenth and sixteenth centuries that the nation-state can be said to be emerging as the natural unit. A certain national consciousness appeared as early as the fourteenth century in the two most highly developed of Western states, England and France—a consciousness that was evoked by their prolonged conflict in the Hundred Years War. Spain, the Netherlands, Sweden, just the kind of sentiment Rousseau had in mind when drafting the doctrine of the General Will. And it was eagerly adopted by the exponents of nationalism.

The eighteenth-century democratic movement, the demand that political privilege should not be so severely restricted, burst forth in the great French Revolution with all the violence of long-pent-up energy a decade after the death of Rousseau. In the mass of pamphlet literature that accompanied the preparations for the calling of the States-General there emerged one of greater worth and influence than perhaps all the others. It was written by the Abbé Sieyes and was entitled *Qu'est-ce que le Tiers État?* Sieyes attacked the exalted position of the privileged classes and emphasized instead the political authority of the people as a whole. Furthermore, he identified the sovereign people not as any random collection that might happen to find themselves within the confines of the state, but as the nation. "The Nation," he wrote, "exists before all things and is the origin of all. Its will is always legal, it is the law itself."[13] Thus the political debate that accompanied the Revolution veered round from the relative powers of the orders of French society to the authority of the French people as a nation. But what of the influence of Rousseau? His direct influence on the Revolution at first was probably small. He was quoted as the author of the concept of the General Will to justify practical policies which were based on the theory of national unity, but only the Robespierrist Jacobins made a conscious attempt to apply Rousseau's ideas systematically.

More impressive in many ways than the development of the theory of nationalism was its practice by the Revolution. The Papal enclave of Avignon and the Venaissin was a contradiction of the idea of the consolidated nation-state and so was annexed in 1791. The invasion by the Austrian and Prussian armies was made not in the manner of the wars of the *ancien régime*, by one dynasty against another, but in an attempt to save the French monarch from his own people: it was a war against the French nation. And, most important of all, the professional armies of the Hohenzollern and Habsburg were met not by an equivalent Bourbon force, but by the French nation in arms. Volunteers flocked from the provinces, and those from Marseilles gave their nationalistic marching-song to France as her national anthem. And later, when volunteers failed, the weight of numbers in the army was maintained by conscription. Warfare was revolutionized in both senses of the term, and nationalism was consolidated into the military dimension. France now became a consciously nationalist state: provincial loyalties were attacked by the reorganization of local government and the imposition of French as the official language in place of such alien tongues as Flemish, German, and Breton and dialects like Provençal. Such a policy needed no other justification than the claim that the nation was the 'natural' political unit. Contrary ideas which emphasized particular provincial differences and demands for local government—called 'federalism' in the seventeen-nineties—were therefore 'unnatural.' But if a nation is the political unit ordained by nature, then it must have natural—that is, clearly defined geographical—boundaries. Thus there arose the aggressive nationalist demands of Danton for the expansion of France to her natural frontiers—the Pyrenees, the Alps, the Rhine.

The nationalist idea spread across Europe in the Napoleonic era. Its importance in bringing about the downfall of the French Emperor should not, however, be exaggerated. Spanish resistance was largely a local hostility to foreign rule; Russian sentiment in 1812 was patriotism rather than true nationalism; while the German insurrections in 1809 and 1813 were Austrian and Prussian rather than truly German in character. One of the most learned authorities on this period, the late Georges Lefebvre, wrote:

> It is proper to notice, moreover, that, if the discontent roused by French domination undeniably contributed to the development of national individualities, patriotic sentiment in its pure and disinterested form, however, influenced only small minorities and played but a secondary role compared with the suffering of the people and the injured interests of different classes.[14]

It was among the German intellectuals that the Napoleonic conquests roused the true spirit of nationalism. The Romantic movement in German literature, which developed in the late eighteenth century under the influence of Rousseau, gave a literary and cultural basis to this emerging political idea. Perhaps the most influential of these writers was Johann Herder, who emphasized the essential differences between various 'folk'—the *Weltanschauung*, or way of living peculiar to each national unit. This became an attitude of mind which pervaded many of the arts and much of the scholarship of the nineteenth century. Music was composed and history was written in a consciously, even selfconsciously, nationalist vein. It also gave added justification for the essentially political movements for national unity and independence which created the German and Italian nation-states and destroyed the Habsburg and Ottoman Empires. For such nationalist figures as Byron and Mazzini are in the true Romantic tradition. A more militant and political tradition, however, was being developed in Germany at the same time, particularly in Prussia. This was voiced by Fichte, who in the winter of 1807–8 delivered a series of lectures at Berlin, entitled *Addresses to the German Nation*, in which he emphasized the test of language for nationality. Fichte died in 1814, and was succeeded in his chair at the University of Berlin by Hegel. And it was Hegel who, though not a conscious nationalist, brought the contemporary threads together to produce a consistent philosophy suitable for the nation-state (see Chapter 1). It was Hegel who gave the state and, by analogy, the nation that mystical, almost divine power which is, perhaps, the ultimate conclusion of Rousseau's concept of the General Will. In the Hegelian system the state is the reflection of the perfect Idea of his metaphysics. "The Nation State ... is ... absolute power on earth," he wrote.[15] In thus stressing the supremacy of the state he laid the foundations for the development of totalitarian nationalism in which the individual counts for practically nothing as against the state. There is clearly a direct connexion between Hegel and Hitler. The breach with the cosmopolitanism and individualism of the eighteenth century was now complete.

The Nineteenth Century

If Pitt rolled up the map of Europe on hearing the news of Austerlitz, his great pupil in statecraft, Viscount Castlereagh, unrolled it eight years later in company with the great statesmen of Europe assembled at Vienna. Their task was no less than to redraw the frontiers of a continent. Succeeding generations of critics have damned the Vienna Settlement for its excessive regard for dynastic considerations, but the almost complete lack of mass nationalist movements at the time is surely sufficient defence for the diplomats responsible for the arrangements. The Settlement was destroyed by nationalism. That is true, but there was little evidence to suggest the likelihood of this fate in 1814–15.

The nineteenth century was the age of European nationalism, but by the time the movement got under way there were already two separate traditions to be followed. The French school of thought had provided the foundations for the liberal ideas of national self-determination and popular government; the Germans, on the other hand, had exalted the state into the be-all and end-all of political life—a position from where it could keep the people of which it was composed in complete subjection. The nineteenth century witnessed the flourishing of the liberal brand in its early years under the influence of Mazzini and the totalitarian kind in the second half when Bismarck dominated the scene.

Throughout the early years of the nineteenth century the forces of nationalism steadily gained strength; and against the failure of the Poles to break free from Russian control there could be recorded the successes of the Serbs and Greeks against the Turks before 1830 and the Belgians against the Dutch after. Indeed, the creation of an independent Belgian state, finally ratified in 1839, revealed, like a crack in a wall, the weakness of the foundations upon which the Vienna Settlement had been built. Then, encouraged and assisted by the deposition of Louis-Philippe in France and the discontent of the masses due to the poor harvests of 1845–47, nationalist ardour burst forth in rebellion in 1848. Demands for national unity were voiced in Germany and Italy, for independence from Austrian control in Italy and Hungary. But the Habsburg and Romanov dynasties and armies were too strong for the enthusiastic but visionary intellectuals of 1848. Reaction and disillusion followed the years of revolutions, and nationalism soured into the militant ambitions of the Hegelians. In Italy, however, the liberal tradition was not killed. In Italy, alone of the large states, a geographical expression was turned into a nation-state by the romantic blend of nationalism—by the enthusiasm of Garibaldi and the inspiration of Mazzini. Mazzini, who has been described as "the greatest prophet of the new idea" of nationality,[16] believed that national and individual freedom were indispensable to one another. Nationality, he insisted, was a people's conscience, "their *individuality*, without which neither liberty nor equality are possible."[17] He thought, moreover, that once all peoples were constituted into properly defined nation-states they would recognize the demands of self-determination in their neighbours as legitimate, and thus territorial wars would end and an era of progress and goodwill would ensue. "In labouring according to true principles for our country we are labouring for humanity; our country is the fulcrum of the lever which we have for the common good."[18] Such sentiments were to find echoes in the declarations by President Wilson of the United States in 1919.

But the hard-headed Germans were soon to make Mazzini's optimism appear romantic nonsense. Treitschke announced that the "grandeur of history lies in the perpetual conflict of nations";[19] Bismarck welded Germany into a united nation-state by the spilling of blood and the martial use of iron in the three lightning wars with Denmark, Austria, and France (1864–71); and, "as the newspapers smelt sensation, the industrialists profit, the soldiers glory and the masses blood, generous desires for fraternity and freedom gave place to a more sinister spirit."[20] This sinister spirit increasingly darkened the political horizon as the nineteenth century gave way to the twentieth, and a truly Treitschkean conflict broke out in the Armageddon of 1914.

The expansion of the various European nationalisms, whose clashes were important contributory factors in the start of the Great War, had some sort of theoretical justification in the concepts of Pan-Germanism and Pan-Slavism. The former believed in the union of all German people in a single state. And many brought not only the German-speaking Austrians and Swiss into this definition, but also the Dutch and Scandinavians. The interest of this movement in the Habsburg dominions clashed with the Russian-dominated Pan-Slav movement, which sought the union of all Slav peoples beneath the wide-spreading Romanov wing; for the Habsburg Empire embraced many branches of the Slav race, including Poles, Czechs, Slovaks, Ukrainians, Croats, Slovenes, and Serbs. The fact that many of the people who would have constituted these Pan-German and Pan-Slav empires would have been incorporated against their wills seems not to have deterred the supporters of these movements. The mutual hostility of the various Slav peoples especially has been adequately illustrated in the tensions in Eastern Europe since Stalin achieved the dreams of the Pan-Slav movement. Poland and Russia above all have been traditional enemies for centuries. In 1914, however, the dreams had not been realized, though both Pan-German and Pan-Slav ambitions were sufficiently real to turn the local problem of Sarajevo into a world-wide clash of arms. For in the crisis over the assassination of the Archduke Francis Ferdinand the German and Russian empires stood forth from behind the scenes to overshadow the original, but secondary, combatants.

The statesmen who met at Versailles in 1919 to redraw the map of Europe and thus compile the final chapter of nineteenth-century history were not only imbued with a sense of the force and righteousness of nationalism, but were haunted by the ghosts of a century past, of the Metternichs and Castlereaghs, who had, in retrospect, so signally failed to take cognizance of this potent idea. President Wilson, especially, that New World Mazzini, was particularly insistent that the principle of self-determination should be taken as the basis for the settlement. Apart from the refusal to allow the union of Germany and Austria, a serious attempt was made to create a Europe of nation-states. The 'ramshackle' Habsburg Empire was split up to establish a completely independent Hungary and Czechoslovakia and to make territorial contributions to the new states of Yugoslavia and Poland. The revival of Poland as an independent state was made possible by the virtual disintegration of Russia following her defeats at the hands of the Germans and the Revolution of 1917. Finland, Estonia, Latvia, and Lithuania were also carved out of the old Romanov Empire, though attempts to create independent republics in the Ukraine and the Caucasian provinces failed.

The difficult problems with which the diplomats were faced in putting the Wilsonian principles into practice are difficulties inherent in the doctrine of national self-determination itself, and will be dealt with in more detail later in this chapter. Briefly, they were threefold. In places nationalist principles clashed with other, particularly economic, interests; in most cases nationalism was made to prevail. For example, the economy of the Habsburg Empire was based on the unity and facilities of communication provided by the Danube. This natural economic unit disintegrated with disastrous consequences to its components when the individual states of Czechoslovakia, Austria, Hungary, and Yugoslavia were established. Secondly, there were many cases, especially in Eastern Europe, where small enclaves of people were embedded in countries predominantly composed of another nation. For example, the Magyars of Transylvania found themselves embedded in Rumania, White Russians in Poland, Sudeten Germans in Czechoslovakia. In these cases the rights of the minorities were specifically laid down in treaties. But these were largely ineffective because many of the states involved made the guarantees unwillingly and the League of Nations hesitated to encroach upon the sovereignty of the state to enforce them. Finally there was the problem of the areas where two or more nationalities were inextricably mixed. In such areas the final decision was made by the obvious method, already used in the nineteenth century, of popular ballots or plebiscites.

Mazzinian principles of self-determination underlay the new map of Europe, and machinery, in the form of the League of Nations, was set up to provide the opportunity for international co-operation, in accordance with Mazzini's hopes, for the good of humanity at large. But a proud nation had been humiliated—a nation whose nationalist tradition was built on the totalitarian grandeur of the Hegelian state and the warlike politics of Treitschke. These elements had only to be fused with Pan-Germanism and the spurious racial theories of Houston Stewart Chamberlain to subject Europe to the ravages of the nationalist creed in its ultimate degeneration.

Totalitarian Nationalism

Although Nazism was the most thoroughgoing, successful, and famous of the twentieth-century forms of totalitarian nationalism it owed much to the example of Italian Fascism, which, in the nineteen-twenties, preceded the German movement. Fascism was essentially a practical attempt to strengthen the Italian state: the theory came later. Mussolini himself was quite definite about this: "We Fascists," he said, "have had the courage to discard all traditional political theories, and we are aristocrats and democrats, revolutionaries and reactionaries, proletarians and anti-proletarians, pacifists and anti-pacifists. It is sufficient to have a single fixed point: the nation. The rest is obvious."[21] The movement was, in fact, little more than a demagogic appeal by a leader to the masses unsettled by economic grievances. State control had crumbled from weakness and corruption. Fascism promised strength and order. They were imposed by violence and force, by the March on Rome in 1922 and the subsequent elimination of Matteotti and the elements of opposition; they were justified by a Hegelian interpretation of the importance of the state hastily constructed for the purpose by Giovanni Gentile. It is the state, indeed, that is emphasized, rather than the nation. In an encyclopedia article, "Fascism, Doctrine and Institutions," written in 1932 by Mussolini with Gentile's assistance, this is made quite clear:

> It is not the nation which generates the state; that is an antiquated naturalistic concept.... Rather it is the state which creates the nation,

conferring volition and therefore real life on a people made aware of their moral unity.... Indeed, it is the state which, as the expression of a universal ethical will, creates the right to national independence.[22]

Nevertheless, Mussolini's power was based on popular support, and he was fully conscious of the popular appeal of nationalism. In 1919 the romantic nationalist Gabriele d'Annunzio had made an unsuccessful attempt to add Fiume to the Italian state. The raid was in the grand Garibaldian tradition, d'Annunzio became a popular hero, and later he joined forces with the Fascists. Once in power, therefore, Mussolini sketched out a policy aimed at satisfying nationalist pride. The Mediterranean was to become an "Italian lake"; Italy's power was to be expanded in both Europe and Africa; in short, the grandeur that was Rome was to be revived in all its might. To put these plans into effect Mussolini launched a vicious attack in 1935 against Abyssinia, which soon succumbed and was then incorporated into an Italian East African Empire. In 1939 Albania was taken, but an attempt to push southward from this Balkan foothold met with fierce Greek resistance. With German assistance, however, the Italian empire was increased by the addition of Corsica, Montenegro, and the Illyrian coast.

The theory of Nazism, although based on the same basic demagogy that characterized Fascism, has important contrasts. In the first place, Germany had a great military tradition, its philosophical tradition was totalitarian, and, most important of all, it was smarting for revenge after the defeats in the First World War. There was, then, a more positive urge towards totalitarian nationalism than in Italy. The second important contrast is that the theory of National Socialism came first. The policy of Hitler and the Nazi Party was an attempt to put the ideas as outlined in his autobiography, *Mein Kampf*, into practice. Finally, the state is of subordinate importance compared with the nation—or, rather, in this case, the race. The aim of Nazism was the supremacy of the Aryan race.

Let us look at the theory of National Socialism a little more closely. It was a mixture of the theory of national self-determination, of the myth of the pure and dominant Aryan race, and of state power exercised by the Fuehrer and the members of the Nazi Party. The basis of the movement, as has already been mentioned, was Adolf Hitler's autobiographical *Mein Kampf*. It is a popular, emotional work, not a learned treatise on political theory; indeed, its "peculiar fascination," as R. H. S. Crossman has written, "is that it elaborates the half-formed ideas of the streets into a comprehensive secular religion."[23] One is not surprised to learn that it was written in prison by a man born in the atmosphere of racial tension and anti-Semitism which pervaded the Austrian Empire in the years before the outbreak of the First World War. The somewhat disjointed outbursts of *Mein Kampf* were given a semblance of academic respectability by the work of Rosenberg. Alfred Rosenberg joined the Nazi Party soon after its formation in 1919, and in 1930 produced his *Der Mythus des 20. Jahrhunderts* (*The Myth of the Twentieth Century*), in which he outlined a philosophy of history based on the conflict of the Aryan with the lesser races.

One aspect of the theory had a validity that could not be denied by even the most hostile of democratic statesmen. For the Nazis made the natural demand of the nineteenth-century Pan-German movement—namely, that all Germans should be united in a single nation-state. The statesmen of the democratic Powers had accepted this principle of nationalism at the 1919 Peace Conference and had used it to justify the break-up of the Habsburg Empire. How, then, could they, without hypocrisy, deny the same principle for the creation of a united German nation? There were, indeed, substantial numbers of German people outside the frontiers of the German state—in Poland, Czechoslovakia, Italy, and above all, of course, in Austria.

But Hitler took the doctrine of nationalism farther than this. He required not only the unity of the German people, but their supremacy. There are, naturally, he argued, ruling and subject nations; the Germans were the former. "The broad mass of the people," Hitler declared, "... wants the victory of the strong and the annihilation or unconditional submission of the weak."[24]

Hitler had, of course, to justify his assertion that the Germans were naturally a ruling—indeed, the master—race. And this is perhaps the most important part of the whole theory. The idea of an Aryan or Nordic race was built up on supposedly sound biological and anthropological evidence; it is, in fact, a myth. The theory of the existence of a master, Aryan race and the necessity for a race to be pure in order to be dominant was first put forward by the Frenchman Gobineau and the Germanized Englishman Chamberlain, and was later taken over by Hitler and the principal philosopher of the

Nazi movement, Alfred Rosenberg. The Germans were identified with the mythical ancient and pure Nordic race, and Tacitus was quoted to prove the purity of the German nation of old. For had the great Roman historian not written, "The Germans themselves, I am inclined to think, are natives of the soil and extremely little affected by immigration or friendly intercourse with other nations"?[25] There was only one factor, in the Nazi view, that prevented the domination of the world by the superior German nation—adulteration of the race. This idea had the added advantage of whipping up that potent unifying sentiment—hatred—against the people guilty of poisoning the blood of the master race. Popular feeling in Germany, Hitler's own personal prejudice, and important themes in Chamberlain's *The Foundations of the Nineteenth Century*, all led to the choice of the Jew as the mortal enemy. The anti-Semitic programme started as a policy of isolation; it ended as a most revolting genocide. Sustained by the theory of the purity and superiority of a primitive race, the German nation thus sank to a level of primitive barbarism in pursuing its own peculiar distortion of the nationalist ideology. For by 1942 a large part of the Nazi dream had been realized, to become a nightmare for the rest of Europe. The Jewish race was being systematically exterminated in the abominable concentration camps at Auschwitz, Treblinka, and elsewhere, and numerous ghettoes had been eliminated. In all, it is estimated that nearly six million Jews perished at the hands of the Nazis. By 1942, also, the German Reich had expanded to incorporate all German-speaking peoples, including those who had previously lived in France, Austria, Poland, and Czechoslovakia. Furthermore, it was ringed by a host of satellites and occupied territories.

The Expansion of the Nationalist Idea

The nationalist idea is a European idea. It emerged with the democratic movement of the late eighteenth century, it matured in the movements for unity and independence in the nineteenth, and degenerated in the movements for domination in the twentieth. But the Europe of the late nineteenth century was an expanding continent; it was spilling over into the backward continents of Asia and Africa. British, French, Dutch, and German men went out to the developing colonies and other underdeveloped lands, such as China, which managed to retain some semblance of political independence while succumbing to economic imperialism. But they did not go alone: they took with them European goods, European administrative and financial methods—above all, European ideas. So nationalism came to the Afro-Asian world. Although native elements like religion, social structure, culture, shape its growth, it stays a basically European idea. One must emphasize the European origin of the nationalist movements for their true nature to be understood. Thomas Hodgkin is quite definite about this in noting the similarity between the African and European movements. "These resemblances," he writes, "seem more natural if the rise of African nationalism is thought of as the final stage in a chain reaction, deriving its operative ideas originally from the French Revolution—the doctrine of the Rights of Man interpreted as the Rights of Nations."[26]

The theory of nationalism has, of course, had a significant effect on the politics of Asia and the Middle East, and increasingly in recent years of tropical Africa. But before passing on to an analysis of each of these areas it will be convenient to make a few general remarks about the expansion of the idea beyond Europe.

The clash between colonials and imperial Governments is a clash between two aspects of nationalism. Imperialism can be, and certainly was at the turn of the nineteenth century, an aggressive and expanding form of nationalism. The Powers scrambled to partition Africa in the eighteen-eighties for the sake of national prestige. This expanding nationalism met with resistance—from the Zulus in South Africa, the dervishes in the Sudan, the Sikhs and Afghans on the North-west Frontier of India, for example. But these were examples of tribal resistance to foreigners, not attempts to create a self-conscious, united nation-state. The demand for truly national self-determination, the clash of native against European nationalism, came later, once the imperial authority had been consolidated.

Nationalism is frequently the expression of a mass inferiority complex. And the European control of underdeveloped areas was well calculated to produce such a feeling of inferiority. The superiority of the European peoples in science, technology, and administration was used to organize the native peoples for European ends, and scant respect was paid to native customs.

It is true that the colonizing Powers educated many of the natives to take part in the task of administration; indeed, such a policy had to be undertaken to make the administration at all effective. But, far from satisfying the aspirations of these people, their Western education only whetted their ambition and produced a potential leadership for the more widespread, largely economic, discontent of the mass of the natives. For these educated native officials not only imbibed the theories of self-determination with their education, but also developed a personal grudge because of their exclusion from all but the minor positions in the Governmental service. As Professor Brogan has pointed out, the task of leadership "falls to the class that the imperial powers cannot help creating, the new, western-educated, poorly-employed, or unemployed intelligentzia. The imperial powers *must* create this class, since they need cheap clerical aid and they cannot make this class literate only in book-keeping and copying."[27]

The idea of self-government is just as natural in the context of Africa and Asia as it is in Europe: that cannot be denied. But the idea of a nation is not. The nationalist movements in colonial areas inevitably grew in the context of the colonial units whose boundaries were the results largely of historical accident or diplomatic convenience. Indonesia, for example, was the creation of the Dutch, while the frontiers between the British and French possessions in West Africa were of a particularly artificial kind. Any attempt to instil a truly widespread national consciousness among the people must therefore be a most difficult task.

The emphasis comes to be placed, therefore, not on nationality but on colour. Yellow, brown, or black, the colonial people feel themselves distinct from the white rulers; and the white rulers often help this feeling by the colour-bar policy. The question is, of course, most acute in Africa, and the colour-consciousness of modern colonial nationalism was well summed up by the Nigerian newspaper *Daily Success*. The Africans, it declared, "know that if they once built pyramids on the Nile, fought with Cæsar's battalions, ruled over Spain and dominated the Pyrenees, they the very same black people can be great again and be slaves no more."[28]

Here again we see the feeling of inferiority emerging: the necessity to recall past glories, however remote. And in such an atmosphere nationalist movements gain a vital fillip to their self-confidence when a colonial Power suffers defeat at the hands of a native force. The might of Japan in the first half of the twentieth century was of outstanding importance in this respect. At the very beginning of the century in her war with Russia "The news of Tsushima and Mukden was felt like an electric shock in Saigon, in Poona, in Batavia, in Canton. For the first time, an Asiatic power had defeated in battle, with modern weapons, a great white power."[29] The withdrawal of the Anglo-French force during the Suez operation of 1956 had similar repercussions throughout the Middle East.

If nationalism is such a powerful force in the colonial territories, and if the native peoples only want to practise what the Europeans preach, it may well be asked why the white Governments have not more quickly abdicated their power. Is the charge of hypocrisy which many colonials make a just one? The problem is too complex for a straightforward yes or no to be given in reply to such a question. In many cases real or supposed economic and strategic interests have been bound up with European control. British interests of this kind in Aden and the Persian Gulf area, for example, made it difficult to submit to a demand for complete independence. In other areas a white-settler population has been firmly established, and, being in a minority compared with the native peoples, they have feared for their privileges, their existence as an identifiable community even, when the sympathetic authority of the metropolitan Government should be withdrawn. Such was the case in Algeria and Kenya. Finally, there is the central problem of colonial self-government. Many territories that have been demanding independence are in fact incapable of maintaining government along modern lines. In these circumstances the imperial Government finds itself on the horns of a dilemma. If it resists the demands until political education has progressed sufficiently for self-government to have a reasonable chance of success it risks bloodshed in riots against the slowness of the procedure. If, on the other hand, it abdicates its authority it risks the spilling of blood or the destruction of free institutions when its guiding hand has been replaced by an ineffective or despotic native administration. Thus, if bloodshed is to be avoided, the timing must be nicely arranged.

So far the expression of nationalism beyond its original home of Europe has been dealt with in a very abstract way. It is time now to describe its operation in specific areas. First let us turn to Asia.

ASIA

For the purpose of this analysis of nationalism it will be convenient to divide the continent of Asia into several sections. The Middle East countries that are geographically part of Asia will be dealt with quite separately. We are then left with the Asiatic provinces of the Soviet Union, China, Japan, India, Pakistan, and the group of countries known as South-east Asia. The record of the achievement of national independence in South and South-east Asia since the War has been particularly impressive: India, Pakistan, Ceylon, Burma, Indochina, the Philippines, Malaya, Singapore, and Indonesia have all achieved self-government, although the situation in Vietnam is still confused.

"When we turn our eyes to Asia," wrote Alfred Cobban in 1947, "India presents us with what may go down to history as the classic case of self-determination."[30] The British rule in India had given the sub-continent unity and peace; it had given it economic development and religious and cultural freedom; but before 1947 it had not given it political freedom. Peaceful development was risked for the sake of national independence. Indeed, it was probably only the common hostility to British rule that gave the Indians any real sense of unity, for the country is a patchwork of different races, languages, and religions. As Rabindranath Tagore expressed it, "It is many countries packed into one geographical receptacle."[31]

The opposition to British rule first became politically coherent with the establishment of the Indian National Congress in 1885. There was now a focus for the manifold grievances of those who objected to the privileged position of the whites. Attempts to remove British authority at the beginning of the twentieth century under the leadership of the Brahmin B. G. Tilak were violent.

Such a policy was in sharp contrast to the ideas of Mahatma Gandhi, the central figure of the Indian nationalist movement. His great achievement was his successful use of non-violent resistance on a mass scale. This passive resistance to British rule, symbolized by Gandhi's own public fasting, was merely one aspect of his general philosophy of seeking truth through love and non-violence—the doctrine of *satyagraha*.

Gandhi's campaign was successful, and a bare six months before his own assassination Indian independence came into effect. The problems arising from the application of nationalist principles to an area like India immediately became apparent. It had long been evident that the large Moslem minority would not willingly associate themselves in a state dominated by Hindus. Indeed, as early as 1906 the All-India Moslem League was established as a body quite distinct from the Congress. And so in 1947 a separate Moslem state, consisting of the predominantly Islamic areas of East Bengal and the West Punjab, Sind, and Baluchistan area, was established under the name of Pakistan. The act of dividing the sub-continent had caused considerable violence, disruption, and ill-feeling. In 1947 millions of people trekked into the state of their religion—Hindus to India and Moslems to Pakistan. Bloody clashes occurred between the two streams, especially in the Punjab; many people also died from famine and disease, which inevitably ravaged the uprooted hordes of peasant families. Moreover, since their foundation, the two states have been at loggerheads—over the use of the waters of the precious rivers that run through both lands, over numerous frontier disputes, and, most serious of all, over the possession of Kashmir. This northern province has a mixed population, though it is predominantly Moslem. Its ruler in 1947, however, was Hindu. The quarrel over the area became so serious that fighting broke out between India and Pakistan, and the already precarious economies of the two countries were forced to bear the added strain of a heavy military expenditure. That particular quarrel has at present subsided, though Kashmir is still partitioned; agreement has also been reached on irrigation plans; nevertheless, relations are still very strained.

The painful birth of India and Pakistan was not paralleled by similar violence when the island of Ceylon was created an independent Dominion. Nevertheless, the latent divisions between the Hindu Tamils and the Buddhist Sinhalese could not be kept in check for long under a native Government. The six million Sinhalese felt themselves unfairly treated in comparison with their numbers, and Mr Bandaranaike was placed in office to rectify this. The reaction to this policy, especially the decision to make Sinhalese the only official language, was violent: serious communal riots broke out in 1958. A year later the Prime Minister was assassinated by a Buddhist monk, many think because the Sinhalese policy was not being pursued quickly enough. The idea of a united Ceylonese nation, cultivated during the colonial period, has been shown to be a myth. Moreover, the cleavage is a wide one, the result of four major differentiating factors: race, language, religion, and geographical separation.

There is one final point of interest to be made about nationalism in India, Pakistan, and Ceylon. They are determined to be fully independent. Although remaining members of the Commonwealth, India and Pakistan have insisted on becoming republics, and there has been a strong movement in Ceylon in the same direction. Furthermore, Mr Nehru pursued a fairly consistent policy of neutralism or non-alignment with the Communist and democratic blocs opposing each other in the Cold War. In this way he maintained and even enhanced his national independence and increased his strength by holding a central position between the two systems.

It must not be forgotten that Russia is not only a European state, but also important both as an Asiatic and an imperialist Power. She has over centuries expanded westward into Europe and, on a far larger scale, eastward across the steppes into Asia as far as the borders of Persia, India, and China. Nor must it be thought that the imperialist policy of the Tsars has been discontinued. For all their anti-imperialist propaganda the Russians remain an essentially imperialist Power. As John Bowle has written, "The revolutionaries inherited the historic conflict of Teuton and Slav, and the legacy of Tsarist imperialism in Asia."[32] It is, indeed, more instructive in many ways to view Communist policy from the perspective of nationalism than Marxism; such a view may, in fact, be more accurate. "The Kremlin's bid for world domination," to quote John Bowle again, "whatever its ideological propaganda, is founded upon Great Russian solidarity, upon Russian isolationism and Messianic feeling for a 'Third Rome,' and upon the territories won by Tsarist conquest."[33]

This is not the place to deal with the Russian domination of Eastern Europe and the consequent rise of National Communism: this question is dealt with in Chapter 3 of this book. We are concerned here rather with the Soviet Union's Asiatic provinces. Taking the Soviet Union as a whole, and if we accept Ukrainians and White Russians as being of a separate nationality, Great Russians represent only about half of the total population. In Asia there are important numbers, reaching millions, of Uzbeks, Tartars, and Kazakhs.

The Russians frequently claim that they have solved the nationalist problem in their empire. After all, all the fifteen Union Republics that constitute the U.S.S.R. have the right, laid down in the Constitution, to secede, and none of them has! Nationalism among the minority races has not, of course, been killed, though it is true that it is being steadily weakened. In some instances the Russians have resorted to full-scale extermination, especially in the 1943–45 period, when various autonomous regions, especially of Turkish race, were eliminated. The Karachais, Balkars, and Chechens of the northern

Caucasus area, the Kalmuk and German enclaves on the Volga, and the Turkish people of the Crimea were all eliminated as autonomous regions because of their hostility to the Russian Government during the War. Not all the people were killed, it is true; many were deported to other areas. This, indeed, is the favourite method of the Russians. A strongly nationalist area can be weakened either by the mass transportation of the people to other areas or of Russians into the area. Vast numbers of Russians have, in fact, been sent into the Asiatic provinces to develop industry, encourage agriculture, and tap the mineral resources. The 'immigration' is being undertaken on such a scale that it has been estimated that only half the population of Kazakhstan are now Kazakhs; the rest are Russians. Finally, and more commonly in recent years, the Russians are using more humane methods of encouraging local cultures and spreading propaganda against political movements. N. A. Smirnov, for example, has written attacking "the reactionary, anti-popular essence of the ideology of Pan-Arabism and Pan-Turkism, used primarily by the American imperialists to enslave the peoples of the East."[34]

While keeping their own subject nations in a decidedly subordinate position the Russians have been an important factor in inciting other nationalist movements throughout the continent of Asia. Indeed, an attack on the colonies of the capitalist countries was the central theme of Lenin's theory of imperialism. For Lenin the insurrection of native peoples against their imperialist masters was an essential phase in the development of the world revolution. And so nationalist movements were to be given every encouragement, not for their own sake, but for the essential place they held in the Communist strategy. The programme got under way very soon after the achievement of the Bolshevik Revolution in Russia. In 1920 a Congress of the Peoples of the Orient was held in Baku, for example, while in 1921 the Communist University of the Toilers of the East was established at Sverdlovsk to train professional revolutionaries.

The Soviet propaganda and agitation were, however, in many ways too successful. Many, such as Nasser and Kassem, saw through the Russian plan to use the nationalist movements for their own, imperialist ends; others, especially in Africa, have achieved independence and have succeeded in retaining their freedom from Communist interference; finally, where a nationalist revolution has turned into a Communist Government—in China—the nationalist sentiment has remained very strong, and China now presents a serious challenge to Russian dominance in the Asian continent. And since the two Powers have both looked upon such march-lands as Manchuria, Mongolia, and Sinkiang as potential spheres of influence, the rivalry is in more tangible forms than mere desire for prestige.

Although at the end of the last century it was thought that China would be partitioned among the great colonizing powers in accordance with the precedent of Africa, nothing more was achieved than the recognition of spheres of influence. Considering the long cultural tradition and the racial homogeneity of the Chinese, it is not surprising that a nationalist movement rose against the dominant position of the Western peoples in their land. In 1900 Chinese xenophobia burst forth in the Boxer Rebellion, and eleven years later Sun Yat-sen founded the truly nationalist Kuomintang Government, having founded the party in 1895. The nationalist policy of integrating the Chinese peoples into a united nation-state, a policy which was pursued in the inter-War years, has been continued by the Communists since their advent to power in 1949. And once again we see the two aspects of nationalism clashing in the expansionist and unifying policies of Peking and the desires for self-determination in Sinkiang and especially Tibet. More recently Chinese nationalism has taken on a dangerously expansionist attitude against India and the independent buffer-states of the Himalaya. Encroachment into Indian territory is serious enough, but if Peking is to adopt such a policy extensively the existence of Chinese nationals throughout South-east Asia may be used as an excuse for intervention in any of the states with large Chinese populations, such as Malaya, Singapore, Thailand, and Indonesia. There are over ten million Chinese in the area.

Chinese nationalism was given a greater upsurge by China's clash with the imperialist designs of Japan, in the first place in the war of 1894–95 and more importantly that of 1937–45. The rise of Japanese nationalism was, indeed, one of the most important events in the history of Asia in the half-century before her collapse in 1945. Of all backward peoples the Japanese learnt the most quickly and effectively to copy and use Western techniques, both against other Asiatics and against the West itself. And the nationalism they developed has been well described as "the most fanatical, primitive and ruthless of Asian ideologies."[35] Since the teeming population could scarcely be contained in their moderately sized archipelago, it was inevitable that Japanese nationalism should immediately assume an expansionist guise. Starting with modest ambitions against her immediate neighbours, Japan at first took Formosa from China, the southern part of Sakhalin from Russia, and established control over the virtually independent peninsula of Korea. After the First World War she obtained the former German colonies of the Caroline, Marshall, and Mariana islands as mandates. Then came her great war with China when she captured Manchuria and vast stretches of China proper. Finally, during the Second World War she overran Indochina, Thailand, Burma, Malaya, the East Indies, the Philippines, and various British and American Pacific islands.

The Japanese conquests during the four-year war with Britain, America, and their French and Dutch allies in the Pacific and South-east Asia had a vital effect on the embryonic nationalisms of the area. In the first place, the conquered peoples were subjected to economic and social chaos, which inevitably predisposed them to support revolutionary movements. Secondly, they were made to realize the weakness of the colonial Powers. Finally, they tasted the flavour of independence by being given important positions in the Japanese administrative system. The result has been the emergence to independent statehood of the previous British territories of Burma, Malaya, and Singapore; the former Dutch East Indies, now Indonesia; French Indochina; and the sometime American Philippine Islands.

But although the Japanese occupation was the catalyst which liberated the countries of South-east Asia, the so-called 'nations' which have thus emerged are misnamed. The frontiers between them represent not distinct ethnic groupings, but the results of convenient arrangements made by colonial Powers. Many of these 'nations' contain large Chinese minorities—there are, in fact, two and a half million Chinese in Malaya, for example, where there are only three million Malays. The artificial nature of the Republic of Indonesia is made evident by the unwieldiness of this massive archipelago of three thousand islands as a political unit, the difficulty the late Dr Sukarno had to subject the whole area to the authority of Djakarta, and the dispute with the Dutch over the control of the western portion of New Guinea (or West Irian). Stanley Mayes summed up the bewildering complexity of the area when he said:

> Thai as the name of an ethnic group, applies not only to the principal race of Siam but also to two-thirds of the people of Laos, to the Lao tribes of Viet-Nam and to the Shans of Burma. South Viet-Nam has 400,000 Cambodians, and Cambodia almost as many Vietnamese. Add

to this mixture of races a variety of languages, different alphabets, and all the chief religions. You will see then why nationalism, the most powerful ferment of our times, is in south-east Asia inevitably a more complex and more unstable kind of brew than in other parts of the world.[36]

The Middle East

During the 1950's interest in nationalism was focused largely on the Middle East; for in the Far East nationalism had passed its most vociferous stage, in Black Africa it was only just developing as a vital force, while in the Arab countries it reached the peak of its assertiveness. We may almost say, for example, that Colonel Nasser was the very type of modern nationalist. Furthermore, the success of Arab nationalism needs no more proof than the list of states that have achieved national independence during the past half-century. It includes: the various states of the Arabian peninsula, Egypt, Iraq, Syria, the Lebanon, Libya, Jordan, the Sudan, Morocco, Tunisia, and Algeria. In addition, Israel has been established as an independent Jewish state, and British and American economic control has been considerably weakened in the whole area.

Nationalism in the Middle East has been largely of the aggressive, self-confident kind. As Walter Laqueur has pointed out,

> The nationalist aspiration that these countries received was thus mainly of the post- and anti-liberal era. This nationalism is distinguished by the overestimation of one's own nation and the denigration of others, the lack of the spirit of self-criticism and responsibility, an ambivalent appraisal of the destiny of one's nation based on a feeling of inferiority, and a general tendency to attribute anything wrong with one's nation to the evil-doing of others, who should consequently be fought.[37]

These 'evil-doers' in the Middle East are the imperialist Powers, Britain, France, and, to a lesser extent, America and Israel.*

The self-assertive and fiercely anti-Western nature of Arab nationalism is a reflection of its basic inferiority complex, itself the result of centuries of subjection to foreign rule. Until the nineteenth century the whole of the Arab world was part of the extensive, though by then crumbling, empire of the Ottoman Turks. During the nineteenth century and the years before the First World War France

---

* The importance of Islam in Arab nationalism is dealt with in Chapter 5.

took over the Maghreb, Italy gained Libya, while Britain, almost in spite of herself, acquired control of Egypt and the Sudan. During the 1914–18 War the remaining Arab territories, with the assistance of such variants of the British military genius as Lawrence and Allenby, managed to wrench themselves free from the authority of Constantinople. But nascent Arab nationalism suffered a sharp disappointment in the decision of the 1919 peace conference to place Syria and Lebanon under French, and Palestine, Transjordan, and Iraq under British, administration—though it is true that most of the Arabian peninsula achieved independence. The prestige of Britain especially was lowered, as the Arabs felt that it was through Britain's lack of good faith that their independence was snatched from their grasp.

British rule was very grudgingly accepted in Iraq, though the opposition had much of its potential sting removed by the obvious speed with which Britain planned the establishment of independence. This was finally achieved in 1932. But the nationalist movement did not then come to an end, as British influence was still strong and the armed forces still retained bases in the country. This anglophobia burst forth in a Fascist-inspired rebellion in 1941, led by Rashid Ali. The rising failed, and Iraq was politically quiet for the rest of the War under the premiership of Nuri es-Said, a great friend of Britain.

In the Levant during the inter-War period the French mandate of the Lebanon and the British of Transjordan were generally accepted by the inhabitants. The French position in Syria, however, was never a happy one. The British arranged for the independence of both Syria and the Lebanon in 1941 to prevent the Vichy Government from exercising control over the area. The situation in Palestine was very complex. It was an Arab country, but was placed under British mandate. Moreover, the mandate incorporated the Balfour Declaration of 1917 and obliged Britain to "place the country under such political, administrative and economic conditions as will secure the establishment of the Jewish national home, while at the same time safeguarding the civil and religious rights of all the inhabitants of Palestine."[38] The Declaration itself had angered the Arabs, but their tempers were seriously roused when Jewish refugees flooded into Palestine as a consequence of Nazi persecution in the nineteen-thirties. This led, in fact, to a serious Arab revolt in the country in 1936–39. A British White Paper published in 1939 held out prospects of a settlement, and there was little trouble during the War.

From the time of Louis-Philippe the French steadily acquired control over the Maghreb—first in Algeria, then in Tunisia, and finally in Morocco. There was little evidence of truly nationalist opposition to the French until after the 1939–45 War. It is true that the Néo-Destour movement was active as early as 1934 and that the Moroccan Istiqlal Party was formed in 1943, but the French position was not seriously challenged.

The situation in Egypt, however, was very different. Indeed, the Egyptian resistance to British influence was the most highly developed of all Arab nationalist movements. The presence of British troops and officials in Egypt after 1918 led to violent disturbances organized by Saad Zaghlul, founder of the nationalist Wafd Party, and the situation became so serious that the British Government had to send Allenby as High Commissioner. He induced the Government to grant Egyptian independence in 1922. But a mere proclamation was not enough, and, in fact, there was little or no change in Egypt's real position. Four Reserved Points, allowing Britain continued extensive authority over such questions as the Sudan, communications, defence, and foreign residents, and the continued exclusion of Egypt from the League of Nations kept her in a position of subservience more restricting than that binding the Dominions. And so demonstrations continued, reaching their climax in the murder of Sir Lee Stack in 1924 and the subsequent severe reprisals. Relations between the countries remained uneasy until the common fear of Mussolini drew them together in the treaty concluded in 1936, by which British troops were to be restricted to the Canal Zone. Thus, during the War, except for an uneasy atmosphere resulting from the forcible imposition by the British of a Wafd Government in 1942, the internal British position in Egypt was secure.

Although Turkey is an Islamic country, the history of Turkish nationalism is quite distinct from the movements in the Arab countries. The Turkish nationalist movement suddenly became a potent force under the leadership of Mustafa Kemal (Kemal Atatürk) when, after suffering the mutilation of both its European and Arabian territories, Turkey had to bear the ultimate humiliation of invasion by the Greeks, who claimed sovereignty over the Greek peoples of Asia Minor round Smyrna. The Turks were roused to unwonted activity and routed their enemies, and the following year, 1923, the Treaty of Lausanne satisfied nationalism by arranging for a compulsory exchange of populations. The spirit of nationalism was also felt internally with Atatürk's widespread schemes of reform. His language reform was particularly important and typical of the nationalist outlook. "Nationalism," to quote Colonel Hostler, "the central pillar of Kemalist ideology, found its expression in a strong demand for the purification of the Ottoman language by replacing its foreign elements with genuine Turkish words, old or new."[39]

The Jews had to wait thirty years for the Balfour Declaration to be put into effect, for it was not until May 1948 that the state of Israel came into existence. It has been the centre of fierce nationalism almost from the day of its birth. The Jews, on their part, under vigorous political leadership, have been busy during the past two decades building a nation. Israel has developed enormously in economic and certainly military strength—and in population, which has trebled since 1948. The Law of Return of July 1950, which gives every Jew the right to immigrate to Israel, has assisted this growth. Moreover, the heterogeneous people have been given unity not only by their common race, but by the common danger from external attack.

This danger to the Israelis comes from the hostility of the Arab world. To the Jews themselves and many people in the West the creation of Israel meant the return of the Jewish people to their homeland after an exile of two millennia; but to the Asian people in general Israel is an imperialist outpost in their continent, and to the Arabs in particular an unwarranted plantation of alien people on land that is rightfully theirs. The state of Israel was born to war, being almost immediately attacked by Egypt, Iraq, Jordan, Lebanon, and Syria. Nevertheless, in spite of the Arab advantage in numbers, the opposing sides soon found themselves at stalemate. In fact, when the Arab-Israeli war came to an end in 1949 the distribution of territory between the contestants was much the same as had been laid down by the United Nations. The Israelis, however, had lost a strip of coastal territory on the Egyptian frontier round Gaza, and this has been the scene of frequent minor clashes. The uneasy truce has been broken more violently twice since 1949: by the Israeli attack on Egypt in collusion with Britain and France in 1956, and by the Arab-Israeli six-day war of 1967, which has renewed the tension in the area.

In the immediate post-War period France was faced with national ist demands for independence throughout her North African territories. The problem had an unsettling effect on French politics and was a constant drain on the French economy, and so where the situation was relatively simple, in Morocco and Tunisia, independence was granted in 1956. But the complexity of the Algerian question postponed a satisfactory solution until 1962.

Disturbances in Tunisia continued throughout the post-War decade. They were undertaken largely by the Néo-Destour, a party fortunate in having as their leader Habib Bourguiba, who has been described as "an African nationalist of genuine stature, a man who might fairly be compared to leaders like Ho Chi Minh—though he is not a Communist—or even Jawaharlal Nehru."[40] A realistic view of the situation was taken by Mendès-France when he became Prime Minister, and in September 1955 an all-Tunisian Cabinet was formed, followed by the formal recognition of Tunisian independence in March of the next year.

The success of Tunisia gave added encouragement to Morocco and Algeria. The hostility of the Istiqlal movement in Morocco, firmly supported by the Sultan Mohammed V, came to a head in 1953 when the French deposed and exiled the Sultan. There followed serious anti-French riots, particularly violent in August 1955. The exiled Sultan was therefore restored, and Morocco emerged, together with Tunisia, as an independent state in March 1956. Spanish Morocco and the international port of Tangier were included.

The granting of independence to Tunisia and Morocco required no more than the acceptance by the French Government that the colonial connexion was no longer tenable. The situation in Algeria was not similar. In the first place, there was the long political tradition that was expressed in the incorporation of the coastal area as an integral part of Metropolitan France on a par with Corsica or Brittany, for example. Secondly, there was the economic question of the possible development of oilfields in the interior. Finally, and the most vexed question of all, there was the problem of the French settlers. There were approximately a million Europeans in Algeria, and they have been fearful of an Arab-Berber-dominated independent state. Virtual civil war raged for seven years, a war actively supported and encouraged by Morocco, Tunisia, and Egypt. The problem sapped French resources and was the immediate occasion of the downfall of the Fourth Republic. Yet, in spite of the seriousness of the problem and the promises and plans of de Gaulle, the French

President took three years to reach a practical solution. Nor was this problem of mere parochial significance. The Algerian war provided fine propaganda for those who wish to depict the Western democracies as heartless imperialists. Moreover, so successful was this propaganda that France's allies were sincerely embarrassed by the situation.

The Kingdom of Jordan that came into existence in 1946 is, of course, an artificial nation. The main direction of Jordan's nationalist hostility is against Israel, the territorial conflict with whom led till 1967 to the partition of the city of Jerusalem between the two states. There are, however, certain strong elements hostile to Britain also. These elements prevented the adherence of Jordan to the Baghdad Pact, and in 1956 secured the dismissal of the British General Glubb Pasha from his command of the Arab Legion and the abrogation of the Anglo-Jordanian alliance. A still more artificial nation, perhaps, is the Lebanon, with its mixture of pro-Western Christians and pro-Arab Moslems. The realization of the artificiality of the prevailing frontiers in the Arab lands gives a firm basis for the ideas of the Pan-Arab movement, of which more will need to be said later. At the moment we need to note only the attempted federation of Syria with Egypt in the United Arab Republic in 1958 as a notable example of this idea in practice.

The dream of a united Arab world seemed for many years to be frustrated by the rivalry between Egypt and Iraq. For a long time after the War Iraq maintained friendly relations with the West, and even entered a military alliance—the Baghdad Pact—sponsored by Britain. When Nasser, so evidently disliked by the West, created his United Arab Republic in February 1958, Iraq made an abortive attempt to counter this by a rival union with Jordan. The close relations with the West, symbolized by the Baghdad Pact, made the monarchy and Nuri es-Said unpopular with the nationalist forces in the country, especially the army. The storm broke in 1958 when revolution swept away both monarchy and the elder statesman Nuri, and the Western alliance was renounced. But the rivalry with Egypt remained, for the supporter of Iraq's incorporation into the United Arab Republic, Colonel Arif, was defeated and executed by his rival, General Kassem. By 1959 Iraqi nationalism had led the country into a delicate position: it remained aloof from the Egyptian-controlled Pan-Arab movement, it had broken its connexion with Britain, and the only other possible friend, Russia, had dangerous interests in the area.

By its geographical position, comparative wealth, and ambitious leadership Egypt stands out as the natural leader of Arab nationalism. And she has assumed this rôle without hesitation. Before we deal with the Pan-Arab movement, however, it is necessary to take a brief look at the growth of the nationalist spirit inside Egypt since the War.

The movement against the British position in the Canal Zone started seriously in 1951 with the creation of a 'liberation army,' with which the fanatical Moslem Brotherhood were associated. Mob violence reached its climax on January 26, 1952, the terror of which day has earned it the name "Black Saturday." The nationalist elements in the army were not satisfied with the Government, and in the July of the same year effected a *coup d'état*, overthrowing King Farouk. One of the leaders of this military revolt, General Neguib, then became Prime Minister, and in 1953 President. The next year, however, he was replaced by Colonel Nasser, who had, in fact, been the real force behind the coup.

Gamal Abdel Nasser was born in a village in Upper Egypt in 1918 of quite humble parentage. He entered the army and organized the Free Officers' Movement, which was the basis of the 1952 revolt. From the time he took control until his death in 1970 he showed himself to be capable of both cool, calculated moves and emotional and visionary appeals. His action in nationalizing the Suez Canal in 1956 reveals this: "In nationalising the Suez Canal Company he sought both to answer the Anglo-American blow to his political prestige and to find the money for the High Dam without going to Russia for it."[41] Two years before this he had revealed himself as a tough negotiator when making arrangements for the withdrawal of British troops from the Canal Zone.

But Nasser's nationalism did not stop at insistence on Egyptian independence and prestige or the modernization of the state. He toyed with the idea of placing Egypt at the head of a great Pan-Arab Empire of Arab peoples of the Moslem faith, stretching from the Atlantic Ocean to the Persian Gulf. These ideas have been set down in his autobiographical *Philosophy of Revolution*. But the concept of an Egyptian-dominated Arab empire did not originate with Nasser. When he took over control of Egyptian affairs he inherited a policy of supremacy among the Arab states that had been exercised by the anti-Zionist Arab League founded in Cairo in 1945. This League is a loose confederation of most Arab states designed to forward the interests and cohesion of the Arab world against the colonial Powers and Israel. Nasser gave the idea dynamic leadership and introduced modern propaganda methods by the use of Press and radio. His practical achievements were quite impressive. He introduced widespread economic and social reforms in a country where they have long been overdue, he secured the evacuation of British troops and the control of the Suez Canal, and his propaganda campaigns assisted the nationalist movements throughout the Arab world. But he had many setbacks too. His army was ignominiously defeated in the Sinai campaign against Israel in 1956 and again in 1967, he failed to gain control over the Sudan, Saudi Arabia remained hostile, and the union with Syria foundered. At one time too he seemed to have ambitions of leading a resurgent Africa: "We cannot under any circumstances," he wrote in his *Philosophy of Revolution*, "remain aloof from the terrible and sanguinary struggle going on in Africa today between five million whites and 200,000,000 Africans.... The peoples of Africa will continue to look to us, who guard the northern gate and who constitute their link with all the outside world."[42]

AFRICA

For the present generation the most exciting aspect of nationalism is its emergence in Africa. There is perhaps no more remarkable political occurrence in the whole international scene. As William Clark said in 1957, "The lights are being lit all over Africa; we shall not see them put out in our time."[43] The African movements were stimulated by the success of the Asian nations in the post-War period, and one may notice features in common between the two continents. But there are also interesting peculiarities in the African movements.

Besides the essentially European ideas of equality and national self-determination, there has developed the concept of *négritude*—a pride in the essential 'African-ness' of Negro culture and traditions. Indeed, nowhere in the world is it more unrealistic to think in terms of discrete nation-states. For the current frontiers are the results of quite arbitrary diplomatic decisions. There have been, it is true, attempts to identify modern nations with medieval kingdoms, but there has, of course, been no continuity of development. Thus Soudan and the Gold Coast perhaps hope to reflect the medieval greatness of the empires of Mali and Ghana respectively. The present frontiers have no ethnological justification. Either countries are collections of distinct tribes, as in Nigeria, where Ibos, Yorubas, and Hausas live together in an uneasy federalism; or tribes sprawl, like the Somalis of Somalia, Ethiopia, and Kenya, beyond the confines of any one state. The realization of the artificiality of the present frontiers, together with the Africans' sense of weakness, have led to a number of schemes for unification—between Ghana and Guinea, Senegal and Soudan, among the British East African territories, for example. Few have proved permanent. Similarly, much more ambitious plans for continent-wide Pan-African union have met with little success (see pp. 197-98). Indeed although there are good reasons for co-operation—a common colour, common cause against remaining white imperialism, the relative weakness of the individual states—there are very serious obstacles too—conflicting race, language, tradition, and religion, and the problems of vast size, primitive communications, and political immaturity.

The political immaturity of Africa is inevitable. Few Africans have been able to take a really active part in the administration of their countries, and the vast majority have had little or no education at all. The nationalist movements, then, have of necessity quite narrow bases. A certain amount of nationalist fervour can be stirred up among the discontented de-tribalized workers in the towns; but the core of the movement has been the intellectual middle class—Senghor the poet, Danquah the anthropologist, Banda and Houphouet-Boigny (both doctors), Nyerere the teacher, Azikiwe the journalist. Yet, narrow as the leadership has been, it has achieved remarkable results. By 1966 thirty-eight countries throughout the whole continent had achieved independence; and, apart from the bloody civil war in Algeria, the anarchy of the Congo, and the Nigerian-Biafran civil war, there has been remarkably little violence.

The movement away from colonial status has been undertaken with incredible speed. It is interesting to compare the attitudes of the imperial Powers to this revolution. As early as 1944 the Brazzaville proposals recognized the eligibility of Africans for French citizenship. In 1958 de Gaulle produced the idea of a French "Community," though no obstacles were placed in the way of the African colonies when each in turn during 1958–60 demanded complete independence. Indeed, generous economic aid has been continued. The year 1960 was, indeed, that of the "wind of change"—a phrase used by the British Prime Minister, Mr Macmillan, in encouraging the independence movements. The British Government pursued a more gradual policy than the French, steadily preparing their colonies for the political maturity needed for independence. In contrast, the Portuguese have refused to concede the principle of independence for their colonies of Angola, Mozambique, and Guinea, and are holding down the nationalist movements with military force.

Where, as in the bulk of Africa, the European colonists have been in a small minority the metropolitan Government has been faced with a straightforward decision. The situation was complicated, however, in Algeria and Rhodesia, where the white settlers were present in large numbers. But if Rhodesia has presented the British Government with a very difficult problem the complexity of the situation is less tangled than in the Republic of South Africa, where the white-black division itself contains the inner tensions between Afrikaner and English and Bantu, Asian, and Coloured.

Of all the areas of black Africa, the western portion achieved independence most quickly. There were a number of reasons for this: several of the territories, like Ghana and Nigeria, were economically advanced; there were few white settlers clinging to control; and the early achievement of independence by Ghana (1957) and Guinea (1958) encouraged their neighbours.

Three of the West African states should, perhaps, be given special mention. During the early years of the African independence movement Ghana was the centre of attention, largely owing to the dynamic, if controversial, leadership of Dr Nkrumah. In 1950 he became the first Prime Minister, and ten years later, when Ghana became a republic, its first President. He also had the distinction of leading the first black African state from colonial status to independence. Furthermore, he developed distinctive policies which he pursued with a forceful personality. In economics he followed a programme of socialism; in internal politics he set himself up as the *Osagyefo* (the Redeemer) and flung his opponents into gaol; in his relations with the rest of Africa he started and tried to develop an effective

Pan-African movement for unity; the modern Pan-African movement may indeed be said to have started with the Accra Conference of December 1958.

Nkrumah's socialism led to close ties with Guinea, led by a kindred spirit, Sékou Touré. When in 1958 de Gaulle offered the African colonies independence or a new relationship with France Guinea alone claimed her independence, even though she would thus stand to lose vital French economic aid. "Guinea prefers poverty in freedom to riches in slavery," declared Sékou Touré. It was a fine flourish, and it is not without significance that all the other French African colonies (except the tiny Somali territory) acquired their independence within two years.

Guinea is a small state of just over 3 million. Nigeria in contrast has a population of about 60 million. Because of its size, wealth, and complexity the development of Nigeria as an independent nation is of great significance for Africa. A federal system of government was developed by the British before handing over power in 1960. The initiator of the Nigerian nationalist movement, Dr Azikiwe, became the first Governor-General.

In Eastern and Central Africa the transition to independence has been less smooth. Tanganyika, it is true, has been fortunate in avoiding difficulties, in large measure because of the wise guidance of Julius Nyerere, who led the country to independence in 1961. Each of the other East African territories is less fortunate. Somalia —formed in 1960 by the union of the former Italian and British territories—has irredentist claims against its two neighbours, Ethiopia and Kenya. Uganda has had to struggle with the problem of the semi-autonomous kingdom of Buganda, which is one of its constituent parts. Finally, in this area is Kenya, which witnessed the fiercest nationalist struggle against the white man. Resentment against the white settlers was at least a partial cause of the dreadful Mau Mau terrorism of 1952–56. Progress to independence was delayed by fear, an emotion expressed in personal terms by the continued detention, for alleged implication in the Mau Mau movement, of Jomo Kenyatta, the doyen of Kenyan nationalism. He finally emerged as the first Prime Minister of an independent Kenya in 1963. While still under British control the East African territories of Kenya, Uganda, Tanganyika, and Zanzibar had developed a useful programme of economic co-operation. But hopes of fuller integration have not been realized, except for the union between Tanganyika and Zanzibar (Tanzania).

During the late nineteenth century the basins of the Congo and Zambezi came under the control of the Belgian and British crowns. In the Congo the Belgians refused to allow any political development. They could not, however, insulate this vast territory from the nationalist activity in neighbouring areas. Serious disturbances occurred in Leopoldville in 1959. Patrice Lumumba emerged as the outstanding Congolese leader, and when the Belgians suddenly conceded independence in 1960 he became Prime Minister. But since the Congolese were quite untrained and the Belgians had made no preparations for the withdrawal of their authority and administration, Lumumba was faced with an unenviable task. The situation, indeed, soon dissolved into anarchy (see p. 196).

Belgian policy towards the Congo in the 1950's lacked intelligence; British policy towards the Rhodesias and Nyasaland lacked sympathetic imagination. These three territories were linked in the Central African Federation in 1953. Under the leadership firstly of Lord Malvern, then Sir Roy Welensky, it was hoped that the federation would become an effective economic unit and that a political policy of racial partnership would be possible. Such a programme, however, ignored the hostility of the African population, who saw in racial partnership merely Apartheid writ large. The programme also ignored the difference between Northern Rhodesia and Nyasaland, on the one hand, where there were but a handful of whites, and Southern Rhodesia, on the other, where the white settlers were (and still are) a powerful force. Disturbances broke in 1959, especially serious in Nyasaland, where Dr Hastings Banda led the demand for secession from the federation. Independence for Northern Rhodesia and Nyasaland became a matter of time. Independence for Southern Rhodesia became a matter of balancing the interests of the entrenched 200,000 whites against four million blacks.

The situation in (Southern) Rhodesia is becoming increasingly more comparable with the condition of the Republic of South Africa than with its northern neighbours. In South Africa, supported by a religious sense of mission and fully backed by the Dutch Reformed Church, the Afrikaner Nationalist Party has developed during the past two decades an increasingly rigid policy towards the 80 per cent non-white elements of the population (African Bantus, Asians, and mixed-blood Coloureds, the Japanese being considered 'white' for political reasons, while the Chinese are affected by Apartheid). In theory, the non-whites are to be allowed to develop their own ways of life in areas of the country specially reserved for them. In practice, however, only a small portion of the poorer parts of the country are allocated for this purpose; complete separation (the literal meaning of Apartheid) is impossible because whites and non-whites are economically inter-dependent; and the Afrikaners, especially during the administration of Dr Verwoerd (1958–66), have developed a totalitarian mentality and police-state system.

The year 1960, which saw so much activity in Africa, will be long remembered as the year of Sharpeville, when a peaceful African demonstration against the oppressive pass laws was broken up by police shooting. Nearly one hundred Africans were killed. By this time Chief Albert Luthuli had become leader of the African National Congress, and his constant campaign for the use of passive-resistance policies led to his being awarded the Nobel Peace Prize for 1960. But with white-dominated lands to the north (Angola, Rhodesia, Mozambique) and a highly organized political police within, South Africa is likely to remain the citadel of white supremacy in Africa for a long time to come.

Conclusions

Now that we have analysed the growth and expansion of nationalism as a political force we are in a position to make a judgment on the idea. The modern mind is divided between belief in the righteousness of nationalism and abhorrence at its excesses; for both the values and the dangers are undeniable.

Support for the idea of nationalism comes largely from liberals who believe that freedom and self-determination along nationalist lines are inextricably connected. The great English Liberal J. S. Mill voiced this opinion in his *Considerations on Representative Government*. "It is in general a necessary condition of free institutions," he wrote, "that the boundaries of governments should coincide with those of nationalities."[44] Moreover, inasmuch as nationalist programmes are demands for government by the native peoples, they are products of political movements that are popular in nature. They demand, therefore, a public consciousness of, and interest in, politics.

And an enlightened popular awareness of political issues is surely a condition to be desired.

The politician, however, is not the only person with an interest in nationalism. For the awareness of nationality has at times originated as a literary movement, and at others the political aspect has been boosted by a consciously nationalist literary school. The scholar, therefore, considers nationalism as being of value. German nationality was discovered by the literary, philological, and historical work of such people as Herder and the Grimm brothers; while in our own day our knowledge of African history is being increased by the attempts to give the African nationalist movements respectable historical foundations.

The attempts to discover the cultural unity and traditions of a nation are valuable tasks. After all, the nation is, in essence, a cultural unit. Indeed, it is the attempt to give what is essentially a cultural entity a political context that many people see as the origin of the evils that derive from nationalism. The two virtues of pride in one's national culture and loyalty to one's country can, in fact, when combined, lead to the vice of national bigotry.

This desire to identify nation and state would not be so dangerous if it were not necessary, in general, for the state to be a homogeneous geographical bloc; for nations are rarely to be found in such units. Throughout history races and nationalities have become inextricably mixed and widely scattered. Professor Macartney, writing in 1934, was quite clear about this; he wrote: "In its pursuit of the chimera of the national state Europe has entered upon a path beset with dangers to itself. It has set itself a false ideal, and one which, right or wrong, it can never achieve.... Minorities will continue to exist."[45] Eastern Europe and South-east Asia are areas in which nationalities have perhaps become most dispersed. In such conditions national self-determination becomes a trick with mirrors, in which one can discern nations within nations. In Cyprus, for example, the Greek Cypriot revolt against British rule provoked a Turkish nationalist revolt against the Greeks. Nor is such a situation peculiar to the contemporary world. In 1848 the Magyar rising against Austria was soon followed by a Croat uprising against Hungarian rule. Even in such a well-established and integrated nation-state as Britain, Welsh and Scottish minorities have developed separatist ambitions.

If, however, the racial facts do not fit the political theory attempts can be made to alter the awkward facts. By migration, deportation, or extermination a multi-racial state can be made a homogeneous nation. It was this slavery to theory that led to the removal of the German inhabitants from the Oder-Neisse territory when the frontiers of Poland were redrawn after the Second World War. The world is, in fact, strewn with millions of refugees, most of whom have been uprooted in the cause of nationalism. Thus has a political idea become the vehicle of inhumanity.

Nationalism is not only inhumane; it is inefficient too. The claims of the nation-state, as Professor Brogan has said, "were palpably absurd in a world of natural great economic units. Its moral and intellectual claims were preposterous in a world that was won over to objective science. The destruction of the natural unity of the Danube Valley was the great crime of the Treaty of Versailles."[46] Economic chaos indeed resulted in the Succession States. More recently the economies of West Pakistan and North-west India, which rely on a common irrigation system, have also been adversely affected by national rivalry and jealousy. Nationalism can also run counter to geographical and strategic considerations. For example, the annexation of the Sudeten German lands beyond the Bohemian mountains in 1938 in accordance with the Munich Agreement rendered Czechoslovakia defenceless before the German attack in 1939.

Finally, nationalism increases the incidence of war and civil strife. Once a nation that is ruled by another becomes conscious of its own nationality and subjection it will endeavour to achieve independent statehood. And if peaceful persuasion fails force will be resorted to. Moreover, since the frontiers of no nation are clearly demarcated there are ample opportunities for conflict between nations over disputed areas. For, as plebiscites are notoriously unreliable, there is no indisputable method of deciding whether, for example, Alsace should be a part of Germany or France or Transylvania part of Hungary or Rumania. Most serious of all, however, is the tendency to aggression in some nations. Frederick Hertz has gone so far as to say that "National megalomania naturally is the greatest enemy of mankind."[47] It is difficult to explain why nationalism in some contexts takes on this aggressive nature, though it has been suggested that, "Broadly speaking, the longer a nation has been established and the more secure it feels itself, the more profound and the less demonstrative its nationalism will be."[48]

*

In analysing the theory and practical application of nationalism a great variety of experience has been discussed, and the student may be forgiven for emerging somewhat confused as to the true essence of nationalism. Indeed, it expresses itself in a number of contradictory ways. As an idea wielded by Gandhi it was a liberal doctrine, whilst with Nkrumah it became an instrument for authoritarian rule. On a different plane, Mazzini believed that nationalism would lead to world peace, while Hitler turned it into a force for aggression. Such paradoxes have clearly emerged from the preceding pages. But we may perhaps acquire a closer understanding of the phenomenon if we investigate the nationalist's attitude towards his country's place in time. Emphasis on past glories is a common feature of nationalist movements, however slight the actual connexion between past and present societies may be—witness Mussolini's references to Imperial Rome, Nkrumah's references to the sophistication of medieval West Africa. Yet the true constant in all nationalist movements is the emphasis on modernization.

Nationalism is not only inhumane; it is inefficient too. The claims two ways. In the first place it may be noted that whenever nationalism has developed a new focus for political loyalty has been desperately needed. In this respect European society of the late eighteenth and early nineteenth centuries and the Afro-Asian societies of our own day have passed through parallel experiences. In every case rise in population, industrialization, and developed communications have led to the breakdown of traditional village communities. People generally in such societies feel uprooted and are therefore psychologically ready to identify with 'the nation' when this is suggested by their leaders. The leaders themselves are often intellectual middle class, disillusioned with the supra-national ideals that provided the framework of their early political education. In Europe neither the cosmopolitanism of the eighteenth-century *philosophes* nor the Concert of Europe of the post-Napoleonic statesmen proved viable concepts. Similarly, in the twentieth century the imperial relationship between the European states and the Afro-Asian peoples had outlasted its usefulness. Since both local and international units were obsolete, emphasis on the intermediary national unit was perhaps inevitable.

Secondly, it must be emphasized that nationalist movements, certainly in their initial stages, are not widespread popular movements. The nationalists are not the masses but the educated élite. The newly forged nation-state needs expert direction and it is significant that nationalist movements have been led by educated middle-class men, frustrated from exercising their talents in high office because of the alien (by class or race) control of the *ancien régime*. Professors in Europe, Army officers in the Middle East, civil servants in Asia, journalists in Africa, and lawyers everywhere have led the nationalist movements and emerged to high office after the successful revolution. At the same time their emphasis on reforming modernization has had wide popular appeal. Nationalism is the impatience of youth to "get on with the job", witness the names adopted by the Young Italy, Young Ireland, and Young Turk movements of the nineteenth and early twentieth century. And so the nationalist leaders are able to mobilize the people behind a programme of developing their own nation.

What is the present position of nationalism in the world? Its strength in Asia and Africa and its rising potentiality in Latin America are undeniable; many would also interpret it as the basic cause of the Russo-American rivalry. Furthermore, the Cold War between East and West has made each side eager to pose as the protector of national liberties. And so where a situation can be dealt with only by force of arms the strategic advantage of retaining control has to be balanced against the political disadvantage of being labelled an imperialist. Britain shrank from the use of overwhelming force against Eoka and Nasser; Russia and China did not hesitate to use massive strength against the Hungarian and Tibetan uprisings. And in so far as Britain submitted to and the Communists shocked world opinion these incidents illustrate the present strength of the nationalist idea. Even in Europe, where nationalist feelings are more mature and therefore less sensitive, the policies and utterances of President de Gaulle have kept the sentiment alive; indeed, he was brought to power in 1958 and remained in power until 1969 largely on a policy of boosting French national pride.

Nevertheless there are signs of decay. The world is shrinking. International co-operation is necessary to support the world-wide economic networks. The economic units are not nations, but sterling and dollar blocs and the economic federations of the European Common Market and the corresponding "Comecon." International war in a real sense has been made obsolete by technological advances in nuclear and missile research. Furthermore, practical attempts are being made to give expression to the common interests of the nations of the world. There are not only frequent U.N.O. meetings and spasmodic attempts at 'summit' conferences, but day-to-day agencies such as the World Health Organization, the World Bank, the International Court of Justice. Most significant of all, however, has been the measure of supra-national agreement in Western Europe in NATO and the Council of Europe and, most interesting of all, the large measure of economic unity achieved by France, Western Germany, Italy, and the Benelux countries in the Common Market. Europe, in short, seems to be passing out of its era of nationalism, albeit in a gradual and halting way. Perhaps it will be merely a matter of time before the rest of the continents follow suit. It will be a happier world when they do.

CHAPTER THREE

COMMUNISM

THE ARGUMENT

The Bases of Communism. Early communistic thought—theoretical foundations of Marxism.

Marx and Engels. Their lives—the theory of Marxism—the growth and development of Marxism.

Lenin. Lenin and the Russian Revolution—the theory of Leninism.

Stalin. Stalin's rise to power—his version of Marxism-Leninism.

Khrushchev. Khrushchev the man—his ideas.

The Expansion of Communism. Introduction—Expansionist techniques—the satellites—non-Communist countries.

National Communism. Yugoslavia—1956—recent developments.

China. The struggle for power—the development of the Chinese revolution—Mao's contribution to Marxism.

Conclusions. The strengths of Communism—the weaknesses of Communism—the essence of Communism.

THE BASES OF COMMUNISM

If by 'communism' we mean an organization of society in which wealth is evenly distributed and no property is privately held, then communism is as old as political theory itself. Indeed, since the most fundamental problem of life in an organized society is the conflict, either potential or actual, between the 'haves' and the 'have-nots,' the self-evident solution is the elimination of this distinction. On this definition of communism the approach to the levelling idea can be made from two different angles. The earlier thinkers tended to emphasize the corrupting influence of wealth, the necessity to relieve the wealthy of their riches for their own sakes or the sake of society as a whole. It is only later that the emphasis shifts to the misery of the poor and the necessity for a fairer distribution of wealth to relieve that misery.

Plato's Guardian class in *The Republic* live a communistic way of life in barracks. This, of course, allows of no family life, and, indeed, the offspring of this class are to be produced eugenically by regulated breeding. "This manner of life," says Plato, "will be their salvation and make them the saviours of the commonwealth. If ever they should come to possess land of their own and houses and money, they will give up their guardianship for the management of their farms and households and become tyrants at enmity with their fellow-citizens instead of allies."[1] Plato based this argument on theoretical assumptions derived from his intepretation of human nature. Nevertheless, his arrangement of society was not entirely based on abstract principles, for he had before him as a practical model the communistic society of Sparta.

The similarities between Platonic thought and Christian teaching have often been noted. The parallel is very striking in the sphere of social theory. Not only was the surrender of worldly goods specified by Christ as an important aid to entering the Kingdom of Heaven, but later the whole of monastic life was founded on this principle. The Rule of St Benedict is quite specific on this: "More than anything else is this vice of property to be cut off root and branch from the monastery ... [a monk] should have nothing at all: neither a book, nor tablets, nor a pen—nothing at all.... All things shall be common to all, as it is written: 'Let not any man presume or call anything his own' (Acts iv, 32)."[2]

The reaction to the evils of early capitalism produced renewed communistic thought in Sir Thomas More's *Utopia*, published in 1516, and, more importantly, in the intellectual ferment occasioned by the English Civil Wars. It is in this period that concern for the poor is emphasized as the leading motive for a more even distribution of wealth. More's *Utopia* superficially is based on *The Republic* of Plato, but is constructed as a satire on the economic ills of the early sixteenth century. More appealed for a return to a community life morally and economically regenerated. The "Diggers," as the seventeenth-century English communists were called, not only publicized their ideas through the pens of Winstanley, Walwyn, and Overton, but actually attempted a form of agrarian communism on a patch of land near Cobham, in Surrey.

But such ideas were premature in 1650 and had no immediate practical effect. There was a parallel movement in France a century or so later, and connected with the French Revolution in much the same way as the Diggers were connected with the English seventeenth-century revolution. In the second half of the eighteenth century such writers as Meslier, Mably, Morelly, and even Rousseau produced plans for a communistic organization of society. It was these ideas that formed the background to Babeuf's communist Conspiracy of the Equals, occasioned by the disastrous economic policy of the Directory in 1796. Gracchus Babeuf planned to take over control of the government and then redistribute population, organize work, distribute food—create, in fact, a controlled society and economy. His self-professed aim was to complete the Revolution, whose object of equality had so evidently not been accomplished, for Parisians were dying of hunger and cold in the winter of 1795–96, while the *jeunesse dorée* blatantly paraded their excessive new-won wealth. In such conditions Babeuf might have expected much support, but his attempted insurrection was a fiasco, largely because the Government was forewarned by informers.

However, although communism in the broad definition given at the beginning of this chapter has a long and venerable tradition behind it, there are many new and, indeed, alien elements in the modern Marxist version of this old idea. The ethical, Christian basis of monasticism and the Digger movement is quite foreign to the materialism of Marx. There is, it is true, a closer similarity when we come to the French communists of the eighteenth century—to Mably and Babeuf. It is nevertheless important to distinguish between the pre-nineteenth-century communists (with a small 'c') and the Communists of the Marxist school (with a capital 'C').

Yet it must not be thought that Marx was an entirely original thinker. On the contrary, every aspect of his thought is firmly based on the prevailing ideas of the time in which he lived. The greater part of Western Europe contributed to the fund of Marxist ideas.

France produced the great exponents of revolution and socialism. Babeuf, and later Blanqui, developed the details of revolutionary technique. Moreover, early in the nineteenth century "St Simon and Guizot were spreading the idea of the class war; Proudhon the notion that property is theft; Fourier the conception of the middle class as commercial despots."[3] It is true that Marx disagreed with many of these "Utopian Socialists," as he called them—especially Saint-Simon and the Englishman Robert Owen—but they provided the intellectual atmosphere of the time and thus coloured Marx's own work, even perhaps in spite of himself.

The early development of political economy as a separate, scientific study the world owes in large measure to Britain—to the Scots professor Adam Smith and the school of classical economists who succeeded him at the turn of the century. The most eminent of these was Ricardo, and it was he who developed the labour theory of value and its inevitable corollary that any profit made by non-workers derives from the exploitation of those who do work. This, of course, is the central idea in Marxist economic theory.

Finally, and perhaps of most importance for the strength of Marxism as a political theory, was the debt of Marx to the German school of philosophy, of Kant and especially of Hegel. Marx's use of the dialectic and his philosophy of history—without the materialism, it is true—derives directly from his early, formal university training in the German tradition—in short, from a detailed study of Hegel. The basic ideas of Hegel have been dealt with very briefly already in the Introduction, and Marx's use and distortion of these ideas will become evident as we analyse his theories in turn. However, the distinction between the Hegelian and Marxist philosophies may be briefly summarized by emphasizing the essentially idealist nature of the former and the blatant rejection of idealism and emphasis on materialism by Karl Marx. For Hegel, thought and ideas are essential reality, and material things mere reflections; for Marx, ideas are secondary reflections in the human mind of material realities. Secondly, the two men had quite distinct notions of the purpose of philosophy. Hegel merely aimed to interpret the world as it had developed; Marx wanted to foretell the future and change the world. This change of emphasis was quite deliberate, as is shown by Marx's statement in his *Theses on Feuerbach:* "Hitherto it was the mission of philosophers to interpret the world; now it is our business to change it."[4]

And underlying this complex structure of sociology, economics, and philosophy there was the widely diffused belief, inherited from the Enlightenment, in the possibility of human progress. From the Abbé de Saint-Pierre, through Diderot, to the Marquis de Condorcet, the French *philosophes* worked out the idea that man's life is one of continual progress. This idea, now so common, was novel in the eighteenth century, when the theories of cycles or gradual decadence were more generally acceptable. Connected with this essentially sociological and historical view was the biological theory of evolution—biological progress, where man finds himself the least primitive of the animals and still capable of evolving to higher realms. "Just as Darwin discovered the law of evolution in organic nature," declared Engels at Marx's grave, "so Marx discovered the law of evolution in human history."[5]

Marx and Engels

In order fully to understand the nature and importance of Marxism it is necessary to take a brief look not only at the intellectual background, but also at the social conditions in Europe, and more particularly England, in the mid-nineteenth century. For Marxism is as much an interpretation of working-class conditions, and their consequences as Marx and Engels foresaw them, as an economic and philosophical system.

When Marx was exiled and came to England in 1849 he left behind him across the Channel a continent which the Industrial Revolution was only just affecting. The situation in England was quite different. Industrialization was well under way: 6000 miles of railway had been laid; factory organization was firmly established. The changes by nineteenth-century standards had been fast, and they had been made by the courage, foresight, ability, and, admittedly, greed of hard-headed businessmen. For the production of as many goods as possible with the largest possible margin of profit was the general aim. Such a mentality made Britain a prosperous country —"the workshop of the world," whose shop window two years after the arrival of Marx was the Great Exhibition. It is true that the working classes shared in the prosperity of the fifties, but their standard of living was very low, and leaner years were to come after the mid-century boom. There was little to relieve the wretchedness of the average factory-hand's life. He would start regular, full-time work when little more than a child and toil excessively long hours in an unhealthy factory. The few hours that he was able to spend at home were devoted mainly to sleeping in incredibly overcrowded and insanitary slums, whose combined water-supply and sewerage was the local sluggish river or stream. The money that could be mustered from the total incomes of husband, wife, and children was sufficient for the provision of only the barest necessities of food and clothing. Meanwhile the successful businessmen were becoming fabulously rich, looking upon their workers as mere tools for the creation of new wealth. The industrial community was thus split into two castes—owners and workers. England was divided, in Disraeli's phrase, into two nations—the 'haves' and the 'have-nots.' Such was the social scene before the eyes of Marx. He saw the gulf widening and predicted an inevitable revolution.

It is time now to survey, in outline, the life of the founder of Communism. He was born in Trier in 1818, the son of a lawyer who was Jewish by race though Protestant by religion. His scholastic record was a brilliant one, and when he graduated from the University of Bonn in 1841, had he so chosen, he could undoubtedly have made a most successful career in law. He married well too: his wife, Jenny, was the daughter of the Prussian Minister of the Interior. But he chose to devote his life to fighting instead of supporting authority. He spent the eighteen-forties as a journalist, being hounded out of Germany, France, and Belgium, and finally settled in two rooms in Dean Street, Soho. The Marx family—Karl, Jenny, and their children until they grew up or died—lived in the cramped and squalid chaos of those two rooms, on the verge of bankruptcy, for more than thirty years, eking out an existence on the fees from occasional articles for the *New York Tribune*, a legacy of £800, and an allowance of £350 per annum from Karl's friend, Friedrich Engels.

Marx worked very closely with Engels, for whom he had a profound respect. "Engels is always one step ahead of me," Marx once said.[6] Engels was also a living contradiction of the socialist principles he upheld, for he was a substantial factory-owner. It was thus that he was able to provide Marx with the annual allowance. Most of Marx's important work was done in the British Museum during his life in London; it was there that he wrote *Das Kapital*, for example. Marx moved to North-west London in 1881 and died there two years later, and his grave at Highgate is a place of pilgrimage for devout Marxists to this day.

The pronouncements of Marx and Engels fill many volumes, written over some forty years. Moreover, the various ideas which make up the theory of Marxism are not expounded in any systematic way. It will probably be most convenient, therefore, to list the main works of the two thinkers and then go on to analyse the various parts of the theory independently of any specific book. One of the earliest of the important works of Marx was his attack on Proudhon, *The Poverty of Philosophy*, published in 1847. Next there must be mentioned the trilogy on contemporary French history: *The Class*

Struggle in France, 1848–50; *The Eighteenth Brumaire of Louis Napoleon*; and *The Civil War in France*. In 1859 he wrote his *Critique of Political Economy*, the Preface to which provides a definition of the materialist conception of history. In 1875 there appeared the *Critique of the Gotha Programme*. Engels too wrote several important books and pamphlets: *The Origin of the Family, Private Property and the State*; *Ludwig Feuerbach*; and his especially valuable *Anti-Dühring*, written in 1877. Besides the correspondence of Marx and Engels, providing valuable evidence of Marxist thought, the two men co-operated in several pamphlets, including *The German Ideology*, published in 1846. Two years later they produced their world-famous *Communist Manifesto*, a pamphlet described by Laski as having "passed beyond the stage where it requires eulogy. It is admitted by every serious student of society to be one of the outstanding political documents of all time.... Its character is unique, not only because of the power with which it is written, but also because of the immense scope it covers in its intense brevity."[7] The *Manifesto* is a work of history, describing how the capitalists acquired power and the working class emerged as a political force; it is a political tract condemning democratic socialism and outlining what should be the true aim of the workers; finally, it is a call to arms, an appeal to the people to take matters into their own hands. Lastly, there must be considered the most substantial of all the works of Marx and Engels—Marx's *Das Kapital* (*Capital*). This was his *tour de force*, written in three volumes, of which the last two were published posthumously. *Capital* is the exposition of Marx's economics and in particular of his idea of capitalist exploitation in his theory of Surplus Value.

All aspects of Marxism are naturally interwoven; each element is an essential part of the whole scheme. But it will be convenient to make a somewhat artificial division and examine each element separately and in turn.

The fundamental philosophy of Marxism is Marx's revision of the Hegelian dialectic. Briefly, Marx held that the world proceeds towards perfection by the clashes between opposites: the 'thesis' inevitably produces the 'antithesis,' which is inherent in the thesis, and the struggle between these two opposites produces a 'synthesis'; this synthesis in its turn becomes the thesis for a new round in the dialectic contest. This process continues until the final synthesis is reached; stability is achieved, in fact, only on the attainment of the absolute perfection. This is the basic doctrine propounded by Hegel. Where Marx differed from him was on insisting on the importance of environment and economic factors and rejecting the mystical idealism of Hegel. In the dialectical development of society, for example, the nineteenth-century thesis was capitalism, a social system which inevitably produces its own antithesis in the industrial proletariat. The consequent struggle between the capitalist and the proletarian will result in the synthesis of the Communist, classless society—and in this instance this is the ultimate synthesis, the most perfect form of social organization.

In this example of dialectical materialism Marx's philosophy of history—the more important historical materialism—has been hinted at. According to this interpretation of history all aspects of man's life are determined by the ownership of the means of production, for even æsthetic appreciation, ethical codes, and religious beliefs are but expressions of deeper economic forces and conflicts. In the Preface to the *Critique of Political Economy* Marx expressed this idea. "The mode of production of material life," he wrote, "determines the social, political, and intellectual life process in general. It is not the consciousness of men that determines their [social] existence, but rather it is their social existence that determines their consciousness."[8] Several important corollaries follow from the Marxist dialectical and historical materialism. In the first place, the state is nothing but an instrument of capitalist class domination, and must therefore "wither away" before the Communist Utopia can properly be said to have been established. Furthermore, the class struggle is seen to be inevitable—and likewise the revolution. Gradual social reform and the levelling out of differences is not a contingency allowed for; indeed, it is diametrically opposed to the dialectical system of progression by conflict. Marx himself summed up his essential contribution to social thought in a letter written in 1852:

> What I did new was to prove: (1) that the *existence of classes* is only bound up with *particular, historic phases in the development of production*; (2) that the class struggle necessarily leads to the *dictatorship of the proletariat*; (3) that this dictatorship itself only constitutes the transition to the *abolition of all classes* and to a *classless society*.[9]

Although Engels could make some pretensions to being a philosopher, Marx's mind was not so well suited to entirely abstract thought. Marx's prime interest lay in economics, and his most thorough work was achieved in this field—especially in *Capital*, of course. According to Marx all profit derives ultimately from the difference between a worker's real worth and the paltry wage he actually receives. This difference is the measure of the worker's exploitation and the justification for the proletarian revolution, which wrests back from the capitalist his illegitimate gains. It is the awareness of this exploitation that provides the spur to the proletarian masses and brings about their combination to effect the anti-bourgeois revolution. This, baldly stated, is Marx's theory of Surplus Value. Such an interpretation contains an element of truth, though Marx overstated his case. The difference between the wages a workman receives and the price that is charged for the article he makes cannot be explained purely in terms of employer's profit. Questions of supply and demand, costs of administration and distribution, all have to be taken into account. Moreover, his prediction that wages in a capitalist economy would always tend to subsistence level has, of course, proved quite false.

This system of Marxist social and economic philosophy has a twofold appeal—to moderately possessed intellectuals as well as to the poorer, working classes; for Karl Marx was both the scientific analyst of bourgeois society and the religious prophet of the classless millennium. It is a religious message to those who have little faith in, or patience for, the Christian promise of posthumous compensation for earthly poverty. The vast majority of these workers have neither the desire nor the intellect to understand the intricate philosophical, economic, and historical foundations of Marx's promises; they merely follow the catch-phrases of those who do understand and believe in them. For Marx was certainly not content to leave his message unsubstantiated by solid reasoning: his system of history predicted the coming of a Communist society, his philosophy explained the process, and his economics justified it. But even the intellectuals are given more than just cold reasoning; for the Marxist interpretation of history and the prophecy of Communism are given, and accepted by the believers, not as hypotheses to be tested in the light of subsequent social evolution, but as revealed truths. Communism has the stark, unarguable inevitability of death itself—it may be postponed, but it cannot be averted.

The various working-class movements in Europe were given direction and coherence by the publication of Marxist doctrines, for all the Socialist Parties, whether democratic or revolutionary, owe a great debt to Marx. The First International, or congress of Socialists, which lasted from 1864 to 1877, was a practical attempt by Marx to establish a real unity among so many diverse elements. But Marx was too inflexible—he did not realize the necessity for adjustments to the particular conditions in different countries; he could not tolerate the possibility that some one else might dominate the movement. There were consequently conflicts between the strict Marxists and German Socialists led by Lassalle, the French Proudhonists and the international anarchist movement of Bakunin.

The strongest Socialist Party in Europe in the late nineteenth century was the German. The attempts by the Germans to revise the Marxist programme brought forth attacks by both Marx in his *Critique of the Gotha Programme* and Engels in his *Anti-Dühring*. By the turn of the century the Marxist influence had weakened. The moderates found a fine leader in Edward Bernstein, while the Marxists were divided by a quarrel between Rosa Luxemburg and Kautsky. The former worked to preserve the purity of Marxism and died for the cause during the Spartacist revolution in Berlin in 1919.

In France there was witnessed in the Paris Commune of 1871 what came to be considered the first practical attempt to establish Communism. In fact, the movement was republican and patriotic, whipped up by the suffering and humiliation of the German siege, rather than truly Communist. Nevertheless, Communists and manual workers did take part, red flags were displayed, and a certain romantic myth grew up, strengthened by the ruthlessness with which Thiers suppressed the Communards. The French Marxist movement certainly continued to flourish under the Third Republic, especially in the trade unions.

If the First International had been marked by the conflict among numerous leaders, the Second, which met from 1901 to 1914, suffered from a complete lack of effective leadership. The attempt to boycott the 'capitalist' World War by pacifism was a miserable failure before the patriotism of the vast bulk of the people. The destruction of the Hohenzollern, Habsburg, and Romanov empires by the War, however, led to revived action by the Communists, marked by the creation of the Third International. But the moderates were too strong in Germany, though the Hungarian Béla Kun had some success in the old Austrian Empire. But, of course, all such achievements paled into insignificance in comparison with the success of the Bolsheviks in Russia.

Lenin

When Marxism appeared in Russia in the eighteen-eighties it came to a land where social and political discontent had already made itself felt in organized reform and revolutionary movements. These movements were based on the disgust of the intellectual classes with the degenerate state of the Government; they were not mass organizations. The most important of these organizations was that of the Populists (Narodniki). Unlike the Marxists, they were interested in the peasants, not the industrial proletariat, though a section, despairing at peasant apathy, resorted to conspiracy and violence and assassinated Tsar Alexander II in 1881.

The man who has been described as "The principal founder of organized socialism in Russia"[10]—Plekhanov—was, in the eighteen-seventies, a Populist. But he soon changed his attitude and became the foremost exponent of Marxism in Russia, revealing himself, in such works as *Socialism and the Political Struggle*, a scholar of ability greater than any of his Russian Marxist contemporaries such as Lenin or Trotsky. Plekhanov disagreed entirely with Lenin on the tactics of revolution; he warned against the premature establishment of Socialism, which, if the people were not sufficiently educated and prepared for it, would lead, he thought, to dictatorship. Indeed, as early as 1905 he accused Lenin of purposely pursuing this end for personal gain.

Although Plekhanov may be looked to as the leading theorist of Russian Marxism, the central figure in the movement was, of course, Lenin, and it is to a brief sketch of his life that we must now turn. "Lenin" was the revolutionary pseudonym of Vladimir Ilyich Ulyanov, born at Simbirsk, on the Volga, in 1870. His early career parallels that of Marx. A first-class degree in law led to the prospects of a successful career in that profession, prospects renounced in favour of a revolutionary career. He joined the revolutionary Socialist movement in St Petersburg, worked with Nadezhda Konstantinova Krupskaya, who later became his wife, and made a name for himself writing fiery articles. In 1895 ill-health sent Lenin for convalescence to Geneva, where he met exiled leaders of Russian socialism, including Plekhanov. His activities on his return to Russia earned him three years' exile in Siberia. On his release he made his way to Munich, where he started the famous journal *Iskra* (*The Spark*), the organ through which he directed his section of the Russian Socialist movement up to the 1917 Revolution. At one point in their exile Lenin and Krupskaya came to London, where they eked out an existence on an uncertain monthly salary of six pounds from the Party in a sordid little house in Holford Square, behind the Euston Road. But Lenin could at least visit the grave of his master at Highgate and work where he had worked under the great dome of the British Museum. Lenin's life in London was interrupted by his attendance at a conference in 1903 in Brussels. It was at this conference that he carried, by a narrow margin, the proposal for a supreme party headquarters to be established outside Russia. This is the origin of the modern political meaning of the words *Bolsheviki* (majority) and *Mensheviki* (minority). But the Mensheviks soon gained control of policy, especially when Plekhanov threw in his lot with them, and Lenin's authority, although secure over the Bolsheviks, was by that much reduced. He returned from exile to Russia during the 1905 uprising, but fled once more to Geneva on the restoration of imperial authority. The year 1912 saw the connexions between the Bolsheviks and Mensheviks finally severed, and also the launching by Lenin of a new journalistic venture—*Pravda (Truth)*—a paper that has become famous as the official organ of the Russian Communist Party. For the next five years Lenin continued his revolutionary work in exile, until the news of the February Revolution* sent him on his now famous, though then secretive, train journey across Europe, to end with his arrival on April 16 at the Finland Station in Petrograd.

The year before Lenin produced the first number of *Pravda*, Nicholas II's chief Minister, Stolypin, was assassinated, and the fate of the Romanov dynasty was left in the hands of the meddling Tsarina and the notorious monk Rasputin. It needed only the outbreak of war to reveal the depth of the Government's incompetence and make the Revolution inevitable. Hunger, misery, and the scandalous disorganization of the Government at home and the disastrous prosecution of the war against Germany caused mounting resentment, which burst forth in strikes and disturbances early in 1917 and led to the deposition of the Tsar. The Revolution in origin was not,

* The two uprisings in Russia in 1917 are variously called the 'February' or 'March' Revolution and the 'October' or 'November' Revolution. The confusion arises because the Russians were using the Old Style calendar, which was, at the time, thirteen days out in its reckoning. Thus the 'February' Revolution started on March 8 and the 'October' Revolution on November 7.

indeed, an organized Bolshevik rebellion, and the Provisional Government set up under Alexander Kerensky after the initial revolution in March was composed of Social Democrats. Faced with this situation, the Marxists maintained their divided opinion: the Mensheviks, believing the orthodox Marxist argument that a truly Socialist revolution could be undertaken only by an industrial proletariat, maintained that the time was not ripe for their intervention, and they stood aside; Lenin, on the other hand, made a determined attack on the Kerensky Government and an equally determined appeal for the support of the people by promising peace for all, land for the peasants and political power for the workers' soviets or local councils. These tactics were entirely successful, and the Bolsheviks' triumph in their bid for power in November was adequate proof of this. Kerensky's fumbling Provisional Government fell before the organized onslaught of the Bolsheviks under Lenin and Trotsky.

The confusion into which Russia had been thrown by the incompetence of the Tsar's Government and the impact of the war with Germany and Austria was, naturally, worse confounded by the anarchy of revolution. The problem of the German invasion Lenin tackled by the surrender of Russia's western provinces of Finland, Estonia, Livonia, Courland, Lithuania, and Russian Poland at the Treaty of Brest-Litovsk; fighting was then confined to the suppression of the counter-revolutionary forces, both internal and invading. 'White' armies of Russians opposed to the Revolution, stiffened by British, American, Japanese, and Czech contingents, fought 'Red' Army units throughout 1918 to 1920. Admiral Koltchak attacked from Siberia, Denikin from the Crimea, while British forces had occupied the Arctic ports of Murmansk and Archangel. To these counter-revolutionary activities was added in 1920 a direct attack by Poland. But all these onslaughts on the Bolshevik position, unintelligently handled, only served to consolidate their power, and Trotsky's newly formed Red Army emerged victorious against seemingly overwhelming odds.

In 1921 Lenin tackled the economic problems in a temporary surrender of his Marxist principles by introducing his New Economic Policy. He allowed a reversion to such bourgeois practices as private trading and ownership. These conditions lasted beyond Lenin's death to 1927, and were excused as providing a better opportunity for Socialist advance later. But Lenin did not live to see these developments. During the last few years of his life he suffered from a recurrence of the ill-health that had inhibited his activity in earlier years, and in 1924 he died.

"Leninism is Marxism of the era of imperialism and of the proletarian revolution," said Stalin.[11] Apart from the very important practical work of organizing and achieving the first successful Communist revolution, Lenin's task was to adapt Marxist theory to the new circumstances of the twentieth-century world and, in particular, to the fact of revolution in an agrarian Russia.

Besides innumerable speeches and articles, Lenin's ideas are contained in five major books and pamphlets. His first important pamphlet was *What is to be Done?*, published in 1902, in which he argued the necessity for organizing a party to lead the uneducated masses. "If we begin with a solid foundation of a strong organization of revolutionaries," he wrote,

> we can guarantee the stability of the movement as a whole and carry out the aims both of social democracy and trade unionism. If, however, we begin with a wide workers' organization supposed to be accessible to the masses, when as a matter of fact it will be accessible to the gendarmes and make the revolutionaries accessible to the police, we shall achieve the aims neither of social democracy nor of trade unionism.[12]

Seven years later Lenin wrote his main philosophical work, *Materialism and Empirio-criticism*, a somewhat stodgy reaffirmation of the Marxist philosophy and a defence of the materialist against the idealist version of the dialectic. The failure of the industrial countries to be rent by the proletarian revolution that Marx had foretold is explained by Lenin in *Imperialism: The Highest Stage of Capitalism*, written in 1916. Perhaps the most widely read of Lenin's works, however, is the pamphlet he wrote during the revolutionary year. "Lenin's pamphlet, *State and Revolution*," writes Professor Sabine,

> despite the fact that it remained unfinished and was planned merely as an occasional piece, may very probably stand as the classic ideological defence of the November Revolution. It summed up the principal ideas about the European War that Lenin had been issuing since 1914, and it brought the contemporary situation in Russia, the imminent seizure of power by the soviets, into the framework of Lenin's Marxism. Granting the point of view and the habitual modes of thought imposed by the dialectic, it was undoubtedly one of the most convincing and persuasive political tracts ever written.[13]

Finally there must be mentioned the pamphlet Lenin wrote after the Revolution, in 1920, entitled *Left-wing Communism: An infantile Disorder*. In it he dealt with the important practical problem of the relationship between Communists and other Socialists in the West. Briefly, he maintained that the Party should keep in touch with the working class in every way possible.

Lenin's contribution to Communist theory may be broken down into three main spheres. In the first place, he reiterated the basic Marxist doctrine and defended it against 'revisionists'; secondly, he produced his theory of the dictatorship of the proletariat and the related theory of the Party; finally, he took the condition of the twentieth-century world into consideration and produced his theory of imperialism.

The Mensheviks were more orthodox Marxists than Lenin, but, partly because of that, they were less practical. Lenin tried to reconcile adherence to the Marxist theory with the profit to be gained by involvement in the revolutionary situation in Russia. Nevertheless, he defended the materialist and revolutionary nature of Marxism with the ardour of a man of unblemished orthodoxy.

Of course, adaptations had to be made. Marx had envisaged a spontaneous revolution by a proletariat in an industrial country. But the October Revolution took place in a Russsia that was one of the most backward, agrarian, and least industrialized countries of Europe—the most unlikely state, in fact, to undergo a Marxist revolution. Furthermore, Marx had taught that, by the operation of the dialectic, the proletarian revolution would sweep away capitalism and establish a classless society; the very organs of state, the instruments of bourgeois repression, would "wither away" (the phrase actually belongs to Engels). But Lenin perceived clearly that a complete destruction of the Tsarist state machinery would lead to anarchy rather than Utopia. He therefore developed the idea of the dictatorship of the proletariat. Thus a strong but democratic Government was provided for to maintain the essential administrative services in the difficult revolutionary and post-revolutionary period—a purely transitional phase until the eventual establishment of the true classless and stateless Communist society—a goal which could be safely reached only by a careful policy of gradualness. In particular, the proletariat must use their dictatorial powers, in this transitional Socialist stage, against the exploitation of the capitalists.

But even this concession to capitalist and non-dialectic methods was insufficient for a successful revolution. The workers must be educated, and, above all, they must be led. It is necessary at times, too, for some small group to exercise the workers' dictatorship on their behalf. These are the tasks of the Party—a carefully chosen élite well versed in Marxist doctrine and revolutionary technique. Lenin was, indeed, fully conscious of the dangers of an undisciplined proletariat: "The spontaneous development of the labour movement," he wrote, "leads to its subordination to bourgeois ideology."[14] So much for the inevitability of Marx's dialectic! But Lenin did provide himself with a cast-iron excuse for the predominance of the Party.

According to Marx the economic levels of capitalist and worker would inevitably diverge until the critical, revolutionary stage was reached. This doctrine rejected the possibilities of gradual reform inherent in the democratic Socialist movement of nineteenth-century Europe. The evident success of these socialistic ideas, especially in the key industrial states of England and Germany, by the beginning of the twentieth century, however, seemed to postpone the coming of the explosive point; to many the situation even seemed to invalidate Marx's thesis completely. Lenin set himself the task of explaining away this apparent contradiction. By the exploitation of backward peoples, he argues, a new colonial proletariat has been created; and thus the standard of living of the workers in the metropolitan countries is raised by an artificial device unforeseen by Karl Marx. Nevertheless, the class struggle is aggravated rather than tempered by imperialism. Internecine clashes are inevitable in the competitive search for overseas markets and raw materials, while the promotion of revolution among the exploited colonials is a legitimate task for conscientious Marxists. It is this line of thought which, when taken to its ultimate conclusion, leads to the doctrine of world revolution. Because of the expansion of the capitalist system into imperialism the question of the exploitation of the proletariat assumes a far greater urgency: the inevitable Marxian revolution must be hastened by what are, in the eyes of the bourgeois, treasonous activities of Communist agents. And finally, to give even greater urgency to this strategy of provoking the world revolution, it was given out that Russia herself would, sooner or later, become the prey of this all-devouring imperialism.

Lenin was not a great thinker; he did not even maintain consistency with the Marxist doctrine that he upbraided others for adulterating. We cannot deny Lenin's immense impact on the world, of course, nor can we deny the great practical work he achieved in organizing the Bolshevik victory in 1917. But towards the end of his life he came to realize that he had imposed on Russia, by his theories of the dictatorship of the proletariat and the Party, a tyranny potentially more evil than the Tsarist system he had fought so long to destroy. "I am, it seems," he said in 1922, "strongly guilty before the workers of Russia."[15] For the dying revolutionary foresaw the danger to his country and his life's work in the rise to authority of the power-greedy and ruthless Stalin.

Stalin

The death of Lenin left something of a vacuum in Soviet government, and a struggle for power ensued, though the chances of anyone but Stalin's succeeding were slight.

Stalin—another revolutionary pseudonym, for Joseph Vissarionovitch Djugashvili—was not strictly a Russian at all; he was born, the son of a shoemaker, in Gori, in Georgia, and was educated at the seminary at Tiflis. He became a professional revolutionary in 1898, at the age of nineteen, and by 1917 had been exiled six times. It was in 1922 that Stalin really sprang to prominence when he was elected General Secretary of the Party, from which position he systematically filled many important posts with his own supporters.

The only possible rival for Lenin's succession was Leon Trotsky. The name Trotsky during the Stalinist regime became almost a dirty word: 'Trotskyite' was a term of abuse on a par with 'capitalist.' His rivalry of Stalin aside, what was the "Trotsky revisionist" version of Marxism? His central doctrine, fully worked out in *The Revolution Betrayed*, though propounded as early as 1906, was the theory of the "permanent revolution." According to this theory Russia, being a backward, agrarian country, would find it difficult to complete the revolution and achieve Socialism. It was in her interests, therefore, as well as those of the proletariat of the rest of the world, to work for the world revolution; for when the industrial countries have achieved their revolutions they will be in a position to assist Russia in the consummation of hers. The reversal of this international outlook by Stalin, Trotsky claimed in his later years, led to the stultifying of the Russian Revolution by the organization of the Stalinist bureaucracy—a development which made a second revolution necessary for Russia if it were to continue along the Socialist path. The publication of these 'heresies' was dangerous to Stalin because they were so valid. He reacted in a typical fashion: in 1928 Trotsky was exiled, and in 1940 assassinated.

In defeating Trotsky in the struggle for leadership in 1924 Stalin had the support of two strong allies—Kamenev and Zinoviev. Stalin had no qualms, as it might be imagined, in taking a new ally, Bukharin, to crush the opposition of his two former allies. A year later, in 1929, Bukharin went the same way. During the thirties Stalin consolidated his control over Russia by systematic terror—by mass trials and the extermination of all possible rivals. The executions rose in a crescendo of slaughter to the climax in 1937, when Marshal Tukhachevsky and seven other generals were shot. Stalin forced Russia into a programme of industrialization and trampled the peasant resistance underfoot by forced collectivization of farms and the destruction of the 'kulaks'—the class of richer, and abler, peasants. Being naturally conservative, the peasants resisted the Government reorganization of agriculture by destroying machinery and cattle, and Russia seemed almost on the verge of civil war in the early thirties. When war came to Europe again in 1939 Russia had by no means recovered from the upheavals and bloodshed she had just suffered. The Molotov-Ribbentrop Pact of August 1939, by which Russia and Germany pledged mutual friendship, gave the Soviet Union two extra years to lick her wounds before entering upon a further struggle. And even when the "Great Patriotic War" was over Stalin refused to allow any relaxation, for the strengthening of Russia *vis-à-vis* the capitalist world had to be pressed on apace. The strain was terrible. Stalin's death in 1953 must have been a relief to many. Nevertheless, by then he had established himself as a world figure and Russia as a foremost world Power. Stalin, more than any other single man, shaped the post-War world.

Joseph Stalin was a practical-minded tyrant. His aims were to achieve and maintain his own personal control and to industrialize the Soviet Union into a world Power of first rank. But, since he owed his position to the Bolshevik Revolution and the strength of the Party of which he was Secretary, he was bound to justify his actions and policy by theory and to attempt to square his actions with orthodox Marxist teaching. His basic standpoint we have already touched upon in noting his opposition to Trotsky's theory of the permanent revolution. It is now necessary to analyse his ideas in a little more detail.

Stalin's ideas are to be found in four main works. His *Marxism and the Nationalities*, written in 1913, was based on the work that he specialized in in his early years with the Party. Immediately after the death of Lenin in 1924 Stalin delivered a series of lectures which were later published under the title *The Foundations of Leninism*. A little later he wrote a book called *The Problems of Leninism*. Together these two works provide the most important contribution of Stalin to Marxist theory. In 1938 he also produced *Dialectical and Historical Materialism*, originally appearing as Chapter 4 in the *History of the Communist Party of the Soviet Union*.

In spite of the eulogies indicative of omniscience that appeared in Stalin's later years, such as the statement that "Socrates and Stalin represent the peak of human intelligence"[16]—in spite of these eulogies, Stalin was an indifferent political theorist. Ryazanov once interrupted him with a few very forthright words: "Stop it, Koba. Don't make a fool of yourself. Everybody knows that theory is not exactly your field."[17] An attempt to fit the events occurring in Russia and the world in general in the first half of the twentieth century into the straitjacket of Marxism would have needed a mind more subtle than Stalin's. The hair-splitting and half-concealed illogicalities associated with modern Communist thinking and labelled 'double talk' and 'double think' first became painfully evident when the movement came under the control of Stalin. Stalin's theories sprang from a realization of two basic facts—namely, that the Russian Revolution had, in practice, been imposed from above, and, second, that Communism was making little progress in the rest of the world in the era immediately following the October Revolution and seemed likely to make no appreciable progress in the foreseeable future. Stalin therefore developed his theory of "Socialism in One Country," though the immediate occasion was Stalin's conflict with Trotsky, the firm believer in the doctrine of the permanent revolution. Basically Stalin's doctrine was a self-confident statement that Russia was strong enough to develop Communism herself without appealing for help to other potentially revolutionary groups in the more developed countries of Western Europe; and, further, that she was strong enough to ignore the hostility of the capitalist states. It was a nationalistic doctrine, which struck a somewhat discordant note against the international proletarian harmony of Marx, Engels, and Lenin, and it led to a policy whereby "Revolutionary movements in foreign countries were staged or called off," in the words of the late Carew Hunt, "in accordance with whether they furthered the immediate policy of Russia."[18] In its international aspect, then, Stalin's theory of Socialism in one country led to a firmer control from Moscow over the national Communist Parties in capitalist states exercised especially, of course, through the Comintern and Cominform. It also led to isolation from and tension with the outside world. Russia was the isolated and besieged citadel of Socialism in a predominantly capitalist planet: "We are fifty or a hundred years behind the advanced countries," declared Stalin. "We must make good this lag in ten years. Either we do, or they crush us."[19]

Thus do the international implications of the doctrine of Socialism in one country lead inevitably to the necessary internal pattern of development and control. If Russia was to be the central and leading figure in the Marxist movement, rather than the backwater envisaged by Trotsky and even Lenin, then she had to be strengthened. That meant intensive industrialization. In order to push through programmes of industrial reconstruction and development it was necessary to produce the state-controlled Five-year Plans. These were blueprints for the reorganization and development of Russia's basic industries and, the fourth one, for her post-War reconstruction. A central planning bureau, Gosplan, was established for co-ordinating the work. Stalin inaugurated five such plans—in 1928, 1933, 1938, 1946, and 1951. The power of the state was thus being intensified, and totalitarianism became the essential feature of the Stalinist regime. And what of the doctrine of the withering away of the state? Stalin turned not a hair: "To keep on developing state power in order to prepare the conditions *for* the withering away of state power," he said, "that is the Marxist formula ... the contradiction is vital, and wholly reflects the Marxist dialectic."[20] And the state became increasingly the man. It was Stalin who industrialized Russia, it was Stalin who collectivized the farms—and it was Stalin who broke all resistance, active and passive, fancied or real, in a consistent policy of terror. "From 1928 to 1939 there were always at least 7 million Russians permanently in prison or concentration camp," writes Suzanne Labin. "In all 17 million Russians perished: 8 millions as a result of conditions in camps and prisons, 1 million as victims of the mass shootings, and 8 millions as victims of the great famine."[21] Yet perhaps the most remarkable aspect of all in this construction of the great totalitarian Socialist state was the adulation of Stalin himself—not only by the official Press, but by a host of sycophantic writers of all descriptions. So excessive was the praise afforded the Soviet leader that *Izvestia* regretted in August 1936 that, "Writers no longer know with what they can compare you, and our poets have no longer sufficient pearls of language to describe you."[22]

It was against this sickening "cult of personality" that Khrushchev rebelled in his famous speech at the Twentieth Congress of the Soviet Communist Party in February 1956.

Khrushchev

Nikita Sergeyevitch Khrushchev, the First Secretary of the Communist Party of the Soviet Union from 1953 to 1964, was born in 1894 in a small village near the border of the Ukraine. He comes from a working-class peasant home and in his early years led a working-class life as a shepherd-boy and coalminer, picking up his education at night school. The young Khrushchev was employed in Party work from 1919, and during the Second World War he organized guerrilla resistance to the Germans in his native Ukraine. Khrushchev never hid his humble origins, and made a point of expressing his interest in and airing his knowledge of agriculture. Following his appointment as First Secretary of the Party he introduced his virgin-land scheme for the agricultural development of Kazakhstan with a self-confidence equalled only by its remarkable initial success. Indeed, he has been described as "Immensely confident, perhaps over-confident; brash and contemptuous in his approach to delicate problems; ebulliently vital..."[23]

Soon after the death of Stalin Khrushchev became First Secretary of the C.P.S.U. That was in September 1953. This appointment was a great step forward, for it was from this position that Stalin had risen to supreme power. But for the moment he was overshadowed by Malenkov as Prime Minister. In February 1955, however, with the assistance of powerful allies, Khrushchev manœuvred Malenkov out of office and placed in his stead a man he could easily control—Marshal Bulganin. It was thought at one time that the reaction against the rule of Stalin would lead to a collective leadership: the sharing out of power among Khrushchev, Malenkov, Molotov, Mikoyan, Kaganovitch, and the rest. Khrushchev's personal attack on the Stalinist "cult of personality" and his emphasis of the Leninist concept of the Party seemed to confirm this interpretation. But Khrushchev eliminated his colleagues, and the way he did it provided an interesting insight into his character. In the first place, of all the leaders who were eliminated, only one, the Chief of Police, Beria, lost his life, and for this Khrushchev was probably by no means solely responsible. Khrushchev deposed and degraded; he did not destroy. But, what is more, the men who accepted degradation were no mean rivals. Malenkov and Beria especially wielded considerable power after Stalin's death; Molotov and Kaganovitch were old-established and respected members of the Party; while Zhukov held a similar position in the Army. Yet they were all removed from office, together with others, such as Bulganin, Serov, and Shepilov, of lesser significance. The only man of standing to remain within the inner circle of government was the wily and imperturbable Mikoyan. Nikita Khrushchev emerged as the undisputed head of both state and Party. Moreover, he made several important adjustments to the theory of Marxism-Leninism-Stalinism, and it is to these that we must now turn.

The most important of Khrushchev's declarations were made in his startling speeches at the Twentieth Congress of the C.P.S.U. in February 1956. In secret session he unleashed a bitter attack on Stalin, revealing him as the tyrant that we in the West had long known him to have been. From the point of view of a serious re-thinking of Communist doctrine, however, the violent 'de-Stalinization' had little importance; for when the essential ideas are crystallized from the torrent of abuse we perceive the all-powerful monolithic Party refurbished and as tyrannical as ever. "In a word," wrote Edward Crankshaw at the time, "the villain of the piece is not Stalin the oppressor of the Russian people, but Stalin the oppressor of the Communist Party."[24] No, the real importance of that historic congress lay in the pronouncements of Mr Khrushchev in public session.

Khrushchev's real contributions to Communist thought are to be found in his rejection of the theory of the inevitability of war between the capitalist and Socialist systems and his doctrine of the "different roads to Socialism." As Edward Crankshaw has pointed out, there were two reasons for Khrushchev's renunciation of the inevitability of war theory—the reason he gave at the Twentieth Congress and the real reason, based on the facts of present-day power-politics. Reporting Khrushchev's version, Crankshaw has written,

> The premise that wars are inevitable, he said, "was worked out at a time when, firstly, imperialism was an all-embracing world system; and secondly, the social and political forces not interested in war were weak and insufficiently organized, and so could not force the imperialists to eschew war." This situation, he went on to say, applied on the eve of both the last two great wars; but now, he went on, the situation had been radically changed by the emergence of a whole group of powerful social forces favouring peace. This meant that there was no longer any question of "a fatal inevitability of war" and Lenin's imperialistic thesis was to that extent outdated—though, he concluded, it was still correct in the sense that "so long as imperialism exists, the economic basis for an outbreak of war will continue to exist with it."[25]

But, as Crankshaw is at pains to point out, it is the outmoding of war as a political method by the invention of the hydrogen bomb and not the strengthening of pro-Communist opinion that has made war unnecessary—more, suicidal. "It is all very well for Lenin," he writes, "thinking in terms of Tannenberg, to look forward with enthusiasm to a series of mighty conflicts which would end in revolutionary triumph and the ultimate victory of global communism. But nuclear fission has made nonsense of such ideas."[26] Indeed, it was the suicidal nature of modern war that was emphasized by Mr Khrushchev when he took the Chinese to task at the 1960 Bucharest Congress for their continued belief in its inevitability. The concept of the inevitability of war has been replaced by the idea of competitive coexistence—economic competition, which, with dialectical inevitability, will lead to the collapse of capitalism. The aim, the end, the goal, are the same; only the methods are different.

The opposition to the doctrine of international conflict was paralleled by a further declaration by Khrushchev that the take-over by the Communist Party of an individual country need not necessarily be accompanied by violence—it could even be achieved through the due processes of parliamentary government.

There is an inevitable corollary to this loosening of the formerly rigid doctrine of progression by conflict. If different methods are foreseen and are permissible the variations will be the result of peculiarities of local conditions—dependent, in fact, on national characteristics, history, economy, and so forth. Stalin had insisted on the control of all Communist Parties from Moscow; Khrushchev put forward the doctrine of the "different roads to Socialism." Each country is now capable, in theory, of setting its own course for the Communist haven. It is interesting to note that, in expounding this idea, Khrushchev appealed to the authority of Lenin. "As long ago as the eve of the Great October Socialist Revolution," he declared,

> Lenin wrote: "All nations will arrive at socialism—this is inevitable, but not all will do so in exactly the same way, each will contribute something of its own in one or another form of democracy, one or another variety of the dictatorship of the proletariat, one or another rate at which socialist transformations will be effected in the various aspects of social life. There is nothing more primitive from the viewpoint of theory or more ridiculous from that of practice than to paint, 'in the name of historical materialism,' *this* aspect of the future in a monotonous grey. The result will be nothing more than Suzdal daubing."[27]

This reversal of one of the central features of Stalinism had complex causes and has led to widespread results. It was part and parcel of the de-Stalinization campaign, of course, and derived from a belief that his policy was mistaken—that rigid control by the Kremlin was impossible. The force of nationalism in Eastern Europe was pulling against the absolute subordination of the satellites to Russian interests. The destruction of the mystique of the infallibility of Stalin and Moscow, however, had a remarkably solvent effect throughout the Communist empire. The most dramatic incident was, of course, the Hungarian uprising. But this phenomenon of National Communism, though inextricably bound up with the ideas of Khrushchev, is a subject in itself and must be dealt with later in this chapter.

THE EXPANSION OF COMMUNISM

As we have seen, the failure of other countries to follow the Russian lead of Communist revolution in 1917 was a grave blow to the optimism of Marx's teaching. Stalin, however, turned the situation to Russia's advantage by controlling, through the Comintern, the various Communist Parties throughout the world and ordering their activities to suit Soviet policy. The Communist Parties became the servants, not of the international proletarian revolution, but of Russia's nationalist ambitions. But this control, before the Second World War, was exercised over the members of the Parties, not over whole nations, for the Soviet Union was the only Communist state in existence. It is true that Mongolia fell under Soviet influence well before the War and became the first Russian satellite, and that the western borderlands of Russia from Karelia to Bessarabia were absorbed by Stalin in 1939-40. But the effective territorial expansion of Communism has taken place since the Second World War. Since 1945 seven East European states and two Asiatic (China and Tibet), besides portions of three other countries (Germany, Korea, and Vietnam), have acquired Communist governments. This is an impressive advance, and we must ask how the successes were achieved.

It cannot be denied that Communism has had a genuine appeal for many people. As an ideology it stands for social improvements and a higher social morality than is to be found in the acquisitive, capitalist society, while in economics it advocates organized planning as against the anarchy of the free market. During the 1930's and early 1940's Eastern Europe and China suffered, with few exceptions, régimes of almost personified injustice, inefficiency, and corruption. For many people Communism represented hope; and if the hoped-for benefits had to be paid for with a loss of liberty there was little of this to be surrendered in any case, especially in China.

Yet the spread of Communism has not been achieved without resistance. Communists have failed to gain control of several states where their popular appeal might have led them to expect power—for example, Italy and Indonesia. Furthermore, a number of these countries that now have Communist régimes would in all probability have governments of a different hue had their native Communist parties not been assisted from outside, especially from the U.S.S.R. During the height of the Cold War it was widely held in the West, especially in the U.S.A., that 'International Communism' represented a well-organized world-wide plot to subject the whole globe to control from the Kremlin. The several national Communist movements have shown themselves too independent for this analysis to be anything but a naïve over-simplification. Nevertheless Russia has afforded invaluable help to the 'fraternal parties', and it is to these activities that we must now briefly turn.

It must be constantly borne in mind that Communism is an international doctrine: it appeals to workers of all lands to unite, while the faithful are kept buoyed up by the belief that the ultimate collapse of Capitalism is determined by the inevitability of History.

Broadly speaking, it is conceived that Communists might achieve power in one of three ways: a spontaneous mass revolution; 'revolution from above' by a small, well-organized Party; and partisan warfare.

The classical scheme, envisaged by Marx, was the spontaneous seizure of power by the armed uprising of the oppressed workers—a vision based on the great *journées* of July 1789 and August 1792 of the French Revolution. In the period immediately preceding the October Revolution in Russia there was much discussion as to the readiness of the Russian people for an uprising. Lenin developed a theoretical position in which parliamentary institutions were denounced in favour of the expression of popular opinion through soviets, while spontaneous action was replaced by party organization and stimulation. Thus the February Revolution was, ironically, more spontaneous than the carefully engineered Bolshevik insurrection which overthrew the Kerensky régime. The relationship of party, soviets, and people was explained by Trotsky:

> When headed by a revolutionary party, the soviet consciously and in good season strives towards a conquest of power. Accommodating itself to changes in the political situation and the mood of the masses, it gets ready the military bases of the insurrection, unites the shock troops upon a single scheme of action, works out a plan for the offensive and for the final assault and this means bringing organized conspiracy into mass insurrection.[28]

And so, not even the Russian Bolshevik Revolution was a spontaneous proletarian uprising: indeed no Communist régime has yet been established in this way.

In 1917, and in the years of civil war that followed, a Communist régime was established throughout Russia by the seizure of the centres of power and the use of force. The technique of imposing a Communist régime on a majority of unwilling or passive people was used throughout Eastern Europe in the 1944–48 period, though foreign force was here an important factor. And this imposition of Communism by outside pressure is the second method. It is true that the régimes in Poland, East Germany, and Rumania, for example, have become increasingly accepted, but there is no denying that the Communist parties of the East European countries would not have achieved power so quickly, perhaps not at all, but for the Russian pressure. This is even admitted officially: "Hardly any of the people's democracies belonged to the type of country with a highly developed capitalist system ripe for socialism...." the editor-in-chief of *Kommunist* has written. "Thanks to the Soviet Army, it was possible for the popular democratic régimes to be constituted and established in these countries without any commotion or civil war worth mentioning."[29]

The third method of achieving power, partisan warfare, has been the successful technique used by those Communist leaders who have, since 1917, succeeded in establishing themselves without outside assistance—namely Tito in Yugoslavia against the German occupation forces, Mao Tse-tung in China against the Kuomintang government, and Ho Chi Minh against the French Imperial forces in North Vietnam. The Chinese example is taken as the model for this way of seizing power. The Chinese prestige derives from the personal authority of Mao as writer and man of action, the complexity and length of his struggle against the Kuomintang, and the great size and importance of China. Mao has shown how a great country can be won by achieving popularity through social reform and military victory through flexibility and surprise: "We use the few to defeat the many—this we say to the rulers of China as a whole. We use the many to defeat the few—this we say to the enemy on the battlefield. That is no longer a secret, and in general the enemy is by now well acquainted with our method. But, he can neither prevent our victories nor avoid his own losses, because he does not know when and where we shall act."[30]

Castro's seizure of power in Cuba was based on these techniques and the Latin American area may well be the scene of similar operations in the future.

Stalin especially, during the last ten years of his life, sought to exploit the opportunities to extend the influence of Communism. The Soviet Government has been accused of cynicism and immorality in such activities. But this depends on one's moral code. In the words of Moscow Radio: "From the point of view of Communist morality, only those acts are moral which contribute to the building up of a new Communist society."[31] Marxist morality, then, is a branch of politics: the furtherance of Communism is the basic aim, and, as Khrushchev declared, "Anyone who mistakes our smile for a withdrawal from the policies of Marx and Lenin is making a mistake. Anyone who believes that will have to wait until Easter falls on a Tuesday."[32]

Violent words have sometimes been supported by violent action as in the military operations in Hungary and Tibet and in the Korean War. But because of the fear of sparking off a nuclear war, direct military action is not likely to be used by the major Communist Powers unless provoked too far by the U.S.A. Political manœuvring, propaganda, and economic warfare offer more subtle and less dangerous methods of strengthening minority national movements in non-Communist states. The attempts by the Communist Parties to become serious contenders for political power in representative assemblies have met with little success, particularly in Western Europe. Open hostility to all other political parties in accordance with strict Leninist teaching has not, in general, paid dividends. The alternative method, which has been tried with varying degrees of success in both East and West Europe, is that of the 'United' or 'Popular' Front. This technique involves the attempt by the Communists to achieve power by allying themselves with non-Marxist left-wing parties. Once in power the vital Ministries are secured—especially the Ministry of the Interior controlling the police—with a view to developing more widespread control from that base. This infiltration technique was used with conspicuous success in Eastern Europe in 1945–48.

Outside the framework of party politics much energy has been expended on propaganda. Of particular interest in this connection are the 'Front' organizations. These are associations like 'Peace Organizations' and 'Democratic Leagues' that are mainly non-Communist in composition, but which are persuaded to publicize Communist policies in their programmes. The true nature of these associations, which were particularly active in the Stalin era, has been clearly revealed by one who did much to organize them, Clara Zetkin. She wrote:

> Such organisations must not be placarded in red with the words "Communist Organisation." On the contrary, they should bear the outward and visible signs of neutral organisations.... It is not merely desirable but essential that representatives of all schools of thought should be admitted to their controlling bodies. What really matters is that the aims and programme of these organisations should be dictated to them (without their realising it) by the Communist Party.

On the economic front attempts have been made to extend Russian influence in Asia and Africa by giving economic aid (especially loans on easy terms) and by sending technicians to help in the running of the equipment supplied.

Another aspect of the economic offensive particularly evident in the post-1945 period was the disorganization of Western industry by Communist-inspired industrial disputes and strikes largely co-ordinated by the World Federation of Trade Unions from its headquarters now in Prague. The W.F.T.U. has as its objects the infiltration of free trade unions, the penetration of the unions in uncommitted countries, and the general prosecution of the economic war against the West. The harm done to the industries of most Western states can be quite out of proportion to the numbers of Party members in the unions; for in directing the activities of their members the Party executives choose very carefully their industries, their factories, their unions, and the positions of responsibility they want to capture in the unions. And when the opposition the Communists have to face is weakened by apathy among the non-Communist unionists and already poor industrial relations, the disruption caused by Communist activity is not then so surprising.

The initial spread of Communism into Eastern Europe in the immediate post-War period was achieved largely under the aegis of Stalinist Russia. Communist Parties in the various countries gradually took over control, and the presence of the Red Army made opposition unthinkable. Czechoslovakia remained a multi-party state until 1948, but in that year, with the mysterious death of Masaryk, resistance to Communist pressure came to an end. However, the mere establishment of Communist governments throughout Eastern Europe was not sufficient for Stalin: he wanted the direct subordination of these states to Moscow. This aim was achieved in two ways— by the creation of the Cominform and by the elimination of the 'national deviationists.'

As a gesture to Allied solidarity the Communist International (Comintern) was abolished in 1943. In 1947 a new body, the Communist Information Bureau (Cominform), was set up to perform a similar function. The parties in France, Italy, Poland, Czechoslovakia, Hungary, Yugoslavia, Rumania, and Bulgaria were to be controlled from Moscow by means of this organization. With the exception of Yugoslavia (see p. 103), this control proved effective. But the parties themselves were divided—between those whose first loyalty was to their country and those who were creatures of Moscow. There followed a series of purges. Rajk in Hungary and Kostov in Bulgaria were executed; Gomulka was imprisoned in Poland. By 1950 ruthless Stalinists ruled Eastern Europe—Ulbricht in Eastern Germany, Rakosi in Hungary, Hoxha in Albania, for example. Eastern Europe from the Baltic to the Rhodope mountains had become a network of satellite states.

The rigid political control by Russia lasted until 1956. Since then control has been gradually relaxed so that the term 'satellite' is no longer appropriate, though strong links (through the military Warsaw Pact and the economic Comecon) and some control still remain.

In Asia the Communist régimes of North Korea and North Vietnam have been set up under the protective shadow of China, though it is doubtful whether they have ever experienced the kind of Stalinist control that existed in Eastern Europe.

Communism is now established in two major Powers and a fringe of minor states. Moreover, even beyond this area it is an ideological force of some significance, and it is to these countries that we must finally turn.

In the immediate post-War era it seemed possible that the sequence of events in Eastern Europe might be repeated in Greece, Italy, and France. Greece was rent by a Communist-inspired civil war, and France and Italy by Communist-inspired strikes and economic dislocation. In France and Italy too Thorez and Togliatti led formidable parliamentary parties. The Communist Parties in these two countries still command considerable support, though the electoral arrangements of the Fifth Republic in France reduced the number of Communist Deputies from 149 at the demise of the Fourth Republic to a mere 10 in the 1958 elections, despite their polling 18.9 per cent of the votes. The 1962 and 1967 elections saw an improvement in their position, however; 73 Communist deputies were returned in 1967.

The Communist Party of Great Britain had an active though small membership in the inter-War period, but it was only after Russia became involved in the Second World War that membership leapt to its all-time peak of 56,000 in 1942. The decline since then has been due to three major factors. In the first place it became increasingly evident, especially after the establishment of the Cominform, that the British party was being used as a tool of Soviet policy. Secondly, many intellectuals were alienated by the dictatorial pronouncements of Stalin and Zhdanov on the arts and sciences. Finally, the Russian action in Hungary in 1956 led to widespread revulsion of feeling and the resignation of 8000 members—though, it is true, this lost membership has since been made good. The party remains particularly strong in the trade union movement and because of this position it has been estimated that they were able to control about 140,000 votes at the Labour Party's Conference in 1958. King Street, the Communist Party headquarters, is still a source of irritation to the British body politic.

The British Government and public are, generally speaking, tolerant towards the Communist minority. In the U.S.A., on the other hand, reaction is sometimes violently hostile, as was witnessed during the McCarthy 'witch hunts' of the early 1950's and the activities of the John Birch Society more recently. Extremism is perhaps inevitable since the U.S.A. is the epitome of that capitalism with which, the Marxists argue, the proletariat must inevitably clash.

Although Marx envisaged his revolution occurring in industrialized countries, the Communist doctrine has perhaps a greater appeal today among the under-developed countries. In the immediate post-War period and during the Cold War, Communism was attractive in the Afro-Asian world as being an anti-imperialist force. For had not Lenin observed that "England's back will be broken, not on the banks of the Thames, but on the Yangtze Kiang, the Ganges, and the Nile"?[33] And when the Communist-inspired Fidel Castro established himself in power in Cuba in 1959 powerful elements of American opinion began to fear that perhaps the U.S.A.'s back might be broken in the Caribbean. However, as imperialism declines anti-imperialism loses much of its force. A more permanent attraction of Communism for Asia, Africa, and Latin America lies in its emphasis on economic planning. Quick, ruthless organization of essentials seems a relevant programme in these poor countries. It is true, of course, that many Afro-Asian leaders, like Nehru, Nasser, and Nkrumah, have been bitter opponents of imperialism and fervent supporters of economic planning without being Communists. Indeed, the factors in favour of Communism in these areas are delicately balanced against the forces of opposition, such as religion, and the fear of Russian and Chinese expansionism.

Both Russians and Chinese have, indeed, worked to encourage the spread of Communism in the under-developed lands. The Russians have befriended Castro, Sékou Touré, Nkrumah, Kassem;

the Chinese have helped the Communists of South-east Asia, in Vietnam and Indonesia especially. Both propaganda and aid have been channelled into the under-developed countries to give a favourable impression of Communism. Soviet financial assistance to Egypt to build the Aswan High Dam (after the U.S.A. had withdrawn its promise of a loan) is a notable example of aid; Chou En-lai's African tour in which he declared that the continent was now "ripe for revolution" provides a recent example of propaganda.

And yet Communism has made remarkably little progress in the under-developed world, apart from China and her Korean and Vietnamese neighbours. Cuba has a virtually Communist régime; Kerala (one of the constituent states of India) has had, on occasion, a Communist-dominated government; while in Indonesia, until the coup in 1966, Sukarno attempted a régime of compromise to satisfy the demands of the very large P.K.I. (Indonesian Communist Party).

National Communism

In the immediate post-War years, as we have seen (see p. 100), Stalin sought to extend Russian control into Eastern Europe by controlling the governments of these satellite states. Since the Red Army was already in most of these countries the task was not too difficult. The Red Army, however, had not liberated Yugoslavia. Under their fiercely independent Communist leader, Josip Broz (Tito), the partisans had liberated their own country. And Tito refused to subordinate himself to Stalin. Within a year of the establishment of the Cominform—actually inaugurated in Belgrade—Yugoslavia was expelled, and 'Titoism' became the hope of the patriots in the satellite states. Stalin did everything in his power, short of actual military operations, to break the upstart Croatian, but without success. In 1953 Tito even aligned himself with the Western world by forming the Balkan Pact with Greece and Turkey. In 1955–56, when Khrushchev was effecting so much de-Stalinization, he reversed his old master's policy towards Yugoslavia. Visits were made in a spirit of great conviviality, with much hand-shaking, speech-making, and smiling. But the reconciliation was shortlived. In May 1958 the struggle was renewed—by the Peking *People's Daily*, which described Tito as an imperialist agent and an enemy of Socialist unity. The Russians followed up the Chinese attack by economic pressure.

What were Tito's crimes? Perhaps the most important was his quite simple but obstinate refusal to be ordered about by Moscow. But there are important practical and ideological ramifications to this simple desire for independence. Yugoslavia stands forth as a living example of Communism successfully developing independently of Russia—indeed, in spite of Russian hostility. It became an alternative and more attractive focus for Communists who wanted advice and not orders for the development of Communism in their own countries. Moreover, although Yugoslavia retains many of the features of Communism common to all such régimes from Cuba to China, Tito has evolved several important new ideas. The Yugoslav system is less authoritarian and bureaucratic in both the government and the economy. Both town and rural workers are given more freedom in their work than their opposite numbers in the Soviet Union, though, admittedly, the distinctions are becoming less acute as the Soviet Union introduces changes along more liberal lines. Perhaps the most important innovation by Tito has been the establishment of Workers' Councils to allow the factory-hands to take part in the running of industry.

Although the quarrel between Moscow and Belgrade remained bitter for many years, the growing rift between Russia and China, which became evident by 1960, led to closer understanding between the reformist Russian and Yugoslav régimes.

During the decade following the end of the Second World War Yugoslavia remained unique among the states of Eastern Europe in achieving both a Communist government and independence of Russia. 'National deviationists' were removed from the governments of other countries, and the 1953 uprising in East Germany against Soviet control was suppressed with military force. Nationalist aspirations in Eastern Europe lay dormant until 1956.

In February of that year Khrushchev denounced the tyranny of Stalin and expounded his belief in the "different roads to Socialism." The implications seemed to be that Moscow would now allow the East European countries each to develop according to their own national traditions and needs. In the autumn of 1956 Poland and Hungary followed through this implication by open revolt.

In Poland Wladislaw Gomulka, who had been imprisoned in 1949 for his 'Titoist' tendencies, was swept back into power by the nationalist enthusiasm. The situation was delicate, for although

Gomulka's belief in Communism could not be challenged, his reinstatement was a clear anti-Soviet move. The Russians wanted to maintain the stability of Poland because of their communications with East Germany. On the other hand, the Poles knew that for the same reason the Soviet Union would not relinquish control over Poland. It was a perfect situation for a compromise, and an arrangement was soon affected. The Soviet military position was confirmed, while a liberalization of the Polish régime was permitted. Political discussion revived and a working arrangement with the Church was established with Cardinal Wyszinsky; Workers' Councils were set up; and collective farms were allowed to lapse. And so, under the steadying hand of Gomulka, Poland has evolved her distinctive national pattern of Communism—quietly and with little violence.

Much more dramatic was the 1956 revolution in Hungary. Disturbances started in Budapest in protest against the police-state régime of Ernö Gerö, and soon spread to the provinces. Imre Nagy, a popular, liberal-minded man, was induced to form a new government. Nagy made it clear that what the Hungarians wanted most was to be freed of Russian control, even to be an internationally neutral state like Austria. In taking his stand on this advanced position Nagy went much farther than Gomulka. Indeed, he went too far. The Russians returned with reinforced armour and crushed the revolution. Nagy was arrested and later executed. Another Russian puppet, Janos Kadar, was installed in his place.

Apart from being a blot on the Communist copybook and proof of the unpopularity and inefficiency of their economic methods, the Hungarian uprising provided a perfect model for National Communism. The enthusiasm for the uprising was incontestable—especially among the young people, the very ones who had, so it was believed, been 'conditioned' to accept the *status quo* of Soviet domination.

Since the death of Stalin, and more particularly the crisis year of 1956, the pattern within the Communist world has become much more complex: internal conditions have become more fluid and the relationship with Russia more independent. Greater freedom inside the former satellites and greater freedom from Russian control are, indeed, connected as two aspects of the general move away from Stalinist dogmatism. Yet they must be distinguished. Whether the emphasis is placed on independence from Moscow ('polycentrism' is the word coined by Togliatti) or internal liberalization depends on circumstances other than doctrinal beliefs. Personal freedom is comparatively developed in Poland because of the strength of the Church and the careful handling of the 1956 crisis by Gomulka. Independence of Russia, however, is particularly emphasized in Rumania because of that country's economic resources and interests. Liberalization of the régime has occurred in all the countries of Eastern Europe: secret police are less in evidence, freedom of speech is more developed, collectivization of agriculture has been stopped or reversed. Growing independence of the U.S.S.R. has been shown by the speeches and actions of politicians and the dissolution of the Cominform in 1956. There are, however, many permutations on these themes. Moreover, it must be emphasized, close relations between Eastern Europe and the Soviet Union still exist, and the freedoms enjoyed fall short of those that are common in the Western world.

China

In many ways the development of Communism in Europe is a reflection of the evolution of the system in Soviet Russia: in large measure the parties have developed under Soviet control. The Communist creed has, however, been shaped very differently in China. This is scarcely surprising, since the country is vast, has its own strong traditions, and has never been subjected to Russian domination.

The Chinese Communist Party was founded in 1921, and with Russian assistance it soon established itself in the governing Kuomintang party. However, Chiang Kai-shek, who was manœuvring for power from 1925, determined to eliminate the Communists. He struck in March-April 1927, in Shanghai, killing many of the leaders. But some, including Chou En-lai, escaped to the hills of the Kiangsi and Hunan provinces, in the south-east; they were joined by some army units. Ignoring Russian advice to pursue the classic Marxist tactic of concentrating efforts on the cities, Mao Tse-tung organized a Communist régime on the basis of politically organized peasantry and guerrilla warfare. Stalin retaliated by recognizing Chiang's régime in 1929.

Chiang launched several full-scale military attacks on the Communists from 1930 to 1934. Very slowly the area under Communist control was reduced. Then the momentous decision was made to evacuate the area. 100,000 Communists, military and civilians, set forth on the celebrated Long March, now part of Chinese Communist folk-lore. After two years of incredible hardship, through 6000 miles of inhospitable and defended country, the Communists reached Shensi province—a bleak, easily defended area in the north of the country.

But Shensi was chosen by Mao not only as a suitable base for operations against the government forces, but also to enable the Communist army to fight the Japanese (who had recently invaded China) and thus win more widespread support as a national movement. In 1936 Chiang was, indeed, forced by one of his own generals to make peace with the Communists in order to present a common front against the Japanese. The Communists, already popular with the peasants because of their land reforms, now began to recruit support among the educated classes. The Japanese war was a great advantage to the Communists: Chiang's forces were discredited by defeats in the field; Mao's won success and fame with their guerrilla tactics.

During the early 1940's, while the war with Japan was still being waged, relations between the Communists and the government steadily deteriorated. And in 1945, with U.S. assistance, Chiang took over the areas that had been occupied by the Japanese, even in the north where the Communists could not passively suffer such an affront. The U.S. Government, recognizing the strength of the Communists and the danger of civil war, sent General Marshall to China in 1946 to try to effect a reconciliation. The attempt failed, and the struggle between the Communists and Kuomintang was resumed. Chiang, however, met with little success. The scale of the war gradually increased as the Communists grew in power. Nor was the Communists' strength based on military success alone: their dedication, reforming zeal, and efficiency set them in stark contrast to the inefficient and corrupt Kuomintang. A final offensive in 1949 forced Chiang to evacuate the mainland and seek sanctuary in the island of Formosa.

The new People's Republic of China was faced with grave difficulties: it had to exert its control over all areas of the country and over all segments of opinion; it was faced with the urgent necessity to introduce agricultural reforms and to initiate planned industrialization. The work was at first undertaken gradually and with moderation. The party exhorted people to work for the new régime; the wealthy landlords and the richer of the peasants were dispossessed, land was redistributed, and collectivization was started. Industrial expansion was more difficult to achieve, since outside financial and technical assistance was not available on any large scale. Even Russia was unhelpful: in 1945 Stalin seized the Manchurian industrial plant, while the Sino-Soviet treaty of 1950 provided for only meagre Russian assistance. (The history of the relations between the Russian and Chinese Communist parties indeed reveals more suspicion than co-operation, despite their adherence to a common ideology.)

A change of pace was, however, noticeable in 1955. The campaign to secure the adherence of the intellectuals was intensified and the collectivization programme was speeded up.

But in 1957 the authoritarian grip in intellectual matters was relaxed. "Let a hundred schools of thought contend." Discussion was to be fostered: "Doctrinaire criticism settles nothing. We do not want any kind of poisonous weeds, but we should carefully distinguish between what is really a poisonous weed and is really a fragrant flower."[34] Encouraged by this invitation of Mao's to debate the shortcomings of the régime, party officials, intellectuals, and journalists released a flood of criticism. The response of the government was to revert to arrests and censorship.

Attention was, however, immediately diverted to the revolutionary economic changes launched in 1958—the "Great Leap Forward" and the Commune system. As Chou En-lai explained in a speech in 1959, the two movements were connected: "In the past year a big leap forward in industry and agriculture and a surging movement to set up people's communes took place in China. The leap forward in industry and agriculture promoted the development of the movement for the people's communes, and this in turn has given new impetus to a still bigger leap forward in industry and agriculture. ... The Chinese people have created the organizational form of large-scale people's communes which combine industry, agriculture, trade, education, and military affairs and in which government administration and commune management are integrated."[35] The plan was to achieve a massive and rapid recasting of the economy and society by severe regimentation and the full exploitation of China's vast resources in man- and woman-power. The grandiose plans were not fulfilled, partly because of poor harvests and partly because of the inherent unreality of the scheme. Nevertheless very great progress has been achieved: economic development is under way by the harnessing of the energy of a people spurred on by a dynamic leadership and ideology. The leadership is that of Mao Tse-tung; the ideology is the Maoist interpretation of Marxism.

Mao's contribution to Marxist theory is perhaps less important for its originality than for the immense claims that have been made on its behalf. Mao has been built up into an omniscient leader in a campaign reminiscent of the Stalinist cult of personality. His words are the key to ultimate truth. As early as 1951 it was declared that "Mao Tse-tung's theory of the Chinese Revolution has significance not only for China and Asia, it is of universal significance for the world Communist movement. It is indeed a new contribution to the treasury of Marxism-Leninism."[36] Even the success of the Chinese women's table-tennis team in 1965 was explained by their being "armed ... with Mao Tse-tung's thought," which "raised their skill by leaps and bounds and greatly fortified their confidence in daring to seize victory."[37] The presentation of Mao since the death of Stalin as the leading Marxist ideologist has, indeed, contributed in no small way to the quarrel between the Soviet and Chinese parties (see pp. 201–202).

What, in fact, has Mao Tse-tung contributed to Marxist thinking? His ideas can be analysed under two main headings—namely, his theory of revolution and his theory of "people's democratic dictatorship."

Mao's ideas on revolution are very pragmatic. He has emphasized the importance of the peasantry in any revolution in a backward, rural country like China; he has developed ideas on guerrilla tactics suitable for a Communist seizure of power in such a country; and he has propounded the concept of self-sustaining rural bases from which these fighters can operate. Such is "the road of Mao Tse-tung."

More important from the strictly theoretical point of view are Mao's pronouncements on the difficult Marxist ideological problem of the transition period from the revolution to the emergence of the true classless Communist society. Where Lenin and Stalin believed in the "dictatorship of the proletariat and peasantry," Mao has expounded—especially in his important essay "On the People's Democratic Dictatorship," published in 1949—the concept of a multi-class dictatorship. Putting far greater reliance than any of his

Marxist predecessors on the possibility of converting the wealthy to a truly co-operative attitude to the Communist régime (with the help of 'brain-washing', perhaps), Mao held out the hand of friendship to the national—*i.e.*, submissive—bourgeoisie. Furthermore, as has been noted above, Mao urged that 'contradictions' within this complex régime should be resolved by open discussion. His "hundred flowers" speech, subsequently published as a pamphlet *On the Correct Handling of Contradictions among the People*, is an important contribution to Marxist theory. However, both in relation to the multi-class régime and the free debate of ideas, the dictatorial element has in practice been more in evidence than the democratic. The experiment of the commune system also emphasized the totalitarian trend of Maoism. The experiment was launched not only as a far-reaching practical reform, but also as a vital theoretical breakthrough in this same area of the transition to Communism: the Russians were given a broad hint that the Chinese had found the formula, which had eluded the Soviet régime, for the very rapid progress to the true classless society—the Marxist promised land.

Conclusions

The great complex of ideas which Marx and his successors produced has, of course, had an immense influence on the world. No other single thinker since Locke and Newton has made quite such an impact. There is much that can be found to be criticized in the Marxist system of thought and these aspects will be considered in due course. There is, nevertheless, clearly much of positive value to human understanding which has made the system such a widespread mode of thought. The merits of Marxism can be discerned in three major areas: firstly as an academic system of analysis; secondly as a practical tool in understanding economic and social needs; and finally as a revolutionary doctrine suited to the needs of the twentieth century.

In the academic field Marx, together with Max Weber, virtually founded the discipline of sociology by his detailed analysis and categorization of social relationships and his explanation of social dynamics. He has come closest yet to the Enlightenment ideal of a "Newton of the Social Sciences": he processed a vast amount of historical, economic, and social evidence, and produced the all-embracing laws of economic motivation, class conflict, and the inevitability of historical progress, for example, which, he claimed, provided "scientific" explanations of social and historical events. In emphasizing the vital importance of economic factors as explanations for political power, social tensions, even personal motivation, Marx widened historians' understanding by a whole new dimension, which no scholar, Marxist or not, would now dream of ignoring. His system of thought has the intellectual attraction of embracing a mass of empirical evidence and modes of thought from a range of disciplines (philosophy, history, economics), and emerging with a set of brilliantly simple propositions. If he created sociology, he also revolutionized history and economics.

However, although Marx's work is very much the product of the scholar's study and has had such a profound influence in this academic setting, the practical implications of his work are also of great significance. Because of Marx's work we now have a clearer understanding of the weaknesses of the capitalist economic system. He saw the relationship between trade cycles, over-production, and unemployment; he foresaw the development of organized labour and of the need for planning. As a result of his diagnosis many changes have been effected in economic systems and not only by convinced Marxists: central large-scale planning and the control of unemployment, for example, are features of even the U.S. capitalist society. Similarly, attitudes towards social ills have been revolutionized. The nineteenth-century *laissez-faire* acceptance of evils and injustice as an inevitable part of the social scene can no longer be sustained as the "welfare state" has become a widespread ideal. Furthermore, when a community accepts the achievement of social justice and equality as its goal it gains in moral fibre, stimulated by a sense of direction and purpose for the common good. Acceptance of Marxist *political* ideals is not necessary for the enjoyment of the benefits of Marxist insights into economic and social problems.

The purely political merits of Marxism lie in its appropriateness as a revolutionary doctrine for the twentieth-century world. The liberal democratic traditions established by the American and French Revolutions of the late eighteenth century could no longer provide the necessary impetus for a movement designed to undermine established régimes, especially in Eastern Europe and Asia: by the twentieth century liberalism had become effete. Marxism, on the other hand, provided a bold, all-embracing theory and the promise of massive economic and social changes. Moreover, Lenin's rejection of the view that a long intermediary stage of capitalist development was necessary for an underdeveloped country gave promise of a rapidity of progress well suited to the economic needs of Asiatic countries.

This does not mean, of course, that non-Communists fail to discern the fallacies in the Marxist structure of thought. Marxism claims to provide an all-embracing philosophy of man's life in society and a guide to action at every turn. Such a claim, not surprisingly, seems too ambitious to uncommitted observers. We must now turn our attention to the inadequacies of Marxism.

Firstly, there are some internal illogicalities in the philosophy. According to the dialectic, a clash between capitalism and the proletariat will lead to the Communist, classless society. But this has not happened. An extra phase—that of the dictatorship of the proletariat—has been inserted. There must be a preparatory stage of 'Socialism,' it is argued, before true Communism can be established. Indeed, the very name Union of Soviet Socialist Republics is a standing indication that the Russians themselves claim to have progressed no farther than the Socialist phase. This is, surely, inexplicable in terms of the dialectic; it is, in fact, a concession to the progression by gradualness that the dialectic so vehemently rejects. Moreover, the importance attached to the activities of the Party in the Revolution contradicts the Marxian prediction of a spontaneous uprising of the proletariat. The dialectic proves to be, indeed, not a framework, but rather a straitjacket for Communist thought. The theoretical rejection of progression by gradual development is a rejection of one of the most obvious lessons of history, and attempts to pay lip-service to it lead Marxists into the contortions of 'double-talk.' In order to prevent any erosion of their philosophical system Marxists must defend the whole structure: dogmatism chases away humility. In the words of Djilas, "The exclusiveness of Marx and Engels was born and intensified by something else that was at the roots of what they had learned: convinced that they had plumbed the depths of every philosophy, they thought that it was impossible for anyone to attain anything significant without taking their own view of the world as the basis."[38] Such an attitude of mind leads, inevitably, to authoritarianism, inflexibility, and singleness of purpose. Yet it is interesting to note that any system of thought is, according to the theory of historical materialism, merely the evanescent product of transient economic circumstances! Thus is the claim of Marxism to an insight into ultimate truth condemned by its own theory.

Secondly, it is difficult for some people to accept Marxist explanations of events and human actions. To talk in terms of historical inevitability seems almost to personify History and endow it with power over human destiny—a sadly fatalistic belief. Moreover, within this framework economic factors are held to explain all. But human motivation is far more complex than such a theory suggests. Neither Marxist economics nor the old German proverb, repeated by Feuerbach, "Der Mensch ist was er isst" ("Man is what he eats"), is subtle enough to provide the magic key to the understanding of human nature. Art and literature, for example, cannot be produced in accordance with an economic theory. Stalin—or, rather, Zhdanov, his lieutenant in these matters—tried to eliminate all 'bourgeois' art forms. Such rigid adherence to Marxism has been recognized as impracticable by the relaxation of literary censorship, especially after the death of Zhdanov in 1948 and Stalin five years later. Nevertheless the difficulties surrounding the publication of such recent novels as Dudintsev's *Not by Bread Alone* and Pasternak's *Dr Zhivago* indicate that ideological barriers still inhibit the artist.

Thirdly, let us consider the weakness of Marxism in the sphere of politics. It is very difficult to envisage how the state can in practice 'wither away.' All the tendencies in this technological age are for the increase in concentrated governmental power. Furthermore, the tendency to authoritarian government has been most pronounced in those very states that have adopted Marxism as their official creed. No régimes in the history of the world have regimented so many people as the governments of Stalin and Mao Tse-tung, while the Berlin Wall is a material reminder that the people do not enjoy the experience.

Finally, in the light of these objections one must question whether the claim of Marxism to be 'scientific' can truly be sustained. Indeed, it may be doubted whether the term can have any valid meaning when attached to Marxism, except only in so far as Marx was making a sincere attempt at producing a science of society. But either his laws showed that the revolution was imminent in nineteenth-century industrial countries like Germany and Britain, in which case they have been proved wrong; or the time-scale is limitless, and the laws are therefore incapable of being disproved and consequently 'scientifically' valueless. Furthermore, scientific enquiry must be objective and dispassionate—free of value judgments. But Marx does concern himself with values as well as truths: in the words of Durkheim, "Socialism is not a science, a sociology in miniature—it is a cry of pain, sometimes of anger, uttered by men who feel most keenly our collective *malaise*."[39]

Communism is a complex movement, and it may be justly objected that the foregoing criticism takes too little account of its manifold variations. How far are such generalizations true only of the basic Marxist doctrine, or how far, conversely, are they reflections of, for example, the Stalinist distortion of Marxism? As we have seen in this chapter, the basic Marxist doctrine, complex in itself, has been subjected to an immense amount of commentary and adjustment. This process started, indeed, in Marx's own time, and led to his comment that he was not himself a Marxist! Although during the Stalinist era it was possible to count oneself a Communist, of a Trotskyite hue for example, without following the Moscow 'party line,' Soviet Russia did dominate the Communist movement and gave it some cohesion, albeit with a not very pure Marxism. Since about 1956, however, there has not even been this unifying force of central direction. The personal authority of Stalin is gone; Russia is no longer the unique example of a state based on Marxist principles. There are some fourteen Communist states in the world today, each evolving its own brand of Communism.

Yet these states claim with some justification to differ in their political, economic, and social systems from the non-Marxist world. What is the essence of the Marxist system of thought that sets these countries slightly apart from the rest of the world, for all their mutual differences? One may distinguish five faces of Communism.

The 'religious' nature of Communism is dealt with elsewhere in this book (Chapter 5), and it is necessary here only to point out the dogmatism of the faith, the great respect for the leading theorists, and the immense zeal and selflessness of many of the followers of the doctrine, especially in their 'missionary' work to convert others.

The zeal of the Communists derives perhaps just as much from their being revolutionaries as Marxists. One must continually remind oneself that the enthusiasm, expansionism, and authoritarianism of Communist movements have been witnessed in non-Communist revolutions, notably the French Revolution of the late eighteenth century. Furthermore, as the revolution in Communist countries recedes in time, as in Russia, for example, the excesses become less noticeable.

The aim of the Communist revolution is social reform; and this may be distinguished as the third aspect of Communism. The more equitable distribution of wealth, the easing of the lot of the working classes, and the destruction of class distinctions have all been clearly evident in the programmes of Communist parties.

There have, however, been contrary tendencies in the rise of the Party as a new exploiting class. It is this interpretation that has been analysed in some detail by Milovan Djilas in his book *The New Class*. "The once live, compact party," he writes, "full of initiative, is disappearing to become transformed into the traditional oligarchy of the new class, irresistibly drawing into its ranks those who aspire to join the new class and repressing those who have any ideals."[40] We are faced with fascinating paradoxes here: Communist régimes are, generally, in the control of a privileged class, operating a system dedicated to the eradication of privilege and class; and in the one country where a real effort is being made to reform this situation—namely, Yugoslavia—Djilas languished in gaol for daring to suggest that such reform is necessary.

And so we come to the fifth face of Communism. When an entrenched group, like the Communist Party, seizes control of a country and justifies its power and programme by reference to an all-embracing doctrine, like Marxism, opposition is intolerable, for opposition would endanger both power and doctrine. But without opposition there can be no true freedom, as so many political prisoners in the Communist states have discovered. While Communism denies freedom it will win little sympathy in the countries of the Western world. This essential distinction between the Marxist and liberal traditions has been expressed in a particularly cogent way by the late R. N. Carew Hunt, who wrote, "In the West there has been a tendency to stress the *political* aspect of democracy rather than its *economic* aspect, and although at times this may have been carried too far, the fault is on the right side, seeing that a people which surrenders its political rights in return for promises of economic security will soon discover that it has made a bad bargain, as it is helpless if the promises are not kept."[41] But is the denial of political liberty an inescapable feature of Communism? This is perhaps one of the most vital questions we have to face in the world today.

CHAPTER FOUR

DEMOCRACY

The Argument

Introduction. The need for analysis.

Classical Greece. Introduction—Greek democracy in practice—contemporary commentaries—comparison with modern system.

The English, American, and French Revolutions. The legacy of the Middle Ages—the English Civil War and the "Bloodless Revolution"—the American War of Independence—the French Revolution.

Utilitarianism and Liberalism. Jeremy Bentham—Victorian Liberalism.

Democratic Socialism. The rise of Socialism—present-day influence of Socialism—relationship between Socialism and democracy.

The Basic Elements. Introduction—equality—popular sovereignty—humanitarianism—the rule of law—liberty.

The Myth of 'Totalitarian Democracy.' Introduction—origins—lack of true democracy.

Conditions for Democracy. Introduction—tradition—fraternity—popular desire for democracy—political responsibility.

Conclusions. Introduction—underdeveloped territories—the Western world—criticism of democracy—its defence.

Introduction

Of all the political words in common use to-day, 'democracy' is perhaps the most difficult to define. It is fairly common knowledge that the word has a different meaning when applied to Periclean Athens, welfare-state Britain, or the German Democratic Republic. But it is not enough to be vaguely aware of differences. If we are to acquire a true understanding of the nature of the democratic form of government, we must understand why so many widely differing political forms are embraced by one word and what differences this linguistic cloak does in fact hide.

One reason for the lack of clarity in the conception of democracy is the fact that it is not an ideology—it is not an organized system of thought comparable to Nazism or Communism: the democrat has no *Mein Kampf* or *Das Kapital* as an authoritative exposition of doctrine. Works which immediately spring to mind as possibilities for filling the gap—Locke's *Second Treatise of Government* and John Stuart Mill's *On Liberty*—are not in fact of the same calibre. "They are brilliant essays, not great works."[1] Indeed, although there are theoretical foundations to our present systems of democracy, the empirical strain is of greater consequence than in other political philosophies.

The aim of this chapter is to sketch the development of democracy as a political form and as a series of philosophical assumptions concerning the nature of man, society, and the state, and to analyse the main aspects and problems of democracy in the world to-day.

Classical Greece

Although modern democracy must find its origins in such medieval institutions as Parliament and the jury and in the political theories of the seventeenth and eighteenth centuries such as equality of men, natural rights, and sovereignty of the people, it is nevertheless useful to start a discussion of this subject in the ancient world. The word 'democracy' itself is Greek in origin—*demokratia*—"the rule of the people." But our interest is more than philological. An analysis of Greek democracy illuminates our twentieth-century equivalent with the light of historical perspective. There are lessons to be drawn from the similarities of, and contrasts between, the two systems.

The conditions under which fifth-century Athenian democracy flourished were, of course, vastly different from those of twentieth-century America, for example.

The political unit in ancient Greece was the *polis*, or city-state—minute compared with the nation-state of to-day. Athens, which in the fifth century B.C. became the most successful and influential of the democracies, was large in comparison with its neighbours. The city itself, together with the surrounding rural territory of Attica, which it controlled, covered little more than a thousand square miles, while its citizens numbered a mere 40,000. To the Greeks democracy meant direct, active participation in government by all the citizens, and not the election of representatives as in our present-day practice. There were three main elements in Greek democracy. Firstly, supreme control of affairs was vested in the Assembly of citizens. In this way all the citizens took part by discussion and voting in the government of their own city. They made laws, elected military, naval, diplomatic, and civil officials, made decisions for or against war and peace, and passed judgment on criminals. For such a method of government to be truly democratic, however, it was necessary, secondly, to ensure freedom of speech in order that all sides could be heard before a decision was taken. Finally, all political offices were open to all citizens, who were chosen for these positions by lot. An elaborate system of checks and controls was erected to prevent the acquisition of excessive power by any individual or body, who might thus endanger the democratic system. There was no permanent Civil Service, for example. The administrative Council of Five Hundred was made up of different people each year to prevent the growth of any corporate feeling, and all the magistrates had to account for their actions to the Assembly at the end of their year's term of office.

The Athenians themselves were proud of their democracy. They believed they had a practical system of government, which drew upon the collective wisdom of the citizens, yet provided against the corrupting effect of power. But, more than that, they believed it was a step nearer than the alternative monarchy or aristocracy to the full and perfect life. For the Greeks believed that "the polis belongs to the class of things that exist by nature and ... man is by nature an animal intended to live in a polis."[2] A man, therefore, can live a full, natural life only in association with his fellows in the city. The more a man can participate in this political life the better man he will become. The most eloquent defence of democracy made by an Athenian—if not the finest of all time—was given by Pericles in his Funeral Oration immortalized through the pages of Thucydides:

> Let me say that our system of government does not copy the institutions of our neighbours. It is more the case of our being a model to others, than of our imitating anyone else. Our constitution is called a democracy because power is in the hands not of a minority but of the whole people. When it is a question of settling private disputes, everyone is equal before the law; when it is a question of putting one person before another in positions of public responsibility, what counts

DEMOCRACY

is not membership of a particular class, but the actual ability which the man possesses. No one, so long as he has it in him to be of service to the state, is kept in political obscurity because of poverty.... Taking everything together, then, I declare that our city is an education to Greece, and I declare that in my opinion each single one of our citizens, in all the manifold aspects of life, is able to show himself the rightful lord and owner of his own person, and do this, moreover, with exceptional grace and exceptional versatility.[3]

In spite of such panegyrics Athenian democracy was not without its critics. Government by the mass of the citizens, it was argued, is open to abuse and leads to weakness. The general run of people are ignorant and liable to be swayed by the emotional appeal of demagogues. Democracy tends to degenerate to ochlocracy—the rule of the mob. But the fundamental question which determined the contemporary attitude towards Athenian democracy was the advisability of government by amateurs. It was the belief that politics is a specialist art needing specialist training that led Plato to take up his antidemocratic attitude. For, in Plato's view, the qualities required for the proper exercise of political power can be acquired only by those with exceptional ability and after long philosophical training—by a small minority, in fact. "Unless either philosophers become kings in their countries," says Plato, "or those who are now called kings and rulers come to be sufficiently inspired with a genuine desire for wisdom; unless, that is to say, political power and philosophy meet together, ... there can be no rest from troubles ... for states, nor yet, as I believe, for all mankind."[4]

The weakness of a government by amateurs proved disastrous in the military sphere when Athens, and, indeed, the whole of Greece, was confronted in the mid-fourth century with the professional and undemocratic, but highly efficient, might of Macedon under Philip. But the Athenians shunned the organized despotism which might have saved them from conquest, and thus "deliberately risked security for the sake of the freedom and variety of life and thought which they prized so highly."[5] The battle of Chæronea in 338 B.C., in which the combined Athenian and Theban army was routed by Philip, indeed, marks the passing away of the era of the independent Greek city-state where democracy had at times flourished. It was replaced now by the autocratic empire of Philip, Alexander the Great, and their successors.

The weakness of democracy against a highly organized military state, at least in the initial phases of conflict, is a lesson from Greek history which has been oft repeated in a modern context. The final task in this analysis of ancient democracy is, indeed, the comparison of that system with our own, some 2300 years after. The differences are fairly evident. A system of direct democracy with every citizen participating in government is impossible in the context of a modern nation-state. A modern state is far too large in both population and area, and its citizens are far too busy to devote whole afternoons to political debate. The Athenian of the age of Pericles led a simpler life, and could thus afford the time for his political activities. Also, many, though by no means all, were assisted in their work by slaves who were not citizens and therefore did not share in the political rights of citizenship. The exclusion of slaves, resident aliens, and women from political rights in Greece is, of course, another distinction between the two concepts of democracy.

Nevertheless, there are similarities. The citizens of the democratic state of the twentieth century do exercise some control over government through elections; freedom of discussion is still a much-treasured feature of democratic political life; and political office is again open to rich and poor alike, preferably amateurs.

The English, American, and French Revolutions

In the modern world the development of political democracy has been centred round the machinery of popular representation. It is true that some Swiss cantons have, though in decreasing numbers, maintained a system of direct democracy for centuries. Such a system, too, was Rousseau's ideal political organization. But these examples are merely the exceptions that prove the rule that modern democratic constitutions must be of a representative nature.

Medieval society was hierarchical and anything but democratic. Nevertheless, the seeds of modern representative democracy were sown in the Middle Ages and were not completely choked by the weeds of royal and aristocratic power, at least in England. The concept of the supremacy of an independent law and the democratic jury system provided the ordinary Englishman with a certain amount of freedom against the arbitrary action of his social superiors. But the political action for the establishment of the rule of law in such documents as Magna Carta, and the development of a parliament in certain respects independent of royal control, was the work, necessarily, not of the ordinary Englishman, but of the upper classes—the barons. By forcing John to affix his seal to the main principles of the Great Charter at Runnymede in 1215, the barons won an important victory for themselves against royal authority. The first third of the Charter defines the feudal rights to which the King is entitled. Of the clauses concerned with the law, Number 39, asserting the right of a freeman to be tried only by his peers or the common law of the land, is the most famous, largely because of the excessive emphasis placed upon it by the lawyers of the seventeenth century in their struggle against Charles I. However, inasmuch as the King's power was defined, the Charter was an important step in the development of the principle of liberty in the land.

Parliament originally was largely baronial in composition. Its strength was, however, increased with the inclusion of representatives from the shires and boroughs, who had the right of sanctioning taxation. This power of the purse became a strong argument against a king wishing to rule arbitrarily. The decision of Henry VIII to use Parliament as a means of prosecuting his quarrel with the Pope and continuing the existence of the Reformation Parliament for the unprecedented time of six and a half years added both to its authority and to its cohesion. Thus, by the reign of Elizabeth, Parliament was an established, regular, and, indeed, privileged part of the constitution, containing a small but organized and vociferous Opposition under Puritan leadership.

In the story of the development of democracy in England Magna Carta and Parliament are indeed vital institutions, though they were, in fact, of less significance in the thirteenth century than they were to become in the seventeenth.

"The second half of the eighteenth century" is now being interpreted as "the period in which democratic ideology rose to influence in western countries. In the American colonies, Great Britain, Geneva, the Austrian Netherlands, Liége, and the Dutch Republic, ideas of democratic government were developing."[6] The movement culminated in the great French Revolution of 1789, but it had an important prologue in the English revolutions of 1640 and 1688.

The English Civil War was, in origin, an attempt by Parliament to restrict the power of the King. In particular, the House of Commons demanded, as was shown in the Petition of Right of 1628, that the King should not resort to arbitrary taxation or imprisonment. Parliament's discontent with Charles's rule festered during the Eleven Years' Tyranny when the King ruled without assembling the Houses (1629-40). And so, when Parliament was again summoned to deal with the financial crisis resulting from the Bishops' Wars with Scotland, the general feeling of discontent soon burst into open hostility and war. The opponents of Charles I—the Eliots, the Pyms, and the Hampdens, the men who claimed that they were upholding the ancient liberties of England as expressed in Magna Carta—were, however, anything but members of a democratic assembly. Only a very small proportion even of the adult male population of the country had a right to vote in the seventeenth century. But once the war had started democratic ideas began to develop, especially in the Army. The starting-point of these ideas was essentially religious—namely, in the demand for religious liberty and the belief in the equality of Christians before God. It is not surprising that constitutional and fiscal quarrels should have been accompanied by religious discontent. As early as Elizabeth's reign the Puritans had taken the lead in Parliamentary opposition, and the High Church policies of Charles and Archbishop Laud confirmed them in their hostility to the Crown. Since they had established their position before 1641 it was inevitable that they should take an important part once the war started. A great deal of discussion took place, in the Army particularly, and some of the more left-wing elements such as John Lilburne and the Levellers soon progressed to the political implications of these ideas. How advanced their ideas were is proved by the nature of the *Agreement of the People*, a paper constitution drawn up by Lilburne's right-hand man, Wildman. It provides for manhood suffrage, frequent parliaments, and freedom of conscience. Although these democratic ideas were not acceptable to most of the Puritan leaders, they nevertheless achieved wide publicity through the mass of pamphlets distributed at the time and through the political discussions held in the Army. The essence of the ideas abroad in the Army in the middle sixteen-forties was given by one representative when he said:

> Really I think that the poorest he that is in England hath a life to live as the greatest he; and, therefore truly, Sir, I think it's clear, that every man that is to live under a government ought first by his own consent to put himself under that government; and I do think that the poorest man in England is not at all bound in a strict sense to that government that he hath not had a voice to put himself under.[7]

Most of these advocates of democracy did not go beyond the religious and political spheres to an economic attack on property. A left-wing section of the Levellers, known as the Diggers and led by Gerard Winstanley, did, however, advocate a communistic form of rural economy, but the movement gained little support.

The English revolution was achieved in two parts, divided by the counter-revolution of the Stuart Restoration from 1660 to 1688. James II, in his enthusiasm to re-establish Roman Catholicism in England, roused hostility and fear by his arbitrary use of the royal prerogative. Within three years of succeeding to the throne, in fact, he had become so unpopular that he did not even dare stay to fight for his inheritance when William of Orange landed at Torbay to claim the crown in his stead. Thus the deposition of James II ensured the preservation of individual liberty and the rights of Parliament. For William and Mary became sovereigns by the grace of Parliament as well as of God, and the terms of the Parliamentary grace were laid down in a series of enactments known collectively as the Revolution Settlement. The Bill of Rights of 1689 provided a framework for constitutional government by enumerating specific restrictions on the sovereign's power: he was forbidden to raise taxes without Parliamentary consent, to prosecute through special courts, alter or suspend laws, or maintain a standing army during peace-time. Other laws provided for the frequent and regular summoning of Parliament, the freedom of worship for Dissenters, the ending of Press censorship, and the security of tenure for judges. But even these important practical considerations were not enough for many tender consciences still wedded to the idea of the sanctity of kingship. The "Bloodless Revolution" had to be justified. This justification was provided by a man who became one of the most influential of British philosophers —John Locke. He argued, in his treatise *Of Civil Government*, that the relationship between the Government and the governed was in the nature of a contract—the Social Contract. By this contract the people give their consent to be controlled by a Government on condition that the Government does not violate the natural rights of life, liberty, and property. Once any of these rights is infringed the contract is broken and the people have a right to rebel to change the Government. James II, it was thus assumed, had broken the contract by abusing his prerogative powers. Although Locke did not think that his ideas necessarily implied a democratic form of government —for the people had a perfect right to choose a monarchical or oligarchical form—the declaration that all government rests on the consent of the people, whose natural rights are sacrosanct, became the basis of the democratic movement of the eighteenth century.

The practical effect of ideas is frequently at variance with the intentions of their authors. That the advocates of democracy in the eighteenth century should have looked to John Locke for their inspiration would have surprised and disturbed that supporter of the aristocratic government of the Whigs. Sir Isaac Newton would have been even more surprised. Yet such was the influence of both these Englishmen. The psychology of Locke's *Essay concerning Human Understanding*, combined with the brilliant simplicity of Newton's laws of celestial mechanics, gave the eighteenth century a touching faith in the potentiality of human reason. One has only to combine this faith with Locke's political concept of natural rights to produce the doctrine that the people as a whole should have complete control over their political destiny.

The practical effect of Locke's ideas was first demonstrated in the revolt of the American colonies. In the view of the American thinkers the colonies were merely "doing a 1688" on George III, though, unfortunately, this revolution was not bloodless. George III, it was argued, had violated the Social Contract, and rebellion was thus justified. Such is the basic theme of Jefferson's Declaration of Independence, drawn up to justify the war a year after its outbreak. It includes these words:

> We hold these truths to be self-evident, that all men are created equal, that they are endowed by their Creator with certain unalienable Rights, that among these are Life, Liberty, and the pursuit of Happiness.—That, to secure these rights, Governments are instituted among Men, deriving their just powers from the consent of the governed,—That whenever any form of Government becomes destructive of these ends, it is the Right of the People to alter or to abolish it.[8]

If the democratic origins of the American War of Independence were based on a misrepresentation of English theory, the American constitution was based on a misrepresentation of Montesquieu's interpretation of English constitutional practice. In his *L'Esprit des Lois* he put forward the view that liberty was safeguarded in England by the balance of power between the three branches of government—the executive (the king), the legislature (Parliament), and the judiciary (the law-courts)—so that no one could completely dominate the others and thus gain complete power. The Americans, however, took this a stage farther in providing for a *separation* of powers by isolating the President from Congress and so forth. But in noting the theory behind the American Declaration of Independence and the constitution, which was finally ratified in 1788, we must not forget the extremely practical importance and influence of these documents. The establishment of the United States of America as an independent state is a vital milestone in the history of democracy. For the first time in history the basic principles of democracy were laid down as fundamental parts of the system of government; individual rights, freedom, and suffrage were all guaranteed. Thus, proudly, America became the first democracy of the modern world.

The democratic ideas of the eighteenth century had their origin in England; they had their first practical application in America; but the centre of intellectual activity in the Age of Reason was France. Yet the opposition to the royal government of the *ancien régime* was, like the opposition to James II, aristocratic rather than popular. Although the French nobility in the seventeen-eighties mouthed democratic sentiments, few sought anything beyond an increase in the political power of their own class. But the destruction of royal authority destroyed at the same time the dam which had kept back the flood-tide of democracy. The French privileged classes, in refusing to submit themselves to taxation to rescue the royal Government from bankruptcy, made the summoning of the States General in 1789 inevitable. They soon found, to their cost, that the forces they had unleashed and had hoped to use were beyond their control. The representatives of the unprivileged established themselves in authority as the National Assembly, and the structure of privileges that had characterized the France of the *ancien régime* was swept away.

From a practical political point of view, however, the French democrats had little success. When the new constitution was finally produced in 1791 the sovereignty of the people was hedged about by very unrevolutionary middle-class qualifications. Only men who paid tax to the equivalent of a silver mark were elegible for election to the Assembly, and although all adult males were 'citizens' all those who did not pay taxes to the value of three days' labour in the year were relegated to the category of 'passive' citizens and were denied the vote. The Jacobin constitution of 1793 swept away all these reactionary restrictions and came down firmly in favour of full democracy. It differed in another respect also from the 1791 constitution—it was never put into operation! Moreover, within six years of its compilation Napoleon was virtually dictator of France.

Nevertheless, the Revolution marks an important stage in the development of democratic ideas. The popular cry of "Liberty, Equality, and Fraternity" and the levelling of all titles to a common 'citizen' was echoed on a more lofty plane by eloquent appeals to the "sovereignty of the people" and the General Will made by young lawyers in the Assembly and in the political clubs. Many of the ideas expounded by the revolutionaries were more or less faithful reproductions of the doctrines of Jean-Jacques Rousseau—that most controversial of political theorists, who coined the exciting phrase "Man is born free, and everywhere he is in chains."[9] The revolutionaries were very conscious of the existence of natural rights —that is, certain rights which man has by virtue of being man, but which by the eighteenth century, at least, had become obscured by the growth of privilege and despotic government—and, copying their American predecessors, they issued a Declaration of Rights. "The end of all political association," it declared, "is the preservation of the natural and imprescriptible rights of man. These rights are liberty, property, safety, and resistance to oppression."[10]

The outbreak of revolutions in America and France, countries so closely associated with England, the one by political ties, the other by geographical location, naturally had a profound effect on English political thought. The Americans found sympathizers among the Whig politicians, notably Edmund Burke, who, in actively opposing the power of George III at home, could quite sincerely maintain the parallel between the English Parliamentarians of the seventeenth century and the American revolutionaries of the eighteenth. He was opposed to the very concept of absolute and irresponsible sovereignty, to Parliament levying taxes on Americans who had no constitutional method of expressing their views about such impositions. Moreover, the revolt stimulated in England a movement for Parliamentary reform along more democratic lines. Burke himself, together with many politicians of like mind such as the Marquis of Rockingham and Dunning, organized a campaign to reduce the power of the Crown in Parliament especially by reducing the amount of money available for sinecures and bribes. This scheme was known as the Economical Reform Movement and, in its own limited way, was quite successful. A parallel movement, demanding reform of the actual system of representation, also came to the fore about the same time and had quite strong support in the country, especially in Yorkshire. The leaders of this movement included the Duke of Richmond, Savile, Wyvill, and Horne Tooke. The colourful career of John Wilkes too was not without its importance in defining and upholding British liberties. He successfully denied the validity of general warrants issued for the arrest of unspecified persons; of the Government's right to reject a duly elected Member of Parliament; and of Parliament's claim that their proceedings should not be published. But the enthusiastic cry of "Wilkes and Liberty" had cooled to a most tepid interest in reform when the events of 1789 in France revived the whole question. The Revolution was welcomed by many of the English radicals, including Thomas Paine and William Godwin, who, in defending the action of the French people, at the same time produced important contributions to democratic thought. Tom Paine, in his popular *Rights of Man*, countered Burke's denunciation of the French Revolution, and insisted on the necessity for universal suffrage and recognition of the sovereignty of the people. Godwin's *Political Justice* was a more academic work, based on an optimistic belief in man's natural powers, and therefore less popular. The publication of these and similar books is proof that France did not have a monopoly of democratic thought in the seventeen-nineties.

Utilitarianism and Liberalism

While the Americans and French were endeavouring to found new political institutions on the basis of Reason and Natural Rights an eccentric Englishman was groping his way towards the formulation of a different principle of government, albeit dependent on the characteristic eighteenth-century faith in human reason. Jeremy Bentham believed that the aim of government should be the provision of "the greatest happiness of the greatest number." This basic tenet of the Utilitarian school of thought, which Bentham founded, like the Contract theory of Locke, did not necessarily imply a democratic form of government. Circumstances, however, brought Bentham to the conclusion that no other form of government would in practice pursue this end. He came to realize that Governments pursue their own interests as much as other people. Numerous devices must therefore be established to ensure that the Government uses its power to produce happiness in such a way as to diffuse this precious commodity as widely as possible. To achieve this he not only advocated reforms which have since been passed, such as female suffrage, secret ballot, appointment of civil servants by competitive examination, but also the abolition of the Monarchy and the Lords and the election of the Prime Minister by Parliament. The test of an institution, indeed, became its usefulness in producing happiness—its utility, hence the term 'utilitarianism.' But as Government activity frequently reduces happiness, it must be kept to a minimum; every one should be allowed to pursue his own form of happiness in his own way. This is the doctrine of *laissez-faire* which became so important in the nineteenth century. The increase of happiness became, therefore, the justification for democracy in the utilitarian wing of the English radical movement at the beginning of the nineteenth century. Moreover, Bentham had collected about him a large number of disciples, who publicized his ideas and consciously put them into practice in England and throughout the Empire; for the Benthamites included such famous writers and administrators as James Mill, Edward Gibbon Wakefield, Lord Durham, Edwin Chadwick, to mention but a few.

In the year that Bentham died the great Reform Bill was passed into law, inaugurating a whole series of measures for Parliamentary reform, which eventually culminated in the emergence of England as a democratic country. The idea, embodied in the 1832 Reform Bill, that the franchise was a privilege given only to the more substantial citizens was gradually whittled away (under the pressure of the Chartists and the more enlightened politicians), until the right of every adult male, and eventually female, to take part in the election of Members to Parliament became an accepted principle of the constitution. The Great Reform Bill of 1832 had been a grave disappointment to the working-class people of the towns especially. They had expected a share in political power, but few qualified for the £10 household franchise required by the Act. This discontent became canalized into the Chartist movement, which demanded the implementation of the Six Points of the People's Charter concerning the method of representation originally drawn up in 1838. Although initially unsuccessful, all but one of their demands eventually became law. Indeed, it was clear to many people that the 1832 system was too illogical to be maintained. The franchise qualifications particularly were quite arbitrary. Relatively few adult males were left unenfranchised after the 1867 and 1884 Acts, while women were included in 1918 and 1928.

Parallel with this reform of British political institutions there was evolving from the basic ideas of Utilitarianism the philosophy of Liberalism. The most brilliant exponent of Victorian Liberalism was John Stuart, the son of James Mill, the close friend of Bentham. In his essays *On Representative Government*, *On Liberty*, *On the Subjection of Women*, he puts forward the idea that the franchise is a duty or a trust to be given to those who prove their worth for citizenship; it is not a right to be demanded by responsible and irresponsible alike. He insists, too, that there is no justification for excluding women from the franchise merely because of their sex. His essay *On Liberty* is a fine plea for freedom of the individual. But Mill was very much aware that freedom and democracy are not synonymous; he feared, indeed, the destruction of freedom by democracy through the ignorance of the masses. "The will of the people," he wrote,

> practically means the will of the most numerous or the most active part of the people: the majority of those who succeed in making themselves accepted as the majority: the people, consequently, may desire to oppress a part of their number, and precautions are as much needed against this as against any other abuse of power.[11]

But he was intelligent enough to realize that no amount of pleading by himself or anyone else could stop the tide of democracy. He therefore advocated the provision of compulsory education so that the franchise, when extended, could be exercised with intelligence and judgment.

Democratic Socialism

The development of ideas and demands of a purely political nature for popular control of the government has frequently (Professor Parkinson would say always and inevitably[12]) been followed by the extension of ideas of equality and popular control in economic matters. The political democracy of the Levellers led to the communistic ideas of the Diggers; the political ideals of the French Revolution to the economic demands of Hébert and Babeuf; and before England had achieved complete political democracy the Labour movement arose with its demands for greater economic equality. The transition is, of course, quite a natural one.

Modern Socialism is a product of the Industrial Revolution, a response to the social and economic problems of a modern and industrial society. Liberalism, neither in England nor on the Continent, was in itself capable of solving these new problems, and had thus by the end of the nineteenth century become politically bankrupt. The social problems of the industrial state provoked a fruitful response among political thinkers throughout Western Europe during the early and middle years of the nineteenth century: Robert Owen in England, Proudhon in France, Lassalle in Germany. Owen was another of the remarkable group of individualist, dedicated English radicals who flourished at the turn of the eighteenth century. He became disgusted with the conditions he saw in factories, and proved by his own reforms in his mills at New Lanark what improvements could easily be made. His attempts at organizing a co-operative movement, trade unionism, and a perfect "socialist community" at Harmony, in the United States, were all doomed to failure. Nevertheless, he set the tone for a breakaway from the *laissez-faire* school of thought. For that reason he is often referred to as the first Socialist. The first great ferment of Socialist ideas arose in France in the first half of the nineteenth century when Saint-Simon preached international organization of labour, Fourier the establishment of self-supporting communities, Louis Blanc the establishment of national workshops, and Proudhon the abolition of private property. In delivering a lecture in 1862, subsequently called *The Workers' Programme*, Ferdinand Lassalle inaugurated Socialism in Germany. Perhaps one of his most important contributions to Socialist thought was his emphasis, in true Hegelian fashion, of the importance of the state. Thus was started the alliance between Socialism and nationalism which was to become such a powerful force in German politics. But the development of the Socialist movement in all these countries, although retaining the individual stamp of these and other thinkers, owes much to the work of Marx. He is the true founder of modern Socialism. The movement bifurcated into democratic and revolutionary Socialism largely because of the different conditions prevailing in the different countries of Europe. Where political democracy had made progress, as in England, or where the Government was willing to introduce social legislation, as in Germany, it was possible for the Socialists to co-operate with the established political parties in power. Where such conditions did not prevail the Socialists had of necessity to adopt a revolutionary programme more in line with strict Marxist teaching. Such was the case in Russia.

In England the Labour Party emerged as a separate political organization at the turn of the century. Its political ideas were basically those of the Utilitarian and Liberal schools of thought. The moderation of the British Socialist movement is well illustrated, in fact, by the "inevitability of gradualness" philosophy of the Fabians. This society, formed in 1884 and including such intellectual giants as the Webbs, Graham Wallas, and Bernard Shaw, aimed to achieve Socialism by the gradual introduction of reform through Parliament. Early working-class M.P.'s, in fact, were elected as members of the Liberal Party and were suitably dubbed 'Lib-Labs.' It was not until 1893, under the inspiration of Keir Hardie, that the Independent Labour Party was established, and it was not until 1918 that it adopted Socialism as its official programme. From its origins, the Labour Party was a hybrid movement of middle-class intellectuals, who gave it leadership, and working-class trade-unionists, who gave it weight. But the Fabian influence has always been strong.

Developments on the Continent ran along similar lines, although attempts at 'Popular Fronts' with the Communists were more successful. The more aggressive theory of Syndicalism in France, too, had more success than its English equivalent, Guild Socialism. These were attempts to circumvent the undemocratic nature of capitalism and the bureaucratic nature of state Socialism. The exponents of this idea, notably Sorel in France and G. D. H. Cole in England, wanted to see the economy of their countries run by the trade unions, by democratic election. They aimed to combat especially the excessive centralization envisaged by state Socialist programmes of nationalization.

The influence of democratic Socialism to-day may be analysed under three heads: the policy of the British Labour Party, the adoption of Socialist principles by non-Socialist parties, and the activities of the Social Democratic Parties of the Continent.

The policy of the British Labour Party is based on two fundamental ideas—namely, that the state should control the country's economy, and that every one should have equal social and economic opportunities. In order to achieve a planned economy certain specified industries and services have to be nationalized and investment controlled so as to maintain full employment and the most efficient use of the country's resources. Recently, however, there has been some rethinking on the question of nationalization, and it seems likely that the Party will be less doctrinaire on this question in the future. Social equality is to be achieved by comprehensive schemes of medical services, pensions and insurances, housing, and education.

The latter policy is, in fact, the welfare-state scheme, and is no longer a monopoly of the Labour Party. For, indeed, no political party dependent on popular support can to-day maintain itself without having a full programme of social legislation. In Great Britain the Conservative social programme is almost indistinguishable from that of the Socialists. In the United States there is no Socialist Party, but social legislation has been undertaken particularly by Democrat administrations. Finally, on the Continent many non-Socialist parties, especially the Christian Democrats, have comprehensive social programmes.

There are Social Democratic Parties in most countries in Western Europe. Since the War they have been at a disadvantage, for they have tended to be centre parties squeezed into a minor position between the Communist and Conservative Parties to their left and right respectively. They also underwent a crisis of conscience, uncertain whether to ally themselves with the Communists or the parties to their right. The tension in the Italian Socialist Party, for example, was so serious that it split the Party in two in 1947, Sig. Nenni favouring support for the Communists and Sig. Saragat opposing any such co-operation. On the whole, however, the democratic Socialist Parties have avoided any alliance with the Communists, and any tendency in that direction was halted, and in some respects reversed, with the disillusionment over the Russian action in Hungary in 1956. Until the mid-1960's there was little strengthening in the position of the Socialists; Right and Centre parties dominated the political scene in the 1950's everywhere in Western Europe except Scandinavia. This situation was underlined by the hat-trick achieved by the British Conservative Party in the elections of 1951, 1955, and 1959.

What is the relationship between Socialism and democracy? In defence of Socialism it is maintained that equality, an essential feature of democracy, is meaningless if confined to a political context, for economic pressure is frequently more dangerous than political pressure to the democratic structure, for "money talks," and it is quite capable of talking politics. Furthermore, a restriction of the principle of equality to the narrow sphere of the franchise is illogical. Professor Pollard expressed this basic idea very forcibly. "There is," he wrote,

> no more reason why a man should be allowed to use his wealth or his brain than his physical strength as he likes.... The liberty of the weak depends upon the restraint of the strong, that of the poor upon the restraint of the rich, and that of the simpler-minded upon the restraint of the sharper. Every man should have this liberty and no more, to do unto others as he would that they should do unto him; upon that common foundation rest liberty, equality and morality.[13]

Finally, it is argued, enfranchisement is little consolation to a man when he is penniless. The struggle for existence then obliterates all other minor political issues. In short, the free political debate that is such an essential feature of democracy is impossible without the premiss of economic wellbeing.

It is argued against Socialism that it involves loss of freedom, another essential ingredient of democracy, through economic planning and control and the restraint of private enterprise. This view is fundamental to the Conservative Party's platform in Britain. Lord Hailsham has written that

> economic democracy, economic freedom, means the sharing, the diffusion, of economic power, that is property, as widely as possible throughout the community. This diffusion Conservatives regard as the very antithesis of Socialism.... Socialism aims at the concentration of power, political and economic, in the hands of a few privileged chiefs.[14]

But charges such as these are countered by the argument that lack of economic control leads to extremes of riches and poverty, and that freedom in this context implies freedom to starve and is therefore not worth attaining. The argument is also put forward that economic control does not interfere with political liberty. Lady Wootton, for example, has written that "there is nothing in the conscious planning of economic priorities which is inherently incompatible with the freedoms which mean most to the contemporary Englishman or American. Civil liberties are quite unaffected."[15]

The Basic Elements

In the previous, mainly historical, sections a certain elementary understanding of the nature of democracy has been assumed without its being defined. It is time now to turn to a consideration of what we do mean when we speak of democracy. Whether democracy is regarded as a form of government, a way of life, or an attitude of mind, it is still necessary to define the essential features of such a government, life, or mental outlook. While accepting that democracy implies a certain mode of life and mental attitude, it must be emphasized that it is essentially a method of organizing society politically; its essential elements are mainly political.

There are, it is suggested, five basic elements without which no community can call itself truly democratic. These elements are equality, sovereignty of the people, respect for human life, the rule of law, and liberty of the individual. It is proposed to discuss each of these in turn.

It has been said of the concept of equality that "No idea is more difficult in the whole realm of political science."[16] It is as well, therefore, to be clear in our own minds what we mean by the word before discussing the other constituent elements of democracy.

Although, historically speaking, the origin of the idea of equality is to be found in the Christian belief of the equality of men before God, and although it has been extended by Socialism to the realm of economics, the egalitarian element in democracy is essentially a political concept. The Pauline doctrine that all men are equal in the sight of God tended to be obscured in the Middle Ages by the feudal stratification of society. It was revived in Luther's doctrine of "the priesthood of the Christian man." But it was not really until the eighteenth century that the idea became widespread. The achievement of universal suffrage in the numerous democratic countries throughout the nineteenth and twentieth centuries is a measure of the increasing acceptance of the principle of equality in the sphere of civic rights. It is sometimes objected that men are not equal; that, in fact, men are different in religious beliefs, racial origin, social position, economic standing, and, above all, intellectual ability. But the democrat does not deny this; he merely claims it to be irrelevant. For equality should not be confused with uniformity. Democratic equality means equality of political rights irrespective of the individual's religion, wealth, intelligence, and so forth—that all individuals should be treated in a political context as if they were equal. This political ideal is summed up in the well-known tag, "one man, one vote."

But even when the idea of democratic equality is restricted to its proper political meaning our analysis has still not gone quite far enough; for from this idea there are several inferences to be considered. It implies, firstly, the absence of political privilege. If any group or class have an unfair chance of attaining political power they will undoubtedly use that opportunity to a certain extent for their own advantage, thus exaggerating the inequality. Democracy, in fact, implies the equal right and opportunity of all citizens to hold political office. In the second place, equality involves the provision of adequate opportunities for every one to play a full part as a citizen in accordance with his interests and abilities. Careers, for example, should be open to talent, not money, class, connexions, or influence. This argument leads inevitably to the vexed question of economic equality. Socialists insist on its importance, others deny it. But this is a question already dealt with in the previous section.

The aspect of equality so far discussed is that which involves the relationship between citizens. But, if we are to be consistent, the idea must not be confined to this internal aspect of the question. It must be extended into the field of international politics—to the relations between individual states. The idea that all states are equal is, in fact, the accepted basis of the United Nations Organization. In the General Assembly "one state, one vote" is the practice. It is sometimes forgotten that this is a democratic standpoint. It is, of course, a difficult idea to accept when faced with the vast difference in power between the Soviet Union and Nicaragua, for example. Yet the preamble to the United Nations Charter makes the standpoint very clear:

> We the peoples of the United Nations determined... to reaffirm faith in fundamental human rights, in the dignity and worth of the human person, in the equal rights of men and women and of nations large and small, and to establish conditions under which justice and respect for the obligations arising from treaties and other sources of international law can be maintained, and to promote social progress and better standards of life in larger freedom.

It is in the international sphere that the moral basis of the doctrine of equality is to-day perhaps most evident. President Eisenhower underlined this when he declared, "We cannot subscribe to one law for the weak, another for the strong; one for those opposing us, another for those allied to us."[17]

One further aspect of the question of equality which needs to be emphasized is the status of women. Only recently, and even now not in all countries, have they attained equality of civic rights with men. All adult women were not enfranchised in Great Britain until 1928, and it was not until 1945 that they received similar rights in France. The campaign for women's rights was started by William Godwin's wife, Mary Wollstonecraft, in the French Revolutionary period, and revived by J. S. Mill in the eighteen-sixties. However, it was not until 1903 when Mrs Pankhurst founded the Women's Social and Political Union that the Suffragette movement, as it came to be called, really got under way. Yet it was rather the sterling services performed by women during the First World War that probably swung the balance in their favour.

Before we pass on to the next aspect of democracy it is necessary to discuss the question whether the doctrine of equality is, indeed, a vital element. To the men of the eighteenth century—the authors of the American Declaration of Independence and the French Declaration of Rights—this would have been an absurd, almost sacrilegious, question. Men were by nature equal, and it was this truth that enabled them to question and fight the monarchical and artistocratic regimes of England and France in the name of democracy. In this the eighteenth century perceived the essential logic of the idea of equality. If men are not equal, then some have a better right to political power than others, and an aristocratic form of government, not democracy, is the logical result. The belief in equality is, in short, the essential defence of the individual against the abuse of political power.

From the idea of equality of political rights it is but a short step to the idea of popular sovereignty, for if every one is politically equal no one has a greater right to political power than his fellow. Political power or sovereignty rests, then, with the mass of the people.

But to make the simple and dogmatic statement that the people are sovereign raises, in the context of the modern state, more difficulties than it solves. For the mere assertion of this idea presents the practical problem of how the people are to exercise their sovereignty without even hinting at its solution. It is patently impossible for fifty million British people to govern themselves, as the will of the people cannot, for practical reasons, be expressed through referenda and plebiscites on every question which comes up for political decision. It is true that popular opinion can and does assert itself to have a direct influence on the Government on occasions. Mass meetings, petitions, newspaper campaigns, can all bring home to the Government the will of the people and sometimes force it to act in accordance with that will, or at least adjust its policy in deference to the popular movement. Perhaps the most significant issue over which public opinion has had effective control in modern Britain was the enforced resignation of Sir Samuel Hoare in 1935. Within a few months of his appointment to the Foreign Office he roused fierce public indignation by his scheme, drawn up in conjunction with Laval, for concessions to Italy in Abyssinia. On occasions such as these it is the people that take the initiative. In referenda and plebiscites it is the Government normally that voluntarily appeals to the populace at large. Amendments to constitutions are the most common reasons for making a direct appeal to popular opinion by means of a referendum. Plebiscites are held to ascertain the wishes of the people in areas where boundaries are being redrawn. But such recourse to direct democracy is a rare occasion, and normally the sovereign people has to rely on representatives to make its will known. And this raises another problem. If the people delegate their authority to govern to some select body, what guarantee is there that the sovereign people will be able to exercise effective control over their delegates? Many political thinkers, Rousseau among them, have thought this problem to be so difficult as to be impossible of solution. They can only regret the process by which the modern state was built up or advocate its virtual destruction by excessive decentralization. In practice, of course, the problem has been tackled by the adoption of the ideas of representation and the rule of the majority.

The idea of a person or body of persons being elected to represent a community is by no means modern. The medieval practice of the appointment of a jury and the sending of representatives of the shires and boroughs to Parliament is proof enough of the strength of the tradition in England. A certain control of the representative in Parliament can, of course, be exercised by the holding of frequent and regular elections and the publication of his activities while in office. But to whom is the representative responsible? Is the M.P. the representative of his constituency only or the whole country? The answer to this question involves an analysis of the general nature of representation. There are two general positions—of the delegate and the representative. A delegate is sent to a meeting to express views which have already been decided upon by his constituents; a representative, on the other hand, is sent to exercise his own judgment for his constituents on any issues that may be raised. A member of a modern parliament is evidently a representative rather than a delegate, for not every question that is likely to be raised at Westminster, for example, can possibly be discussed at constituency level before the candidate is elected. Furthermore, a parliament is a national assembly concerned more with national than with local matters, and a representative's loyalty to his country must be placed before any parochial feelings. The classic expression of this idea was made by Edmund Burke in 1774 when he rejected the claim of his constituents to control his actions once elected. "Parliament," he said,

> is a deliberative assembly of one nation, with one interest, that of the whole; where not local purposes, not local prejudices ought to guide, but the general good, resulting from the general reason of the whole. You choose a member indeed; but when you have chosen him, he is not member of Bristol, but he is a member of Parliament.[18]

The will of the people in a modern state, then, is expressed through their representatives. The representatives decide what, in their opinion, the people want, and if their judgment in this is faulty the people can express their disapproval at the next election. But it is a practical impossibility for the whole population to agree on any political question, even for a few hundred representatives to do so. When there is a difference of opinion we accept the decision of the majority. This is convenient, but it is not necessarily just or democratic. There are, indeed, great dangers in the concept of the rule of the majority. If a section of a community—racial, religious, or social—is a permanent minority, it might easily suffer oppression at the hands of the majority without a constitutional method of redress. Also, there is no justification for believing that mere numbers prove wisdom. The true interests of a community, as Rousseau saw, might best be served by following the judgment of the minority. Nevertheless, majority rule is the only practical method in the modern state, and, provided other elements such as tolerance and the rule of law are present, there need be little cause for fear. Indeed, it is the rejection of majority rule that is to be feared, for the alternatives are unanimity or minority rule—the one leading to anarchy since agreement would be impossible, and the other to oligarchy. Thus would democracy be destroyed. One or two practical considerations regarding the principle of majority need to be mentioned, for even when one has admitted the validity, or at least utility, of the idea, its practical application remains a problem. In the first place, when we speak of the will of the majority, are we thinking in terms of a majority of the electorate or a majority of the representatives? They need not coincide. For example, in the 1951 election in the United Kingdom, the Labour Party polled over 200,000 *more* votes than the Conservatives, yet won 26 *fewer* seats. The British system of one man one vote, one M.P. one constituency, also has the unjust result of reducing the effectiveness of the smaller parties. In the 1959 election, for example, the Liberals obtained 5.9 per cent. of the votes, but just under 1 per cent. of the seats. These disadvantages are eliminated in the proportional-representation systems. There are two main methods. In the one method votes cast for unsuccessful candidates are taken into account for the election of representatives on a national basis without constituency in a second 'scrutiny.' In the other method voters indicate their order of preference for the various candidates, and second and later choices are taken into account. The representative assembly thus becomes a true reflection of popular political opinion. Unfortunately, the multiplication of the number of parties tends to Governmental instability. The efficiency of politics is not directly related to mathematical perfection.

Democracy cannot work if tolerance of other men's ideas and respect for other men's lives are not instilled into the mind of society. So important has this element become that it has even been suggested that it is the fundamental difference between democracy and authoritarianism. "Nowadays," declared the *Observer* leader-writer, "a drowning man on a raft is the occasion for all shipping to be diverted to try to save him; this new feeling for the sanctity of human life is the best element in the modern world. It is the true distinction of the West."[19]

The concept of tolerance started as the idea that a man's religious beliefs were his own personal concern and not a proper sphere for interference by the state. This belief was first expressed in a forcible way by Locke at the end of the seventeenth century in his *Letter concerning Toleration*. This was published in 1689, and argued the essential separation between the religious and civil spheres, between faith and coercion. Force, moreover, he argued, is ineffective—it can only make a man *say* he accepts a belief; it cannot change his soul.

At the same time that Locke was defending toleration in theory, his political allies, the Whigs, were introducing the idea in practice by their Act of Toleration, passed in the same year, 1689. The idea spread to France, where it became a crusade at the pen of Voltaire. It was not long, too, before the principle was taken out of its religious context and transferred to the realm of politics and law. Respect for a person's religious views became respect for his political opinions; respect for his political opinions became concern for his happiness and very life. Humanitarianism was born.

This respect for the dignity and worth of the human body and mind is as precious as it has been restricted in both time and place. Cruelty has been a natural human attribute the world over. Indeed, until quite recently it was widespread even in the Western Hemisphere, and of its continuation in many parts of the world to-day we are made all too frequently aware. As Professor Salvadori points out, "Europeans enjoyed 'autos-da-fé,' Indians suttees, Persians bastinados as much as the ancient Near East people had enjoyed crucifixion, as much as the modern nazis gleefully enjoyed the liquidation of a race, or modern communists the liquidation of a class."[20] Most countries to-day pay at least lip-service to the principle of humanitarianism by subscribing to the United Nations Declaration of Human Rights, though it is little short of hypocrisy for many signatories. This document consists of thirty articles outlining in precise language the inalienable rights of mankind in every sphere, civil, personal, economic, social, and cultural. Moreover, it has been translated into many different languages and widely distributed. Ignorance can, therefore, be no excuse, and in the practical application of these principles of humanitarianism we have a useful yardstick for measuring the strength of a state's democracy.

Democracy, as has been said, is essentially a political idea; but it involves also the legal relationship between Government and governed. It is a common contention that government should, as far as possible, be based on an impersonal law rather than on the unpredictable whims of men. This, briefly, is the idea behind the rule of law; it "implies a set of doctrines all designed to secure that coercion of the individual by the state can be used only where it is required by previously existing and generally known rules."[21] Our first task is to analyse this set of doctrines.

These doctrines can be reduced to two main principles. The first is that no one should have any legal privileges, that every one should be subject to the ordinary law of the land, should have the same rights, and be subject to the same punishments. The second principle is that no one should be in danger of arbitrary coercion by the Government. It is the term 'arbitrary' that is the operative word here. The concept of the rule of law admits that it is necessary for the Government to use coercion, but it insists that the citizen shall have the opportunity to know the law and thus to avoid being coerced—that is, he must be able to keep within the law. This situation is made possible, not by the method of passing laws, whether by dictatorial decree or due Parliamentary process, but by the nature of the laws. To preserve the rule of law it is necessary for new legislation to be based on well-known principles and for it not to be retroactive. A law must therefore be, in Blackstone's words, "a rule, not a transient sudden order from a superior or concerning a particular person; but something permanent, uniform and universal."[22]

It has also been suggested, by Dicey particularly, that the rule of law implies a third principle—that of the supremacy of the courts of common law in all judicial matters. This standpoint involves the belief that separate courts of law and a separate legal code for administrative problems contravene the rule of law. It is now realized, however, that the failure of England to develop a separate system along the lines of the French *droit administratif* is proving a danger rather than a safeguard to the rule of law; for administrative tribunals are springing up with extensive powers but without the normal legal safeguards. This lack of safeguards against bureaucratic injustice recently led to the suggestion that England may profitably learn from Scandinavian practice. In Scandinavia an official known as an *ombudsman* is appointed by and made responsible to Parliament to report on any complaints raised about official misconduct or maladministration. No judicial or administrative functionary is exempt from the *ombudsman*'s authority. With the appointment of the Parliamentary Commissioner (see p. 204) England has gone some way to benefiting from the Scandinavian experience. Nevertheless, although there are potential dangers, the rule of law remains one of the main pillars of Western democracy.

The rule of law is essentially an aspect of the liberty of the subject, and it is to the broader questions of freedom—perhaps the most fundamental of all the elements of democratic theory—that we must now finally turn.

The idea of liberty is the outcome of the basic political problem: how to balance anarchy and authority. In the demand for liberty not yet tasted or the pride in liberty enjoyed, few conceive of the principle as involving the complete destruction of political authority. Civil society is, indeed, based on the need for the restriction of man's natural freedom, if only to prevent him from using it to restrict the freedom of his fellows. But the lovers of liberty wish these restrictions to be kept to a minimum, and perceive a greater danger in the modern world from authority than from anarchy. The demand for personal liberty derives not only from the idea that man is by nature free—that political restrictions are artificial—but from the idea also that man's individual personality can develop only when unfettered, and that this free development of the personality is beneficial to both the individual and society. The former justification for liberty is the *a priori* eighteenth-century argument: that men were endowed at their birth with liberty was a self-evident truth to Jefferson. The idea that individual liberty is useful is a doctrine that belongs to Mill and nineteenth-century Liberalism. In his essay *On Liberty* John Stuart Mill provided a tripartite argument for liberty. To deny liberty to any individual, he argued, is tantamount to making the unjustifiable assertion that one's own opinion is infallible; secondly, even errors contain a proportion of truth, and the suppression of truth is never defensible; finally, truth itself tends to suffer if not contested.

The struggle for liberty has been a long one, and, of course, the process is by no means complete. It is a threefold struggle. In some cases liberty has been acquired by the abolition of institutions restraining personal freedom, such as laws against religions, remnants of feudal obligations, and so forth. At other times liberty has been attained by the creation or strengthening of institutions against the arbitrary authority of oppressors. Such was the case in the development of Parliament. But even when offending institutions have been destroyed and necessary ones established by those fighting for liberty, their goal may still be unachieved if the people as a whole are apathetic. The third aspect of the struggle is, then, to make the achievement of liberty a popular demand. For some people will reject the opportunity for freedom because of the responsibility it entails; they prefer to be told what to do by an authoritarian regime.

Some even fear the possibility of freedom. Such an attitude was expressed by André Gide many years ago. "I can assure you," he wrote, "that the feeling of *freedom* can plunge the soul into a sort of anguish."[23] The fact that some people do not want liberty has led to the assertion that "it may be necessary to compel a man to be free."[24] This, of course, is a contradiction in terms, even allowing for the subtleties of Rousseau's theory of the General Will. But it is more than that; it is positively dangerous. It was the attempt on the part of the French revolutionaries, the Jacobins in particular, to force the Frenchmen of the seventeen-nineties to accept their interpretation of freedom that led to Mme Roland's famous cry: "O liberty! O liberty! what crimes are committed in thy name!"[25] But such liberty is not part of democracy. The distinction between these two interpretations of liberty has often been made. They are often referred to as negative and positive freedom. The former implies merely the absence of coercion or restraint, while the second implies the positive ability to pursue a good line of action. Knowledge and virtue are therefore prerequisites for positive freedom, and it is in the interpretation of what knowledge and what virtue are required that the danger lies.

The liberties one expects from a democratic regime are reasonably well defined. They include freedom of speech, freedom of the Press, freedom of conscience, freedom of assembly, and freedom from arbitrary arrest.

Democracy consists of the peaceful resolution of differences, of a distillation of at least an approximation to the truth through the clash of opinions. Democracy also consists in the Government's acting in accordance with the wishes of the people. All this involves free and uninhibited discussion—freedom of expression in speech and in print. Apart from the fundamental love of liberty for its own sake, there underlies the belief in freedom of expression the conviction particularly that only by fearless debate will truth emerge. The classical exposition of this point of view was made by Milton more than three centuries ago. "And though all the winds of doctrine were let loose to play upon the earth," he wrote, "so truth be in the field, we do injuriously by licensing and prohibiting to misdoubt her strength. Let her and falsehood grapple, who ever knew truth put to the worse, in a free and open encounter."[26] Where Milton defended freedom of expression from a religious standpoint, John Stuart Mill, two hundred years later, made an equally impassioned plea for the same liberty in the belief that it was an essential condition for the morally mature individual.

In the practice of politics the concept of freedom of expression is found not only in discussion among citizens; it also underlies the whole idea of organized Opposition. Parliamentary Opposition is essential to democratic government, for democracy involves debate, and it is impossible to have a debate when there is no one to put the other point of view. A Government can easily become self-righteous and irresponsible—undemocratic in fact—if it is not continually reminded that it does not possess a monopoly of good ideas or, further, that some of its ideas and actions are positively pernicious. This truth is the basis of the epigram that it is essential for the other side to be put, even when there is no other side!

Freedom of expression, however, is not, and should not be, absolute. Instances when it is necessary, for the benefit of the community, to restrict this liberty are covered by our laws against incitement to sedition and those protecting individuals against libel and slander. But, except in difficult cases of interpretation, such laws are not considered as real restrictions on liberty.

Freedom of expression, naturally, implies freedom of opinion, of which freedom of conscience on religious belief is a special kind. Religious intolerance has caused immense suffering in the past. The attempt to stamp out Islam in Spain, the campaign against the Huguenots in France, the struggle between Catholic and Protestant for domination in Germany, to mention but a few examples, caused untold bloodshed and human misery. Religious tolerance was born of the humanism of the sixteenth century and nurtured in the Protestant communities of the North Atlantic. The practice of religious toleration, however, frequently asserted itself because Governments or communities found it more convenient, rather than from any conviction of its being morally desirable. Henry IV of France, the first monarch to tolerate opposing religious ideas in his realm, issued the famous Edict of Nantes in 1598 because France had suffered so much from the internecine religious wars and only by a period of religious peace could be expected to recover. From such tentative beginnings liberty of conscience, closely linked with the whole principle of freedom of thought and with humanitarianism, blossomed forth in that most sensible and least fanatical of all ages—the century embraced by the English and French Revolutions.

In a democratic society one is, or should be, free to express one's ideas in any medium—through the Press, on radio or television, or at a public meeting. The freedom to meet in public assembly is, therefore, an important concomitant to freedom of expression; and any attempt to restrict this right by legislation—a common enough policy in Britain at times in the past and in other countries to-day —is a serious threat to personal freedom. Speaker's Corner is a valuable democratic institution.

We must consider finally the important freedom from arbitrary arrest. This right is closely connected with the rule of law already discussed. It is most closely associated in England with the famous writ of Habeas Corpus, originating in the Act of 1679, which demands the release of a prisoner if he is not brought before a magistrate and charged with some specific breach of the law, thus ensuring trial in a court of law. Arbitrary detention in prison without trial is, therefore, impossible.

On the essential connexion between liberty and democracy we can perhaps leave the last word with J. S. Mill. "No society," he wrote in his essay *On Liberty*, "in which these liberties are not, on the whole, respected is free, whatever may be its form of government; and none is completely free in which they do not exist absolute and unqualified."[27]

The Myth of 'Totalitarian Democracy'

It is a basic fact of the present international scene that the Communist nations and so-called 'Western' states represent opposing political ideals; political propaganda on both sides is concerned to show the excellence of their own and the faults of their rival's system. Yet a superficial study of the principles being mutually defended and attacked would provide little evidence of the cause of this animosity. The Western democracies, on this superficial view, are defending equality, freedom, and so forth against the Communist peoples' democracies, who, in turn, claim to be the true practitioners of the same principles. It is true, perhaps, that the emotions roused by the Cold War have tended to exaggerate the differences between the two systems; nevertheless, these differences do exist in a very real sense. The claims of the régimes in Russia, China, East Germany, and the like to be democracies are, in fact, false claims. And in so far as the exponents of those regimes are sincere in the use of such terms as democracy, freedom, and equality they are using them to convey a different set of meanings from those generally accepted. This causes confusion, but it would not necessarily be harmful if all who used this new set of meanings were sincere and did not rely on the traditional undertones of meaning in these words for propaganda purposes. Because confusion is caused it is necessary to point out how this different kind of 'Democracy' grew up, and to analyse the reasons for denying its right to be considered alongside our own Western system of liberal democracy.

Liberal and totalitarian democracy have a common origin in the eighteenth century. Rousseau took the idea of popular sovereignty and welded it into a doctrine—almost a religious faith—in his concept of the General Will. But his basically liberal intention was distorted. The establishment of a harmonious political society, which is fundamental to Rousseau's General Will, was the ideal sought after by the Jacobins during the French Revolution. The rule of the Committee of Public Safety was the first totalitarian democracy. During the first half of 1794 Robespierre and Saint-Just were trying desperately to establish a republic of virtue. The policy of Terror came to be justified as a necessary method of eliminating the vicious—in other words, the opponents of Robespierre and his policy! The guillotine became an instrument of lustration; the France of the Year II of Liberty was being forced to be free. The purely political nature of the ideal society envisaged by Rousseau and attempted by Robespierre was given the characteristic economic aspect which it has retained to this day by Mably's theory of property and Babeuf's attempt to round off the Revolution with communistic reforms in his abortive Conspiracy of the Equals in 1796.

It is necessary to sketch in the origins of the totalitarian form of democracy if only to point out that the system does belong essentially to the Western political tradition, and that "its origins go much farther back than nineteenth-century patterns, such as Marxism, because Marxism was itself only one, although admittedly the most vital, among the various versions of the totalitarian democratic ideal, which have followed each other for the last hundred and fifty years."[28]

The common origin of liberal and totalitarian democracy has inevitably resulted in some resemblances between the two systems, though the resemblances are somewhat superficial. In the first place, they both start from the individual; their common goal is the improvement of the lot of the individual human being. In this respect the democrats of both schools sit together on the left-hand side of the fence distinct from the totalitarian of the right, whose aim is the perfection of some collective entity, whether race, nation, or state. Moreover, such elements as equality, liberty, and sovereignty of the people, which are the essential constituents of liberal democracy, are to be found also in the rival system.

But the features which the two systems of democracy have in common fade into insignificance when the differences are brought to light. The fundamental difference lies in their different attitudes to politics. "The liberal approach," writes Professor Talmon,

> assumes politics to be a matter of trial and error, and regards political systems as pragmatic contrivances of human ingenuity and spontaneity.... The totalitarian democratic school, on the other hand, is based upon the assumption of a sole and exclusive truth in politics.... It recognises ultimately only one plane of existence, the political.[29]

This basic, ideological standpoint colours the totalitarian's interpretation of such democratic ideas as liberty and sovereignty of the people. Liberty especially is given a different interpretation; for the totalitarian it means the pursuit of the ideal—the communist, classless society, for example. But, to achieve a completely "free" society in this sense, those who do not agree with the aim or who are apathetic must be "forced to be free." This, of course, is a blatant denial of liberty in the accepted sense. And there is plenty of evidence of the practical denial of true liberty in the totalitarian democracies in the world to-day. Censorship of the Press, imprisonment for holding and expressing religious or political ideas in opposition to the current ideology, the prohibition of opposition political parties, have all been features of Communist régimes. The prohibition of opposition parties and the consequent single-party rule are also a practical denial of the sovereignty of the people; political power does not rest with the people but with the Party—it is the Party that controls the elections and the state machinery, and the form of government is thus oligarchic rather than democratic. Furthermore, if the Party monopolizes all real political rights (being forced, even if not a Party member, to vote for the Party is scarcely a 'right') the principle of equality cannot be said to be observed in such states. The Governments of totalitarian democracies point with pride to the 99.8 per cent. ballot or the 99·4 per cent. vote for the Communist candidate. Such figures are supposed to represent democratic public interest and support for the official candidates. But when one realizes that pressure can be brought to bear upon those who fail in their duty to vote or who vote against the official candidate, these statistics are placed in their true perspective. Of the five basic elements of democracy we are thus left with humanitarianism and the rule of law, and these are hardly features of Governments which rely on secret police and concentration camps or prisons for political offenders.

If none of the five elements of democracy exist in the so-called 'peoples' democracies' we cannot but conclude that the belief that they are democratic societies is a myth. Indeed, the very term 'totalitarian democracy' is a contradiction in terms, for any state which claims a total control over the lives and activities of its citizens is a standing denial of the very essence of democracy.

Conditions for Democracy

It should not be too readily assumed that democracy can flourish in any society. In 1919 and 1945 the victors of the World Wars looked out on a scene made safe for democracy; the forces of despotism had been worsted. Yet twenty years after the Versailles Settlement democracy had been eliminated by Hitler in Germany, Mussolini in Italy, Stalin in Russia, Franco in Spain, Salazar in Portugal; while it had been seriously undermined by corruption, incompetence, and uncertainty throughout the new small states of Eastern Europe. A comparable situation faces us to-day. Eastern Europe, though under a different régime, is still undemocratic. But this is to a certain extent an artificial situation. A more serious blow to the optimism of the democrats has been the failure or only partial success of their system in the Afro-Asian countries. It is, perhaps, not too much of a caricature to suggest that some Americans in the immediate post-War years believed that it was only necessary to establish democratic constitutions throughout the world to cure the world's political ills. It has been adequately proved since that democracy cannot be exported like Marshall Aid. Certain conditions have to be present in a society before democracy can take root, for it is not only a form of government, it is a way of life. Difficulties have been encountered in Japan, Indonesia, Burma, Ceylon, Pakistan, and many of the African and Middle Eastern countries. Dr Sukarno,

General Ayub, Dr Nkrumah, and others of their kind have been seen as the Francos and Mussolinis of the later twentieth century.

Democracy is something more than a series of formulae; it cannot be imposed overnight, for a mature democratic society is the result of a tradition built up, sometimes painfully, over a long period of time. The strength of democracy is, in fact, in direct proportion to the strength of the traditions of freedom, the rule of law, and so forth. Moreover, the progress of democracy in the native territories which have been emancipated from their colonial status will also be dependent on the strength of the democratic element of the past colonial administration. The need for the gradual building up of a democratic tradition before granting final independence is, indeed, one of the fundamentals of British colonial policy. Any attempt to force the pace, it is realized, might be fatal to the whole scheme.

Of the threefold cry of the French Revolutionaries no mention has as yet been made of fraternity. It is not unimportant. Fraternity implies the acceptance that other people have a right to live different lives or hold different opinions. A group of people who are pursuing one way of life and who happen to be in a majority must not use their weight of numbers to force the minority to renounce their individual beliefs or practices. But there are two sides to the medal: if the majority act in a tolerant way the minority must resign themselves to accepting the decisions of the majority.

One final point must be emphasized. Actual oppression by a majority or active rebellion by a minority are not required to destroy a sense of fraternity and thus undermine a democracy. The mere *belief* that oppression or rebellion would occur in certain circumstances is all that is required to destroy confidence in the fraternal spirit of one's fellows. For fraternity is the belief in the goodwill of one's fellow-citizens. In a state where suspicion, distrust, and a spirit of dissension exist fraternity is by very definition absent, and democracy cannot flourish.

The third prerequisite for democracy is that the people should want it; it can be disastrous for democracy to attempt to thrust it upon an unwilling people. A lack of desire for democracy may be expressed in two different ways. There may be a positive antipathy or, as shown above, even fear of freedom and responsibility; alternatively there may be negative apathy. One of the greatest commentators on democracy, Alexis de Tocqueville, believed that a positive urge for freedom especially was the most vital condition for the establishment of a democratic society. He wrote:

> There are nations which have tirelessly pursued freedom through every kind of peril and hardship. They loved it, not for its material benefits; they regarded freedom itself as a gift so precious and so necessary that no other could console them for the loss of everything else.... I attempt no analysis of that great emotion for those who cannot feel it. It enters of its own accord into the generous hearts God has prepared to receive it; it fills them, it inspires them; but to the meaner minds which have never felt it, it is past finding out.[30]

Closely connected with this desire for democracy is an educated sense of political responsibility. This condition may be further analysed into four components—namely, a positive interest in public affairs, the use of one's political rights for the public good, a certain minimum of education in order to be capable of making a responsible and independent political judgment, and, finally, the existence of lively political debate to stimulate thought. We are now venturing to a certain extent beyond the practical to the ideal. We cannot deny the name of democracy to communities which do not possess a completely developed sense of responsibility and political education, for, in that case, democracy would indeed be Utopia—in the sense of the original Greek words—nowhere! Nevertheless, if the above conditions are completely lacking democracy will be of puny growth.

An interest in public affairs may exist in both a democratic and a non-democratic country. If it exists in a non-democratic country and there is sufficient scope for its expression it will often lead to movements for the establishment of a democratic constitution. If it exists in a state which is already democratic, then it will be an important source of strength for the maintenance of that form of government. If, on the other hand, this interest is completely lacking, even in a minority, then democracy will probably not be achieved, or, if already established, will wither through lack of nourishment.

A proper balance is, however, as necessary in politics as in any other social activity: an interest in politics which is fanatical is not conducive to democracy. One's own opinions and interests must be pursued with moderation, and decisions and measures which conflict with one's own interests must be accepted, if they are reasonable, with resignation. The mentality which stretches political interest to a fanatical belief in one's own opinion is not a democratic mentality; it is not a sense of responsibility.

In order to attain a responsible, independent attitude to politics it is probably necessary to be literate. This was the belief behind Robert Lowe's famous remark on the passage of the Second Reform Bill in 1867: "I believe it will be absolutely necessary that you should prevail on our future masters to learn their letters," which has become popularized as "We must educate our masters."[31] To make a responsible political judgment a person needs to be able to think things out for himself by reading and reasoning; he needs to be literate. It is, however, necessary to add two footnotes. First, the education provided for the citizen must, for obvious reasons, be free from state interference and propaganda. Second, it must be admitted that experiments are being made in democracy in illiterate communities, such as India and even Nepal; but they will probably achieve greater success when plans for more widespread education get under way.

The final condition is essentially an aspect of a question already discussed as a basic element of democracy—freedom of discussion. Independent political judgment can be exercised only when there is more than one opinion to choose from. The clash of opinion in debate is therefore essential to democracy. People must not only be free to express their ideas and exchange views, they must have the opportunity to undertake these debates on a wide scale and by every possible medium. Every side of important political issues must be given to the citizens so that they have an opportunity to come to their own personal decisions. Newspapers, radio, television, public meetings, must all be utilized for this purpose. Furthermore, such debate must be of more than academic interest. It must be possible for every idea, if the people so wish, to be given practical application. It must be possible, by force of argument, for a small group to win over followers and gain sufficient strength to become an important factor in the political life of the country. In such a way will the political life of the country be continually in flux and remain vital, and stagnation be prevented. For stagnation produces apathy, and apathy leads to the decay of democracy. There is some cause for concern in this respect in the Western world to-day. People in general are apathetic about political issues: like the Romans of old, their interests are concentrated on *panem et circenses*—or, rather, refrigerators and television. The people of Britain voted Conservative from 1951 to 1964 because they "have never had it so good," rather than from a consideration of the fundamental issues of democracy which arise over international and colonial problems. The electorate tends to vote into power the politicians who promise prosperity, and politicians promise prosperity in order to be voted into power.

Conclusions

Democracy is not a perfect form of political organization, and even within the democratic framework there are many problems still to be solved in both the well-established and the newly formed democratic countries. In this final section it is necessary to examine the problems of establishing a democratic constitution in underdeveloped lands, the state of democracy in the Western world, and the values of democracy over and against other forms of government.

Representative democracy is a form of government which owes its development especially to the political ideas and practices of the Western Hemisphere. It is a feature of the mid-twentieth-century world, however, that the idea of national self-determination has been linked with the idea of democracy in the countries emerging from colonial status. The question must inevitably be posed of how far Western political ideas are suited to the communities of Africa and Asia with such different social and political backgrounds.

The concurrence of the demands for democracy and for national independence can itself obscure the issue of the suitability of democracy. The two demands are by no means identical, for it is possible for a colony to be governed along democratic lines and its democracy be destroyed after the achievement of independence. Imperial states who, like Britain, profess democracy, have thus been placed in a dilemma. Are they to grant independence and risk the destruction of youthful democracy by the establishment of authoritarian régimes? Such has been the danger in recent years in Ghana or, less seriously, British Guiana (Guyana), for example. The alternative is to withhold the grant of independence until, in the opinion of the Imperial Government, the colony is capable by itself of maintaining democracy. However, this may inflame nationalistic feeling and lead to tension. Such was the danger in Kenya and Nyasaland, for example.

In fact, the record of democracy in Asia and Africa since the

Second World War does not reveal very many successes at all, and India is perhaps alone in maintaining its democratic institutions intact. The health of a democracy can be to a large extent gauged by the freedom allowed to and the sense of responsibility shown by the Opposition. If Opposition politicians are flung into gaol for criticizing the Government, then democracy is in danger. This situation has occurred, for example, in Ghana. What, then, are the factors against democracy in the under-developed territories? The answer is twofold. Firstly, the conditions for democracy are frequently wanting: education is very restricted, and a tradition of political activity by the masses is almost entirely lacking. Secondly, the immediate needs of these peoples are economic, not political. Many are existing on a starvation level, and therefore have little interest in anything beyond the immediate problem of living. Also, in connexion with this economic problem, a veritable revolution is necessary to raise the standard of living above the bare subsistence level, and it is doubtful whether this can be achieved without undemocratic control and planning, unless massive foreign grants and loans are made available. The most effective way of nursing young Afro-Asian countries successfully through early stages of democracy is, therefore, by the provision of generous economic aid; where this is lacking democracy is likely to be in danger.

The difficulties being encountered by former colonial territories are hardly surprising when it is realized that the practice of democracy in its own home ground of the Atlantic community is not without its problems.

Although Parliament is a pre-democratic institution, it has become an essential part of democratic machinery. But the problems of the relationship of the other elements of government and of the organization of the procedure within Parliament still have to be solved.

The classic exposition of the institutional requirements of democracy was made two hundred years ago by Montesquieu. He maintained that, as far as possible, the legislative, executive, and judicial functions should be kept distinct, and checks and balances be put into effect to prevent the concentration of power in the hands of one individual or body. "There is no liberty," he wrote, "when the legislative and the executive powers are to be found in the same person or in the same organ. There is no liberty if the power to judge is not separated from the legislative and the executive powers."[32]

Many to-day are afraid that this principle is being ignored, though there is some confusion concerning the nature of the concentration of power. Some point to the excessive powers of the executive as exercised through the Cabinet as the source of unbalance; legislation is determined by the leaders of the Government party, not by debate in the legislative assembly. There are other observers, however, who interpret the destruction of the balance of power by a completely opposite tendency—namely, by the excessive respect for the sovereignty of the people and the consequent emasculation of the executive power. This is the theme of Walter Lippmann's *The Public Philosophy*. "The evaporation of the imponderable powers, a total [dependence] upon the assemblies and the mass electorates," he writes, "has upset the balance of powers between the two functions of the state. The executive has lost both its material and its ethereal powers. The assemblies and the mass electorates have acquired the monopoly of effective powers."[33]

The value of the idea of the separation, if not the balance, of powers may be doubted, and perhaps a greater danger to democracy from within lies in the excessive powers of the political parties. In Britain especially it is now practically impossible to enter Parliament without being a 'bona fide' candidate of one of the two major parties. This means that the candidate has to support the party programme irrespective of his own opinions on any single item of that programme. Furthermore, to retain his position in Parliament, and certainly to advance it, the M.P. must remain loyal to the party. If he does not the party whip will be withdrawn and he will become a political outcast. Finally, in order to ensure party solidarity on any major issue discussed in Parliament, the 'party line' is decided in private committee beforehand. Freedom to speak and vote according to his conscience has therefore become a rare, rather than an automatic, privilege for the M.P., to be exercised only when politically unimportant issues are at stake. Party discipline has become a restraint on democracy: it restricts the M.P.'s freedom of opinion and speech; it makes a mockery of Parliamentary debate. In such a situation, of course, the rôle of the Opposition becomes doubly important; for they, alone almost, become the trustees of Parliamentary democracy. They must be capable of providing an alternative administration, and the Government must not be allowed to forget it. Although there is growing concern in Britain about the danger to democracy which the party machines represent, there is also the realization that weak, fragmented parties raise problems of their own. This arrangement in France led to chronic instability under the Fourth Republic and reduced the Assembly to political impotence in the Fifth. During the twelve years of its existence, for example, the Fourth Republic had twenty-five Governments. The Assembly became a kaleidoscope of parties—Communists, Social Democrats, Christian Democrats, Radicals, Gaullists, Poujadists, to mention but the most important. Coalitions became inevitable, and dissensions within the Government became the order of the day. To remedy this situation the powers of the executive, especially the President, *vis-à-vis* the Assembly have been considerably strengthened by the constitution of the Fifth Republic. Again, it is some practical *via media* that is evidently necessary.

The need for party organization and Governmental efficiency has come about because of the increased activity of the state. Here, in fact, is the crux of the matter and the great paradox: the increased power of the masses has led to a demand that the state should provide them with a better life; this, in turn, has necessitated state interference and organization and a consequent loss of individual liberty. Economic considerations are superseding political awareness. Democracy is undermining democracy. Moreover, liberty can be destroyed in a democratic society in two other ways. Democracy implies government in accordance with the wishes of the people, and the people, through an appeal to their emotional instincts, may insist on a restriction of liberty. McCarthyism provided a good illustration of this danger. The final contradiction inherent in the concept of democracy is the potential contradiction between liberty and equality; for liberty leads to differentiation, while equality implies a tendency to standardization. Again, it is a just balance that is needed. Excessive differentiation will lead to the subjection of the community by one group. "On the other hand, on the egalitarian side, we find ... that despotism has always accompanied the victory of movements aiming solely at equality.... The greater the equality striven for, the more the power needed to enforce it."[34]

It is evident that the defence of liberty, even in a democratic community, requires great vigilance and care; and before we pass on to our concluding remarks it is necessary to pose the question whether it is justifiable and expedient to restrict liberty in defence of liberty. Since a democratic society by very definition allows freedom of expression, it is inevitable, though unfortunate, that some people should use this freedom to denounce democracy—and freedom itself. In recent years, the question has been posed in the following form: "Should Fascists or Communists be allowed to spread their anti-democratic propaganda in democratic states?" The forcible suppression of a movement which is working for the overthrow of democracy is perfectly justifiable, for self-defence is the first law of nature in politics as in the jungle. Moreover, liberty and tolerance are justifiable in a political context only if they are mutual. In practice, however, it is recognized that recourse to repressive measures is itself dangerous; it can become a habit. And it is a mark of political wisdom in a democracy to recognize when to refrain from hunting down a movement already rendered impotent, and when to resist the urge to suppress a movement not yet dangerous.

If there are so many dangers and weaknesses in democracy and so many opponents to it, it may well be asked whether it is such a worth-while form of government after all. Now that we are coming to the end of our survey of democracy we are in a position to draw together the threads and face this vital question. It is proposed to consider, firstly, the arguments which have been put forward by the opponents of democracy, some contradictory of others, but none the less formidable. An attempt will then be made, finally, to counter these charges.

As Plato pointed out long ago, government is a difficult, if not the most difficult, art. It is obvious, according to this argument, that it is a job for specialists. The mass of the people are not possessed of the qualities for making sound political decisions. Yet even the decisions which the people cannot for practical reasons make themselves are made by politicians who are dependent on the support of the people. Thus, when a political judgment is required, "The decisive consideration is not whether the proposition is good but whether it is popular—not whether it will work and prove itself but whether the active talking constituents like it immediately."[35] Furthermore, as there is frequently little to choose between alternative courses of action, the mass of people will vacillate between them and fail to provide a consistent policy. Democracy therefore tends to destroy the valuable feature of consistency in government. It is, in short, inefficient.

It is also levelled against democracy that it exalts mediocrity; for the geniuses must always be in a minority, the ordinary masses in a majority; and the representative of the masses "has all possible temptation, instead of setting up before the governed who elect him, and on whose favour he depends, a high standard of right reason, to accommodate himself as much as possible to their natural taste for the bathos."[36]

It is suggested, again, that democracy is a fake—a veil of respectability drawn over the naked power of the man or men who manipulate the people's votes. Shaw put this idea into the mouth of his Trade Union official, Boanerges: "I say to them 'You are supreme: exercise your power.' They say, 'That's right: tell us what to do;' and I tell them. I say, 'Exercise your vote intelligently by voting for me.' And they do. That's democracy."[37] But trade unionism is not the only source of power behind the scenes of democracy. Family connexions, social background, and wealth, all exert influence, while public opinion is largely moulded by a national Press controlled by a mere handful of businessmen and journalists. Democracy, according to this argument, is an expression of popular opinion as manipulated by these powerful forces, rather than the expression of independent judgment.

Finally, the opponents of democracy reject its underlying optimism. Democracy is based on the assumption that the exercise of sovereignty by the people as a whole will result in political wisdom or, at least, common sense; for the people are fundamentally sensible and careful of their own interests. This is rejected by the critics of democracy. The concentration of sovereignty in the people, they argue, is just as dangerous as the concentration of sovereignty in any other single person or group, and even more likely to result in errors. "No more than the kings before them should the people be hedged with divinity."[38]

Yet, in spite of these attacks on democracy, it still survives, and it is still very much respected. These facts must obviously be explained.

In the first place, it is necessary to answer the charges against democracy. The belief that politics needs experienced specialists is not denied in a democracy. The effective government of Britain, for example, is in the hands of the Cabinet and the Civil Service—highly experienced and well-trained men. What a democratic government does imply is the control of these specialists and the denial of any right to their assumption of complete power. It is an essential part of the doctrine of the democrat that the knowledge and efficiency of the expert must be tempered with the common sense of the masses.

The charge of inconsistency can also be answered. In so far as different lines of policy are tried, this is a virtue rather than a fault, for it prevents stagnation. It is only when the power to make changes is abused that the problem becomes serious. And whenever this does occur the people are revealing a lack of political responsibility—acting, in other words, undemocratically.

Thirdly, the attacks made on the power of popular opinion by such people as Matthew Arnold and J. S. Mill were made largely in defence of culture and good taste. But democracy is concerned with political, not æsthetic judgments.

The next accusation—namely, that the people vote merely in the way that the demagogues tell them—is again a criticism of a perverted rather than a true democracy. The people have the opportunity at regular elections to express their opinions. They have, too, plenty of opportunity of weighing arguments and evidence to arrive at an unbiased decision, for every point of view is given ample expression in different newspapers, magazines, and radio and television programmes. If they do not vote according to their consciences they are neglecting their responsibilities as citizens of a democratic state, and by that much is democracy undermined.

The final question, whether the people can be trusted with absolute sovereignty, is one of faith. There is no argument against faith. The democrat has it; the anti-democrat has not.

But the fundamental justification for democracy can be perceived only when one has pierced the emotional haze of almost religious faith in mankind which underlies the concept of popular sovereignty, and penetrated the fog of argument surrounding the detailed questions concerning the administration of democracy. It then becomes clear that democracy is a method of distributing and thus diluting power. For, since "All power tends to corrupt, and absolute power corrupts absolutely,"[39] the concentration of power in the hands of a small governing élite, which would lead in theory to the ideal of efficient government, is in practice too dangerous. It is true that there have been examples of truly benevolent despotisms, but the evidence of history proves that they are exceptions and that the risk is thus too great. Democracy is a compromise of safety.

CHAPTER FIVE

RELIGION

The Argument

Introduction. The connexion between religion and politics—Christianity and politics.

Nationalism. The connexion between religion and nationalism—examples of the connexion—religion and nationalism at variance.

Communism. Communism as a 'religion' and its similarities to Christianity—the essential hostility of Christianity—comparison with Catholicism—relations with the Catholic Church—relations with the Orthodox and Islamic Churches.

Democracy. Introduction—the two diverse trends—evidence for and against the trends—Christian Democracy.

The Papacy. Practical influence—Papal political theory.

Introduction

Political theory is concerned with the relationship of the individual with the community as a whole; it is concerned to justify certain existing relations and to point the way to a nearer approximation to the idea of a good society. Political theory is thus closely allied to social and ethical theory. So too is religion. The great religions of the world are concerned with the problems of what is right and good and how men should behave towards each other. It is inevitable, therefore, that the basic questions that have been discussed by political theorists should also have exercised the minds of theologians. Conversely, Bishop Berkeley, for example, was quite certain of the necessity to approach politics from a religious point of view. He wrote, "Whatever the world thinks, he who hath not meditated upon God, the human mind, and the 'summum bonum,' may possibly make a thriving earthworm, but will most indubitably make a sorry patriot and a sorry statesman."[1] Moreover, precisely because politics and religion overlap, Church and state have frequently clashed over the interpretation of their respective spheres of authority. Christ stated quite categorically, as St Matthew tells us, "Render therefore unto Cæsar the things which are Cæsar's; and unto God the things that are God's."[2] On the surface this appears to be advice that is simple enough to follow, for the Church is concerned with ideals, whereas the state must busy itself more with practical administrative realities. There are questions, however, where the jurisdictions of the two spheres coincide, and unless there is mutual respect and agreement the coincidence will become a violent clash. "There must," in the words of Leo XIII, "exist between these two powers, a certain orderly connection, which may be compared to the soul and body in man."[3] For there are several issues, as Pope Leo stated, that belong "to the jurisdiction and judgment of both" the ecclesiastical and civil power.[4] These include public policy on the family, marriage and divorce, education, crime and punishment, the righteousness of any given war, and the distribution of wealth. No analysis of the important political forces at work to-day can therefore afford to neglect the impact of the various great religions on the political thinking of the world.

Although the essential connexion between religion and political thought is fairly evident, the practical force of religion in politics to-day is perhaps not immediately clear. This contrasts vividly with the medieval position, when politics was almost a branch of theology. As has already been indicated in Chapter 1, the great thinkers for over a thousand years—Augustine, Aquinas, Luther—all worked from the assumption that the will of God was the ultimate social and political authority. The Renaissance and the rationalism of the late seventeenth and eighteenth centuries brought political thinking down to earth in more senses than one: the foundations of sovereignty became, with Machiavelli and Hobbes, force and expediency instead of divine authority. Political thought, except for the specific contribution of the Churches—in particular the Roman Catholic—has remained secular since that time.

The general turning away from religion, and in particular from Christianity, in the Western world has created its own special problems in the political sphere. The other-worldly nature of religion has, in the past, served to buttress people's souls against the hardships and disappointments of their present existence. It has served to soothe social tensions and give people an ideal to look forward to. Anticipation of something better, more worth while, relieves the lowliest of the deadweight of life endured as a struggle for bare existence at little more than starvation level. Those who have no religious faith require some other moral support and turn to one of the several political doctrines for assistance. Nationalism and Communism are both, to a certain degree, synthetic substitutes for religion. But to exalt these political theories to the rank of a religious faith is to put a tremendous strain on them, a strain which they can surely not bear for long. In particular, the consolation which Christianity, for example, promises for the life hereafter the modern 'secular religions' promise for the life on this earth. While this optimism in human material progress—for that largely is what it is—is seen to be justified by events these faiths will flourish, but once the mood changes to pessimism these faiths are doomed. Their weakness as 'religions' in short lies in the fact that they can too easily be proved to be wrong or unjustified by events on this earth.

The strength of the secular, political 'religions' is frequently based on the power of a state. The strength of Communism is based on the power of the U.S.S.R. and its allies; the strength of Arab nationalism is based on the power of Egypt and its allies. It is possible, therefore, to make a reasonably accurate estimate of the practical relevance of these doctrines in world politics. This is not so with the true, theistic religions. The mass of people are generally apathetic: they would not willingly risk their comfort, certainly not their lives, for their religion. Even the comparatively highly organized Roman Catholic Church cannot force any of its members into a political action against their will. It is equally true that the majority of Russians are apathetic Communists—even hostile to the system. But the Kremlin has a coercive power that the Vatican does not possess. An assessment of the political importance of any religion must, therefore, always be very tentative. As Professor Brogan has written, "It is difficult, therefore, to know what importance to attach to mere religious statistics, to maps showing religious distribution in high colours or to political calculations based on the presumed existence of religious blocs whose strength and political attitude can be assumed."[5] The influence of religious feeling, in any case, will differ according to both the area and the religion under discussion.

Nevertheless, although we cannot define with a mathematical accuracy the strength of religion in modern world politics, we can be quite aware that the connexion is an important one. The resistance of the Roman Catholic Church to Communism in Eastern Europe, the political influence of the Vatican, the work of the Christian Democrat Parties in Western Europe, the force of Islam behind Arab nationalism, have all inspired discussion during recent years. The importance of a sense of religion in the countries of the West was perhaps never more obviously emphasized by lay statesmen in the modern era than in the joint declaration of Sir Anthony Eden and President Eisenhower during the former's premiership. "We are conscious," they declared, "that in this year 1956 there still rages the age-old struggle between those who believe that man has his origin and his destiny in God and those who treat man as if he were designed merely to serve a State machine."[6]

The emphasis in this book is on the essentially Western tradition in political thinking; for, although nationalism, Communism, and democracy have spread throughout the world, they are in origin based on ideas developed in the Western Hemisphere. Similarly, the emphasis in this chapter will be on the religion of the Western world —namely, Christianity.

In discussing the essential connexion between Christianity and politics we need do little more than underline what has already been said above concerning the general close relationship between religion and politics. The Christian feels a moral obligation to campaign for the establishment of a civil society and of international relations on Christian foundations. It is his duty to lay down certain fundamental principles upon which, in his view, political decisions should be based. He should, too, be quite clear to what end society is striving. Dr Temple summed up the Christian position in this way: "The aim of a Christian social order is the fullest possible development of individual personality in the widest possible fellowship."[7] If the Church is Established, as the Church of England is in England, the state, of course, has a certain moral obligation to uphold the principles outlined by its Church. In practice, in fact, it is difficult to ignore Christian principles in the West—they are so firmly embedded in our ways of thought.

With the exceptions of the social concept of feudalism and the cynical ideas of the Renaissance, the whole Western tradition of political theory from the age of Seneca to that of Milton was essentially Christian in its preconceptions and language. The great political debates of these 1600 years were carried on largely in theological terms. The debates concerned the divine authority of the state and the duty of passive obedience by the citizen; the relative authorities of the spiritual and temporal powers; the divine authority of kingship; and the freedom of religious opinion. This religious Christian tradition, it is true, has been partially eclipsed by the progress of modern psychology, economics, and science in particular. But it has not been destroyed. It is impossible entirely to rid ourselves, even if we wished, of our traditions; but, apart from this innate tendency to think in general Christian terms, consciously Christian political theory is still being written. There is certainly no unified body of thought—a fact deprecated by those who would see a unified Christendom standing out against atheistic Communism. The general division produced by the Reformation is still with us. Catholic thought, exemplified by Papal encyclicals and the writings of such distinguished thinkers as Jacques Maritain, tends to be more dogmatic than the much vaguer, pragmatic writings of the Protestants, most eminently represented by Dr Reinhold Niebuhr.

There are signs that the Christian Churches are bringing their political thinking more into line with the needs of the time. The identification of the Church in the eighteenth century in Europe with the worldly aristocracy and their interests, and the failure of the Church to help the ordinary people in their struggle against the evils of the Industrial Revolution, led to a serious lack of confidence on the part of the working classes. In eighteenth-century England they turned to Methodism; in twentieth-century France, for example, they turned to Communism. In this perspective, of course, the revision by the various Christian Churches of their political and social doctrines is of vital political significance.

NATIONALISM

Nationalism is the most widespread of the substitutes for religion which have been discussed in outline above. It appears as a potent force in all four quarters of the globe with peoples of every colour, and is itself often strengthened by the orthodox religions. For membership of a Church gives a people a sense of unity and a realization of distinctness from other peoples; it can therefore frequently be an essential part of the feeling of kinship which is the essence of nationalism.

Just as nationalism can lead to the disintegration of a formerly unified country, so too can the religious basis of nationalism assist in this direction. However illogical from the economic, administrative, and military points of view the division of Ireland into Eire and Ulster or of India into the Pakistani and Indian republics may be, we cannot deny the force of the desires which has resulted in these situations, desires which are mainly religious. An Ulsterman feels himself different from his southern neighbour because he is Protestant in his faith and the other Roman Catholic. The creation of the Moslem League in the old Indian Empire and the subsequent splitting away of the independent Moslem state of Pakistan was the result of fears of Hindu domination once the British withdrew. The death roll of 1,000,000 in the riots which followed when the British did leave in 1947 was sufficient proof of the intensity of religious feelings in the sub-continent. Religious feeling has also surely exacerbated the conflict between Jew and Arab in Palestine and Greek and Turk in Cyprus. In Cyprus the feeling of and demand for unity with Greece found its leader in Makarios—an archbishop of the Greek Orthodox Church.

It can hardly be said that the newly developing Afro-Asian nationalism is based on a strong feeling of religious unity. There are signs, however, of a sense of religious hostility—a rejection of Christianity as the religion of the white man and the imperialist. Dr Murray has made this quite clear:

> Abroad, the growth of self-conscious nationalism in Africa and the Far East and the resuscitation of the old ethnic religions has almost recreated for the Church in India and elsewhere the conditions of the Roman Empire of the first century. Christianity, so closely identified with the white ruling classes, has suffered with them in their eclipse.[8]

The missionary work of Islam, on the other hand, is achieving greater success, for it is the religion of the successful Arab nationalist movement.

Islam is, indeed, one of the important unifying elements of Pan-Arabism. The Moslem religion is by tradition an anti-Western force. It started in rivalry to Christianity in the Middle East, and as it expanded into Europe it clashed with Western Christendom in a series of great struggles—at Constantinople in 717 and 718, at Tours in 732, during the Crusades, at Las Navas de Tolosa in 1212, Mohacs in 1526, and Lepanto in 1571. Indeed, only after the relief of Vienna in 1683 was the Islamic threat to the continent of Europe finally removed. This tradition thus adds to the desire for independence as well as to the feeling of unity. Islam is not, of course, a highly organized political unit. The peoples of Persia, Afghanistan, Pakistan, Indonesia, and of the Moslem provinces of the Soviet Union who are not Arab by race have little, apart from their religion, in common with their co-religionists of the Middle East. There are, too, essentially religious differences within Islam—between the great sects, the Shi'is, the Sunnis, and the Wahhabis. Even in the Arab lands there are political rivalries, between Egypt and Saudi Arabia especially. Nevertheless, what feeling of kinship there is between the Strait of Gibraltar and the Persian Gulf is due to a sense not only of common race, but also of common religion.

The people with perhaps the most highly developed sense of religion in the world are the Tibetans, though the Chinese have done much to crush this spirit since 1959. The lamas had great authority, the Dalai Lama being supreme in both spiritual and secular matters. The Tibetan resistance to the Chinese, which persisted throughout the 1950's, was as much a Buddhist movement as a rising against foreigners. The Dalai Lama fled to India, and the Chinese broke the local resistance largely by ruthless action—executions and transportation—against the lamas before prosecuting similar policies against the population at large.

The alliance between religion and nationalism is, perhaps, fairly evident—more in evidence than the hostility between the two. Yet hostility is more natural, for, vague as the frontiers of the great religions are, they cut across the equally vague frontiers of race and the conversely rigid frontiers of the modern state. Indeed, as Professor Field pointed out, "The great moral and religious systems that have most influenced human conduct, Christianity, Stoicism, Buddhism, and others, have always taught that morality is not a matter of frontiers, but that in some sense benevolence and other duties are owed equally to all human beings just because they are human."[9] The Roman Catholic Church, for example, is a great supra-national institution; it provides the common faith of numerous European and Latin American states, besides large minorities in many countries throughout the world. Islam, although providing a basis for Arab unity, is also an important supra-national religion, extending, or has already been mentioned, beyond Arabia into Asia and the Far East.

The modern nation-state is based not only on a differentiation between it and other nations, but on the complete adherence of the parts to the whole—of the individual citizens to the state. The nation-state is all-embracing, and finds it difficult to accept divided loyalty in its citizens. It is here, perhaps, that religion is the most formidable in its hostility to nationalism. The Pope, for example, has been described as "a kind of special world monarch who rules a synthetic moral empire that overlaps and penetrates the sovereignty of all earthly governments."[10] The problem of reconciling loyalty to one's state and to one's faith is, it is true, older than the phenomenon of nationalism. The early Christians were faced with the conflict of loyalties between Caesar and God; the Catholics in Elizabethan England between Gloriana and Rome; modern Communists—for in this respect Marxism is in the nature of a 'secular religion'—between the nation of their birth and Moscow. But nationalism has extended and intensified the problem. The faith which demands a portion, if not all, of the citizen's loyalty may have its headquarters either inside or outside the state—it makes little difference, except that in an open conflict the state is more able to crush the religious force if it is centred within its own frontiers. Brezhnev can bring greater pressure to bear on the Russian Orthodox Church than can Gierek on the Roman Catholic Church.

Communism

The religious nature of Communism—indeed, its resemblance to Christianity—has frequently been pointed out. Marx has been called "the Calvin of economic theory,"[11] though by the more fanatical of his adherents he would be elevated to a position analogous to that of Christ Himself. Political decisions are taken in accordance with the contemporary interpretations of the utterances of the master and his disciples. The Communist gospel is a large and diffuse collection of works. It consists of the expositions of the dialectic doctrine not only by Marx himself, but also by his famous disciples Engels, Lenin, Stalin, and now, of course, Khrushchev and Mao Tse-tung, besides a host of lesser glossators of the sacred texts.

The diffusion of the belief is in the hands of a relatively small élite—the members of the Communist Parties, whose task is much the same as that of a clergy. Moreover, the best of this élite reveal the qualities of the best of the Christian priesthood. For many of the

Party members have a genuinely sincere faith. Those who worked for the original October Revolution in Russia, those who worked to consolidate the Revolution, and those who have worked and are still working for the extension of the Revolution—all have shown a remarkably selfless attitude to the cause. They have worked tirelessly, many have suffered imprisonment and even death in the manner of missionaries, crusaders, and martyrs. The loyalty required from adherents to Communism is of a very strict kind. Those who cannot give such undivided support are sinners to be pitied; those who wish to revise the dogma are schismatics to be abhorred; and traitors who actively oppose the Revolution are heretics to be destroyed. Perhaps no one has emphasized the parallels more than Professor Parkinson: he has written, "If the political characteristics of Theocracy are to include a Founder, a Mythology, a Sacred Book, a Priesthood, a place of pilgrimage and an Inquisition, Communism must be ranked among the great religions of the world."[12]

Finally, there are communistic elements in Christianity, for both Communism and Christianity have a highly developed social conscience; both exalt the poverty-stricken lower classes. The simile concerning the camel's negotiation of the eye of a needle is as applicable to the Communist as to the Christian faith. From this starting-point of the poverty of the masses both doctrines promise a better life for the future—in the true Communist, classless society and in Heaven, respectively.

The parallels with the Christian religion are therefore very close —close enough, indeed, for eminent Churchmen to express their support for Communism. In England Dr Hewlett Johnson, the late Dean of Canterbury, provided the most famous example of this attempt to combine the two faiths. Such people are becoming increasingly common in Latin America.

Many people, however, would prefer to dub such clerics notorious. This hostility is based on the belief in the essential antithesis between Communism and Christianity.

Fundamentally, of course, Communism is hostile to any religion in being a materialistic philosophy: economic motives are the be-all and end-all of individual and political action. There is nothing for the Marxist beyond this life: there is no Divinity, there is no human soul. Spiritual values and needs are explained as mere reflections of material desires. In such negative ethical circumstances it is scarcely surprising that the individual, so important in Christian teaching, should be lost in the all-important class struggle and trampled down beneath the all-powerful State which has come to be the means to victory in this struggle. All moral judgments are, indeed, dependent on the relation of an action to the achievement of the final end of the classless society. Lies, the breaking of promises, the repudiation of treaties, are all permissible—indeed, obligatory—if they assist in the achievement of this ultimate aim. All this, evidently, is quite contrary to the teaching of Christianity. Nothing could be more categorical than Pope Pius XI's statement on this: "This sovereign reality, God, is the utter and complete refutation of the arrogant and baseless falsehoods of the communists."[13] More challenging, however, was the Report of the Committee on the Christian Doctrine of Man at the Lambeth Conference of 1948. This stated:

> The most highly organised, consistent, powerful, and destructive form of secularism is beyond doubt Dialectical Materialism, and the type of communism in which it is embodied. This is perhaps the one live alternative to the Christian interpretation of man. Between the two there can be no compromise and it seems to be increasingly probable that it is between these two that the world must choose.[14]

Before passing on to a consideration of the relations of Communism with the various religions within the Soviet bloc we must examine one further point of comparison that is sometimes made— namely, the parallels between Marxism and the Roman Catholic Church. This attitude of mind has been neatly summarized by Denis Brogan. He writes, "If you don't like the Kremlin, you say it is a Marxist Vatican; if you don't like the Vatican, you say it is a Catholic Kremlin; if you don't like either, you call down a plague on both houses, thus assuming that they are, in fact, much of a muchness."[15] What is the foundation for this comparison? Both doctrines are international and therefore supra-national in their scope; they ignore the boundaries of states. Their adherents look to a central authority—at Moscow and at Rome—for direction. Furthermore, this direction is given in a dogmatic form—by the General Secretary of the C.P.S.U. assisted by the Politburo of the Central Committee of the Party and by the Pope assisted by the Curia.

Again, as with the general parallels with Christianity, this is a superficial analysis which ignores important facts. It ignores, it goes without saying, the fundamental point that Communism is a materialist, anti-religious philosophy—that Marx himself said that religion is the opium of the people. This attitude ignores too the difference in power exercised by Brezhnev and Paul VI, for example. Mr Brezhnev has not only the power of the various international Communist organizations to call upon, he has also the military strength of the Warsaw Pact at his command. The Pope, on the other hand, has spiritual authority only; he has no temporal power to enforce his decisions, even if he should want to. The double allegiance of Communist and patriot, outside the Communist bloc, is sometimes difficult, but a Roman Catholic patriot is quite common.

Conflicts, or at least uneasy relations, are inevitable between Communism and Catholicism. Not only are there the fundamental differences between them which have just been discussed, but the fact that they are both international organizations seeking adherents to a rigid faith makes them inevitable rivals. This is, moreover, truer of Catholicism than of Protestantism, as the latter is less of a unified force and has a less rigid doctrine.

The practical relationship between Communism and Catholicism has been revealed in Communist countries outside Russia. The bulk of the adherents to Rome living under Communist control are the fifty million in the East European states of Poland, Hungary, Czechoslovakia, Rumania, and Yugoslavia; and there are a dwindling number of converts in China.

In Eastern Europe Church and Party are in a state of equilibrium; neither can afford an all-out attack on the other. It is well known that there is no love lost between them—the imprisonment of the Primates of Poland and Hungary, Cardinals Wyszinsky and Mindszenty, in the Stalinist era proved that. Moreover, much Church property has been confiscated and education secularized. But there is a general working agreement that the Party members should confine themselves to politics, and the clergy to matters of the spirit. In particular, Pope John XXIII, during his short but extremely active pontificate, pursued a positive policy of conciliation to help those behind the Iron Curtain. The position in Poland is especially illuminating. A large proportion of the population, even members of the Communist Party, are Roman Catholics. Gomulka knew that an attack on this body of opinion would be dangerous: he came to an agreement with the Primate when he came to power in 1956, and he was careful to see that the Czestochowa crisis in the summer of 1958 blew over with no serious repercussions. On the other hand, the Cardinal realizes that the post-1956 regime is preferable to a neo-Stalinist dictatorship, and is therefore careful not to provoke the Polish, and more particularly the Soviet, Government.

In China the situation is rather different, for all religions are considered counter-revolutionary, and even Confucianism and Taoism have been attacked. But the fiercest persecution has been suffered by the Roman Catholic Church. Faced with the strong faith of the members of the Church, the Peking Government set up a rival, schismatic Church entirely under its own control. The Vatican has, of course, made a series of protests and excommunicated the bishops of the rival Church; but the Chinese pressure is being successful.

Just as there have been second thoughts on the direct attack on the Roman Catholic Church in Eastern Europe, so has there been a change of policy towards the Orthodox Church in Russia itself. The Church in Russia still exists; it certainly has not been destroyed by the succession of purges and persecutions it has suffered since the Revolution, especially in the years immediately after 1917. The Russians are a religious people, and the traditions of centuries cannot be wiped away by a mere generation's activities of the Communist Party or even the Komsomol, the Communist youth movement. It is true that the attraction of the Church is weakening, yet, inasmuch as the Government's propaganda in favour of scientific, atheistic materialism has had only a limited effect, it is proof of the inadequacy of Marxism as a substitute religion for the mass of the people.

The truce between Church and state in Russia is an uneasy one, and continues only because it is politically convenient for the Government. The leniency of the Soviet Government in recent years towards the Moslem peoples living in the southern regions of the U.S.S.R. derives too from essentially political motives. Russia's policy of backing Arab nationalism against the West, and her attempt to establish influence in the Middle East, would be considerably hampered if the Arabs' co-religionists in the Soviet Union were being persecuted.

Democracy

There is nothing in Christian teaching as such that should make it predisposed to any particular form of government. It is quite possible for a dictator or an oligarchy to rule in accordance with Christian principles as much as a democracy. Indeed, the emergence of democracy, especially in the French Revolution, for example, has often been opposed by the Church as being a revolutionary movement; while democracy has been hostile to the Church as being an ally of the privileged. Nevertheless, authoritarian regimes tend to ignore the sanctity of the individual soul and violate the decencies of humanitarianism. Western democracy, on the other hand, is based on the essentially Christian doctrine of respect for the individual. Furthermore, most modern dictators, Hitler and Stalin perhaps especially, have demanded adulation to the point of worship impossible for a Christian to recognize. That is not to say that all who have supported or do support democracy have been Christians or that all Christians are democrats—rather that Christianity has been so firmly instilled in our ways of thinking in the West that we accept many of its fundamental concepts without fully realizing their origin. The doctrine of the fatherhood of God and thus the brotherhood of man not only makes every individual intrinsically important, but provides him with the equality of brotherhood in relation to his fellows.

Yet it is frequently asserted that the Roman Catholic Church is alien to democracy and that the Protestant forms of Christianity are in sympathy with it. The reasons for this general conclusion can be well summed up by two quotations. The first is from Count Coudenhove-Kalergi's *Crusade for Pan-Europe*, while the second is from Dr Murray's Hibbert Lectures for 1957.

> Catholicism is the fascist form of Christianity of which Calvinism represents its democratic wing. The Catholic hierarchy rests fully and securely on the leadership principle with the infallible Pope in supreme command for a lifetime.... Like the Fascist party, its priesthood becomes a medium for an undemocratic minority rule by a hierarchy ... Catholic nations follow fascist doctrines more willingly than Protestant nations, which are the main strongholds of democracy.... Democracy lays its stress on personal conscience; fascism on authority and obedience.[16]

The weakness of Protestantism—which is also the weakness of democracy—lies in the place wherein also lies its strength. Depending as it does on persuasion and not force, it is characterized by suspense of judgement, not because of lack of conviction but in order to be sure that it can count on the convictions of a sufficient number of people. This induces a certain spirit of agnosticism which cuts the nerve of effort, and while Protestants are making up their mind the Roman Catholics have entered in at once with complete assurance. Similarly with democracy. The totalitarian states can act and strike at once while the democratic states are seeking to be sure of the suffrage of the majority.[17]

This, then, is the thesis: Catholicism is totalitarian, it is dogmatic and hierarchical; Protestantism is democratic, it is more flexible, being based on the Lutheran principle of "universal priesthood." There is, of course, much evidence for this argument in practice as well as in theory. The Catholic Church in the France of the *ancien régime* was one of the privileged estates against which the Revolution was a protest; the Pope was a powerful opponent of the Risorgimento in nineteenth-century Italy; in the twentieth century Pius XI made concordats with both Hitler and Mussolini, as Pius VII had in 1802 with the first of modern totalitarian dictators, Napoleon Bonaparte. Furthermore, the Latin states of both Southern Europe and South America have tended to be governed by authoritarian régimes. On the other hand, political liberty evolved from the seventeenth-century demand for tolerance by Protestant sects; the citadel of democracy in the modern world, the United States, has developed from the Puritan colonies of New England; Protestant England has been the bulwark against tyranny for centuries—against Philip II, Napoleon, and Hitler. Furthermore, the Anglo-Saxon states of the North Atlantic and Scandinavia and the Netherlands are democratic in their Governments.

Although this dual tendency is in the very nature of the two wings of Western Christianity, it is a tendency that has been the result of, and has been emphasized by, historical conditions. The very nature of the Reformation made the Roman Catholic Church conservative and the Protestant Churches progressive. For Rome was forced into a defensive position by the attacks of the Reformers under the leadership of Luther and Calvin. The Counter-Reformation was a counter-attack on the Protestant position, but the relationship had already been established: the Pope was the defender of traditional beliefs, and thus inevitably became a conservative. In different conditions these tendencies can be reversed—in the true interests of Christianity if one takes a charitable view, or because the Vicar of Bray is such a widespread personality if one does not. Because the Dutch Reformed Church in South Africa is so closely associated with the interests of the white inhabitants it has shown a markedly undemocratic attitude towards the Apartheid question despite its Protestantism. In post-War Europe, conversely, the mainly Catholic Christian Democrat Parties proved solid bulwarks against Communism and in defence of democracy because of the hostility of the Papacy to the materialist doctrines of Marxism. Moreover, the generalizations concerning the political tendencies of the Protestant and Catholic countries of the Western world are weakened by the authoritarian tradition of Protestant Prussia-Germany and the democratic tradition of Catholic France.

The work of the Christian Democrat Parties is too important to be passed over in a mere sentence. After all, they claim specifically to approach political questions from a religious standpoint.

The chaos and devastation of the Second World War inevitably created enormous social problems, and these problems in turn stirred up widespread social discontent. The Europe of the late nineteen-forties was ripe for Communist exploitation, and the Christian Democrats provided the only real counterbalance to the Communist threat in Western Europe. They showed that adherence to a materialist philosophy was not the only way of helping the working classes in their plight; that Christianity was not bankrupt as a social force. The strength and distribution of Christian Democracy as a post-War political movement have been shown by Professor Fogarty, who writes:

> Across Western Europe, from Flanders to Venice, there lies a belt of high religious observance, where people are more likely than elsewhere not only to profess religion but to practise it; a sort of heartland of European Christianity.... There are large Protestant as well as Catholic populations in this area, and the tendency to high observance applies to both.... And it is in the eight countries which lie within or touch on this belt—Holland, Belgium, Luxemburg, Switzerland, Austria, Germany, Italy, France—that Christian Democratic movements have in recent years taken their most clear-cut and self-conscious form, and have had the solidest support. Parties officially known as Christian Democratic, and grouping both Protestants and Catholics, held in 1955 nearly two-fifths of the seats in lower houses of parliament in these countries.[18]

Some of the greatest statesmen of post-War Europe have been leaders of Christian Democrat parties of their countries: Konrad Adenauer in Western Germany, Alcide de Gasperi in Italy, MM. Bidault, Robert Schuman, and Pflimlin in France, to mention only the most eminent.

It is true that Sig. de Gasperi is dead, that Dr Adenauer has now retired from office; it is true also that in Belgium and especially in France the Christian Democrats have suffered an eclipse. Nevertheless, weakened as it is, Christian Democracy is an important force in European politics still.

Although the movement has attained significance in the mid-twentieth century, its roots lie in the nineteenth. The idea of combining religious and social questions even found an echo in Victorian England in the Christian Socialist movement of Charles Kingsley and F. D. Maurice. It arose as a reaction against the materialism of the dominant nineteenth-century political doctrines such as Liberalism and Socialism. In the twentieth century, of course, it has found more formidable opponents in Fascism and Communism.

Christian Democracy is not based on a single class: it appeals to employer and workman alike. It is not confined to one country: as has already been noted, it is powerful in eight different European states. Moreover, there is no real international organization: the annual Congresses of the N.E.I. (Nouvelles Equipes Internationales, or International Union of Christian Democrats) have increased understanding, but there has been little real co-ordination of policy. With so little unity, it might almost be thought presumptuous for Christian Democracy to be called a 'movement' at all. Indeed, the traditions and backgrounds of the Christian Democratic parties of the various European countries are so different that they spread over quite a large proportion of the political spectrum from left to right of centre.

Yet there are certain fundamental principles on which all these parties—French M.R.P., German C.D.U., Belgian P.S.C., and the rest—base their policies. In the first place the emphasis is on the individual person and the development of his moral being and the avoidance of his subjection beneath the state. "Where there is a problem to be solved," declared the Belgian P.S.C. in 1945, "the party has only one standard for the choice of a solution. Will the formula proposed lead to the full development of the greatest possible number of personalities?"[19] But the human person is a member of a vital unit—the family, whose preservation and strength is fundamental to the social thinking of all Christian Democrats. The state has the dual rôle of maintaining the rights of the family while at the same time refraining from any action that might be construed as interference. The freedom of the individual is, in fact, in the Christian Democratic philosophy, defended largely by the interposition of various social groupings—the family, the village, the factory, for example—between the citizen and the state. This is the theory of the plural society. The concept of industry as a community —the concept of management and labour having common interests —is, of course, an important one. In practice this has led to the participation of workers in industrial and works councils, through which they take a share in management. The whittling down of the importance of the state by the emphasis on the human person and the community has also been extended by implication into the international sphere, and the Christian Democrats have been among the foremost supporters of the movement for European unity. The ideal, for them, is, of course, the restoration of a united Christendom.

Such, then, is Christian Democracy. It includes Christians of the Protestant Churches, though the majority of the adherents to the movement are Roman Catholic. Many of its principles, too, are based on Roman Catholic political theory, and it is to this body of thought that we must finally turn.

The Papacy

Apart from the Catholic Christian Democrat Parties, Roman Catholics throughout the world—over 500 million—look to the Vatican for guidance; and this guidance is given on political and social, as well as spiritual, matters. Of course, the advice is not always put into practice: the Pope has no way of enforcing his policies, and in some areas, notably those under Communist control, the episcopate has to trim its sails to the prevailing Marxist wind. Nevertheless, the pronouncements of the Vicar of Christ have a weighty influence. The authority of the Vatican is naturally strongest in social questions which border on the province of ethics. Questions of education and marriage are especially prominent in this respect, and cause Catholics to take a firm stand against the state if it sets up contrary systems.

The Pope makes his statements of policy mainly in encyclicals. As he is unable to control the political actions of the vast numbers who are members of the Church of Rome, and as conditions are so different in China or Mexico from those prevailing in Germany or France, for example, the contents of most encyclicals concerning political questions tend to be couched in very general terms. They are, in fact, conscious attempts at an organized body of political theory and its general application. The most important contributions by the Papacy to political thought in modern times have been Leo XIII's encyclical *Immortale Dei*, on the nature of the Christian state, issued in 1885; the same pontiff's *Rerum Novarum*, the first really important declaration on social questions, in 1891; Pius XI's reconsideration of *Rerum Novarum* in 1931, the encyclical *Quadragesimo Anno*; the Church's attitude to Communism was explicitly stated also by Pius XI in his encyclical *Divini Redemptoris*, in 1937; and the late Pope Pius XII's Christmas Message of 1942 dealt mainly with the rights of man.

Catholic political theory is a thriving school of thought. Its basic principle is the idea of natural law, an idea which underlies all political pronouncements from the Vatican and which has been thoroughly analysed by such lay writers as M. Jacques Maritain. Underlying the Catholic concept of natural law is the belief that there is a natural harmony between human instincts and emotions and that any conflict that may occur in practice is the result and revelation of sin. The task of the state, in this context, is to provide the necessary conditions for this natural harmony to operate in political and social questions, to provide the conditions for man to be in harmony with himself and with his fellows. The bare idea of the existence of a natural law is, of course, a very old one, and one of the problems which have exercised the minds of philosophers of this school of thought throughout the centuries is the method of knowing the provisions of the natural law. The modern Catholic view is that, although natural law concerns the absolute factors common to human nature, it is so complex that our knowledge of it must always be imperfect, and our attempts to follow its principles in practice must always take the form of empirical adaptations to changing conditions. This problem of acquiring an understanding of natural law has been well expressed by Jacques Maritain. He writes, "An angel who knew the human essence in his angelic manner and all the possible existential situations of man would know natural law in the infinity of its extension. But we do not: though the eighteenth-century theoreticians thought they did."[20]

The social and economic problems resulting from the Industrial Revolution at first received little attention from the Papacy. Towards the end of the nineteenth century, however, the need for the Church to make its position clear became more and more pressing. Although the Roman Catholic doctrine, as laid down especially in Leo XIII's *Rerum Novarum*, attacks the extremes of poverty and riches and the failure of the state to carry out its social function of protecting the poor, it rejects at the same time the socialist answers to the problems. For Papal social teaching is based on the triple pillars of respect for the individual, property, and the family. The commodity theory of labour is an attack on the dignity of man and is utterly rejected. Furthermore, every man must be given the opportunity of acquiring property; for it is the purposeful direction of his work for the acquisition of property that gives man's life purpose and dignity, while the ownership of property is, in any case, a human right and an essential feature of natural law. Property also is necessary as a foundation for family life. The family is a natural, almost sacred institution, and prior in both time and nature to the state. The family is just one, though admittedly the most important, of the corporate bodies interposed between man and the state. These bodies are all-important in Papal social and political theory. Social and economic ills can, according to the Church's teaching, be alleviated largely by the organization of industry, for example, as a truly unified body. Declared Pius XI:

> On account of the evil of 'individualism,' as we called it, things have come to such a pass that the highly developed social life which once flourished in a variety of associations organically linked with each other, has been damaged and all but ruined, leaving thus virtually only individuals and the state, to the no small detriment of the state itself.[21]

There is the vexed question too of how far the priest should involve himself in social and economic problems in order to help his flock, for more harm might come to the ministry than good to the laity from such activities. In France, for example, the exploits of the worker-priests, who have even involved themselves in trade-union affairs, were condemned in 1953 by Pope Pius XII, a condemnation reiterated by John XXIII.

The state has only limited power. In the first place, all authority is derived from God, Who delegates certain powers to certain institutions. The state, as much as any other body, thus has a rightful claim to only such powers as are necessary for the exercise of its particular function. Moreover, as other institutions, such as the family and the Church itself, have authority of their own, the power of the state in relation to these bodies is naturally limited. Finally, natural law restricts the power that can be rightfully exercised by the state over the individual. It is true that, as the authority of the state is, like all other authority, of divine origin, the individual owes it absolute obedience; nevertheless, once the state abuses its power, arrogates to itself more power than has been divinely sanctioned, and violates natural law, then the subject has every right to resist. Little more can be said of the Roman Catholic basis of the state: no specific form of government, neither democracy nor dictatorship, monarchy nor republic, is particularly favoured. Government, in the words of Leo XIII,

> may take this or that form, provided only that it be of a nature to insure the general welfare. But whatever be the nature of the government, rulers must ever bear in mind that God is the paramount Ruler of the world, and must set Him before themselves as their exemplar and law in the administration of the state.[22]

And that, surely, is the basic attitude of religion to politics.

CHAPTER SIX

CONCLUSIONS

The Argument
The Theoretical Basis of the Modern Political Crisis. The twofold problem—the problem of sovereignty—the problem of obsolescence.
The Possibility of Solutions. Reasons for hope—suggested lines of thought—summing up.

The Theoretical Basis of the Modern Political Crisis

We have analysed the various political theories abroad in the world to-day, and are now in a better position to estimate the part played by these largely outworn theories in producing the tensions of contemporary international politics. For the theories that have been discussed in this book *are* obsolete; their basic ideas belong to a past age. Our modern age, as was suggested in the Introduction, has failed to keep its political thinking in pace with political practice. And it is to the reasons for and significance of this failing that we must now finally address ourselves.

Twice within our own generation it has been pointed out that civilization as we know it has been in danger of being destroyed. In 1939 the threat in its military shape was from total war, and in particular total war as waged in the new, and as yet barely tried, dimension—the air. To-day, three decades but a lifetime of experience away from the age of Hitler, we again have the feeling—if we ever lost it—of uncertainty, now born of the unknown but well-foreseen horrors of all-out nuclear war. In the sphere of international politics the threat of Fascism has been replaced by the complex forces of democracy, nationalism, and Communism, which, in their rivalry, threaten to sunder not only Western civilization, but the whole world. Such parallels with the situation in 1939 are useful, but in the minds of some political theorists they are not fundamental. To them the crisis of the twentieth century, a crisis which is the same to-day as it was when Hitler invaded Poland, has resulted from the failure to adjust our political ideas and preconceptions to the realities of our present-day world.

There are two separate though interconnected problems: first, the tremendous power now exercised by the state, and, second, the failure of the accepted political theories to interpret the political facts of the twentieth-century world. The most serious problems arise from the following situations. Increased administrative efficiency has made the absolute sovereignty of the state extremely dangerous; the development of communications and the increasing interdependence of states have made the concepts of nationalism and national self-determination obsolete; and the application of welfare-state policies makes nonsense of the Marxist dialectic. The leading countries of the world have undergone vast administrative and technological revolutions. Gone are the days when the whole of the British Foreign Office boasted a staff of a mere thirty, from the Secretary of State down to "Ann Cheese, Necessary Woman"![1] Gone too are the days when it took a Prime Minister-elect a fortnight of mad rush to travel from Rome to London. Yet the political philosophies of these days—of Bentham and Marx respectively—still have to do service for the modern world. The nature of the resulting chaos is the subject of this chapter.

One of the most vital questions in political theory concerns the basis of power in a state, or sovereignty. Until approximately three hundred years ago the concept of absolute sovereignty—of the complete control of the lives of the citizens by the Government—was a very new one. The great authority on this question, Bertrand de Jouvenal, makes this quite clear; he writes, "That any human will whatsoever possessed an unlimited right to command the actions of subjects and change the relationships between them—that, for a whole thousand years, was something which was not only not believed but was not even imagined."[2] It was in the seventeenth century that the traditional checks to absolutism were gradually destroyed and "The idea of an entity completely empowered to regulate all behaviours made a resounding entry into political science."[3] By rejecting the authority of God, the sanctity of the law, and the rights of the individual the political theorists of the seventeenth and eighteenth centuries, from the great English philosopher Thomas Hobbes onward, conditioned people's minds to accept the possibility of absolutism. The possibility held forth by the Hobbesian philosophy has been eagerly accepted by the twentieth century and put into effective practice in such totalitarian states as Nazi Germany and Soviet Russia.

The process by which, in theory, the people have lost their individual rights *vis-à-vis* the state is an ironical one. At one time sovereignty resided in the king, and as sovereignty became absolute by the process already described the king became absolute. But with the rise of the democratic movement it was claimed that the people were sovereign, and inevitably their sovereignty was absolute too. This is clearly indicated in the French Declaration of Rights of 1789, which contains these words: "The source of all sovereignty resides essentially in the nation."[4] In practice, of course, the people cannot exercise their sovereignty all the time: fifty million people cannot rule England; two hundred million cannot govern Russia. It is necessary for the people to delegate their sovereignty to politicians or a dictator who can exercise this power. Government then tends to become totalitarian, and the absolute sovereignty which belongs in theory to the people is in practice used against them, with all the consequences so familiar to us who have witnessed the operations of dictators.

The danger of the complete subjection of the individual to the state has, as is well known, been vividly exposed by both Orwell in his *1984* and by Aldous Huxley in *Brave New World*. Even under the Stalinist regime, however, the control of the individual was not so complete as these forecasts. Indeed, although what has happened is frightening enough, it is what is likely to happen if the present tendencies continue unchecked that Orwell, Huxley, and their like are trying to warn us against. The strength of the state *vis-à-vis* the individual citizen—in short, totalitarianism—has been made possible, not only by the theoretical concentration of sovereignty, but also by the practical achievements of increased state efficiency and popular apathy at the destruction of individuality. The theoretical concentration of sovereignty had little effect on the individual until the state machine, taking advantage of modern technological and administrative developments, could effectively pry into the individual's private life. The dangers of a totalitarian regime are in direct relation to its efficiency. For example, it is possible to break a man's morale by spiriting away to an unknown concentration camp his wife or his mother only if a police organization is available to find and transport the innocent victim quickly and quietly. Again, it is possible to undertake a systematic policy of genocide only if one has available such modern refinements as gas-chambers for the disposal of lives and ovens for the disposal of bodies. Finally, a dictator depends for the success of his policies, and even for his continued existence, on the efficiency and loyalty of his secret police—a condition which can only be assured by the existence of an even more efficient and loyal élite of secret secret police to keep the secret police under surveillance and see that they carry out properly their duties of surreptitious housebreaking, shadowing, and falsification of evidence. Thus Beria was more to be feared in the Stalinist dictatorship than Fouché in the Napoleonic, the investigations of Hitler's Gestapo more than the inquiries of Cromwell's Major-Generals. Moreover, the individual has become very reliant on the state, both as a defence against anarchy and as the dispenser of social and economic security. To impair the state's authority thus seems to many like killing the goose that lays the golden egg. It is only when freedom has been lost that its true value is recognized. But then it is too late.

It is often said that a people obtains the Government it deserves. But a people is limited in the type of government it can develop or choose by the background of political thought provided by the philosophers. The people as a whole cannot be entirely blamed for not progressing beyond the political ideas of the time. Walter Lippmann has made this point very clearly:

> Much depends upon the philosophers. For though they are not kings, they are, we may say, the teachers of the teachers. "In the history of Western governments," says Francis G. Wilson, "the transitions of society can be marked by the changing character of the intellectuals," who have served the government as lawyers, advisers, administrators, who have been teachers in the schools, who have been members of professions like medicine and theology. It is through them that doctrines are made to operate in practical affairs. And their doctrine, which they, themselves, have learned in the schools and universities, will have the shape and the reference and the direction which the prevailing philosophy gives it.[5]

What is needed to-day is, then, not just a change of popular attitude, but the provision of a new attitude for the people to change to. Modern politics creak inefficiently because they are based on antiquated foundations. British Rail could not be run with replicas of the *Rocket*. Yet modified political models of that era are still in service—the liberal democratic ideas of Bentham, nationalist ideas of Mazzini, or the Communist ideas of Marx. The individual is too dependent on and subservient to the state, even in a democracy, for *laissez-faire* liberalism to be a true reflection of democratic practice. Secondly, the idea of unrestrained national self-determination is quite unsuited to the modern world, the countries of which are, in practice, closely interconnected by economic necessity and political expediency. Such an idea is, moreover, dangerous when a nationalist conflict can so easily turn into a nuclear war. Finally, although a century ago it appeared that industrialism would lead to an increasing gulf between employer and workman, the wealth made available by the Industrial Revolution has in fact been reasonably well diffused, and the working class too has joined in the general rise in the standard of living in the industrialized countries.

Failure to accept this dichotomy between theory and practice has led to serious problems: to uncertainties of policy in the democracies, narrow-minded nationalist wars and quarrels destructive of true economic and political interests, and the continuation of the Marxist myth of the inevitability of the conflict between capitalism and Communism. If all these difficulties, stemming from obsolete theories, were overcome it is evident that the world would be freed from many, if not all, of its most urgent political problems.

The question naturally arises, why has political theory failed to keep itself up to date? This is a difficult problem, and any suggestions must inevitably be tentative. In the first place, grand, all-embracing treatises are now academically suspect. Scholarship to-day consists of detailed, technical advances on the fringe of knowledge. Philosophy itself, once the collator of human knowledge and wisdom, has become, with the emphasis on logical positivism, a discipline for the expert in much the same way as physics or medicine, for example, always have been. The political philosopher has been affected by this trend as much as any of his colleagues. Secondly, there is a general lack of contact between the people as a whole and the philosophers—a feature of the modern world which Crane Brinton has drawn our attention to in his inimitable way: "the tension," he writes,

> between the intellectuals and the intellectual classes on one hand and the rest of us—those whose main concern is with things, with the handling of things or with the direct management of men—does now

seem to be especially acute. 'Egghead' has a nastiness ... which neither 'longhair' nor the earlier 'high-brow' had.[6]

Thus, although there is an urgent need for rethinking our basic political ideas, such a process is not readily acceptable to the practical-minded public. People too are disillusioned. Science has made such wonderful strides, yet our political wisdom remains stationary. The optimism of the eighteenth century that a Newton of political science would emerge and lay bare the simple, all-embracing laws of social mechanics has been destroyed by the realization that human personality is so much more complex than gravitation. There is, therefore, no longer a widespread interest in political speculation, for "After all, what kills ideas is disillusion," Lord Radcliffe has said. "And this is an age haunted by fear and disillusion."[7] Finally, in a country with a thorough ideological basis, theoretical speculation is dangerous to the stability of the state. The original political thinker is thus in danger, for such a person is guilty of the crime of 'revisionism' and must suffer the appropriate punishment. "On the one hand the ideological discrimination in Communist systems aims at prohibiting other ideas; on the other, at imposing exclusively its own ideas. These are two most striking forms of unbelievable, total tyranny."[8] Such is the conclusion of Milovan Djilas, a man who has suffered imprisonment for revisionist ideas.

The Possibility of Solutions

Nevertheless, there are grounds for optimism. After all, this is not the first era in history that has been sterile of original political thinking. The general conditions that prevail to-day mirror quite closely the conditions under the Roman Empire; yet political speculation revived. The growing realization of the need for renewed political thought is also in itself an encouraging sign. This realization is fed by the belief that political thinking is stimulated and made more necessary by political crisis. To-day we are living in a perpetual crisis. As John Bowle has written, "It would be against strong precedents if the supreme challenge of the hydrogen bomb—the greatest threat which humanity has ever had to meet—should evoke nothing more than a parade of political bankruptcy."[9] Indeed, there are some stirrings—increasing interest, increasing sense of responsibility, increasing activity. It is to be hoped that they are not false alarms.

The main suggestions for the solution of these problems seem to argue the need to resolve two sets of almost paradoxical ideas. Firstly, there is the realization that any new political thinking must take advantage of the great popular confidence in science and technology. Human progress in the modern age has been made possible by the application of science to the conquest of disease and the expansion of wealth. The term 'scientific' has come to be almost a synonym of 'dependable.' And yet a political theory, to be successful, must be based on an ideal or a myth; it must excite the imagination as well as satisfy the intellect. One suggested method of combining science and myth is by the development of a refurbished natural law. For the concept of natural law is based on the essentially biological principle of the preservation and development of the human race. The revival of a natural law theory would also solve one of the other basic problems of modern political thought. Natural law insists on the natural and indefeasible rights of the individual. The heyday of the natural law school of thought was the eighteenth century, and it is no coincidence that it was also the age of humanitarianism, of the practical belief in the rights and sanctity of the human individual. Since the time of the French Revolution we have lapsed again into barbarity, into the practice of torture and extermination. The individual has been submerged beneath the so-called interests of the community and the state. Natural rights have not been entirely forgotten, it is true, but they must be accepted without reservation throughout the world, and the individual must re-emerge as an important entity in himself. Yet, side by side with this need to protect the interests of the individual, there is a need to establish a supra-national world Government. The independent sovereignty of the nation-state is as much an anachronism in the twentieth century as was the independent existence of the petty states of the German Confederation in the nineteenth. From an economic point of view especially a world authority is necessary. In the first place, the world is now economically interdependent to such a degree that the economy of Western Europe, for example, can be jeopardized by a *coup d'état* in the Middle East. Also, because there is no effective umpire for international clashes a large proportion of the resources of the world is wasted on that vicious circle known as the arms race. From the military and political point of view also an accepted political theory of world government is urgently needed. We have, in the United Nations Organization, the institutions for the achievement of the rule of law in international affairs. But on the really important issues such as nuclear disarmament or Communist repression in Hungary and Tibet or the continuing war in Vietnam, the Organization has achieved nothing. Even on smaller issues, such as South Africa's refusal to allow trusteeship status to South-west Africa, its authority has been flouted. What is still lacking, then, is a willingness to accept the authority of these institutions. This lack of willingness is not due to the absence of force—the absence of an effective United Nations army, for example. After all, what is required for a supra-national Government is respect, not fear. The real reason for the comparative failure of U.N.O. lies in the fact that the very idea of such an authority is at variance with our preconceived political ideas. A new political theory must condition us to accept such an authority. It must not be thought that the concept of an effective international organization is a new one. From the disruption of the Pax Romana numerous wise heads have been exercised over the question of the maintenance of international peace. In the sixteenth century Henry IV (or his Minister Sully) produced his "Grand Design" for Europe; in the seventeenth the Dutchman Grotius provided in his *De Jure Belli ac Pacis* the foundations of international law; while, in the eighteenth, Kant, in his *Project of Perpetual Peace*, foreshadowed the ideas which were to underlie the League of Nations. None, however, received practical support.

Political ideas play a great part in shaping events, for good or ill. Political theory, then, affects us all, and, indeed, we all affect political theory. It must not, cannot, be left to the professional theorists and politicians, the Isaiah Berlins and Michael Oakeshotts, the Wilsons and the Heaths. Healthy political thought is the result of the interaction between the professionals and the public. "It is, indeed, useless," writes John Bowle,

> for unpractical idealists to expect a sudden change of front from the top, or to imagine that the voice of reason or enthusiasm can have any swift effect.... It is, of course, necessary to attack public opinion. Only a massive shift in accepted ideas among their peoples will enable statesmen to push through policies suited to the facts.... Today the ideas of world order, and of the obsolescence of warlike power politics before the facts of applied science, have not yet sunk in. It is our duty to try to see that they do.[10]

The duty is a difficult one to perform, but we can all at least avoid complacency, be conscious that what is is not the same as what ought to be, and strive in the knowledge that the judgment of future generations will depend on our success or failure. We have succeeded to a mortgaged fund of political ideas, but let us not hand on a ruinous inheritance.

CHAPTER SEVEN

EPILOGUE

The Argument

Introduction. The perspective in 1970.
Racialism. Nature and origins—White racialism—Black racialism.
The Main Events. Nationalism—Communism—Democracy—Religion.
Conclusions. New political thinking.

Introduction

The penalty of writing at a high level of generalization about contemporary events lies in the frequency with which apparent patterns are dissolved by shifts in relationships. Many of the patterns of 1960 seem to have little relevance now in 1970. The frozen ideological confrontation between Communism and capitalism of the Cold War era has thawed, and Communism has in the process splintered into a large number of national varieties. In Africa the youthful optimism of anti-imperial nationalism has degenerated into internal and international feuds, while throughout the whole world revival of national pride and egoism have seriously weakened the moves towards regional collaboration.

The main purpose of this chapter is to trace the events that have illustrated the impact of political ideas during the period that has elapsed since the book was first written in 1960—a period of great activity, especially in Africa and the Communist countries, and in the struggle for Civil Rights and more effective participation in democratic countries.

Perhaps inadvisedly the early editions of this book contained no coherent treatment of the doctrine of racialism. It is becoming increasingly evident, however, that the belief in distinct human races is having an immense influence on human behaviour, especially as expressed in the form of discrimination by colour. A short section is now introduced with the purpose of examining the bases of racialism as a doctrine, showing the practical difficulties raised by the colour problem in South Africa, the U.S.A., and Britain and providing cross-references to other parts of the book where the matter is treated under other headings.

RACIALISM

Racialism is the belief that mankind can be sub-divided or classified into a number of different groups and that some of these groups are innately superior to others. As a doctrine that proclaims differentiation and superiority it is thus akin to nationalism in its arguments and appeal. However, whereas a nation is usually conceived of as a cultural unit, identified by a common language and tradition, a race is defined as a biological unit, identified by the inheritance of particular physical as well as intellectual characteristics.

In the eighteenth century biologists busied themselves classifying plants and animals and in the nineteenth Darwin expounded his theory of evolution by natural selection. It was but a short step to the use of such scientific explanations on man. Mankind must be classified, it was argued, since it is self-evident that men *look* different. Three major groups stand out: the Negroid with dark skin and curly hair; the Mongoloid with yellow skin and slanting eyes; and the Caucasoid with pale skin and straight hair. And incredibly sophisticated sub-divisions have been made from this basic triad. It did not take long for writers to start arguing that a superior race exists, that superiority was to be equated with purity, and that this superior or Master Race was the Aryan branch of the Caucasoids (see pp. 42–44). Racialism as a conscious ideology thus started as a scientific hypothesis. It became transmuted into policy by the notorious Nuremberg Laws in Germany in 1935, the Law for the Protection of German Blood and Honour being based upon "the knowledge that the purity of German blood is the necessary prerequisite for the existence of the German nation."[1] And it became dehumanized by the systematic annihilation of the Jews as the declared source of adulteration threatening the pure Aryans.

Revelation of the full horrors of the Nazi policy of the "Final Solution" brought about a recoil action against the theory of racialism. Biologists were quick to point out that no firm scientific foundation can be provided for this attempt so to classify mankind.

No categorization holds good in all cases; "mongrel" people are by no means inferior to those who have not intermarried with peoples of other kinds; no group of people is *innately* inferior or superior—peoples differ rather because of cultural and environmental reasons. In the words of the UNESCO statement of 1950, "Scientists have reached general agreement in recognizing that mankind is one: that all men belong to the same species, *Homo sapiens*."[2]

However, as was pointed out in Chapter 1, once a belief is firmly implanted in men's minds it is difficult to eradicate, especially if it meets a psychological need. And so, despite the horrors of Nazism and the authoritative pronouncements of UNESCO, racialism persists. Why is this so? There are two main reasons. The first explanation lies in the general psychological make-up of man. Man needs the psychological security that derives from identification with a group: he fears anyone who is different just because he is different and particularly because the outsider seems to undermine the cohesion of the group. The general tendency to racial prejudice and discrimination results from such an attitude of mind. It is, furthermore, reinforced by the process of stereotyping, whereby people lazily label all members of a particular group with preconceived characteristics: for example, all Negroes are held to be lazy, noisy, over-sexed "Spades". Highly prejudiced people are, however, only a small proportion of any population. They have been identified as those with authoritarian personalities: they are so drastically insecure that they feel compelled to dominate. A group in a society that is weak, either because of its small size or oppressed position, is a perfect target for such people, especially if the group is easily identifiable. A person's most easily identifiable characteristic is, of course, his colour. And this brings us to the second reason for the continuation of racialism. Racialism in the world today is almost synonymous with the subjection by white people of people with darkly pigmented skin. The white man's feeling of superiority is the result of a long history of effective political and economic superiority over coloured people. Indeed, the black man in the U.S.A. was placed until a century ago at the nadir of human social inferiority—he was a slave. In other countries the relationship has been the less extreme form of imperialist and colonial. Economic and technical advantages placed the white man in a superior position to the coloured man in the days of imperialism. Moreover, the economic division remains even in this post-imperial age. In the multi-racial states like the

U.S.A. and South Africa, the white man is more prosperous; and it is a situation that is reflected on a global scale, for the underdeveloped countries are mainly those inhabited by the coloured members of the human race.

One country in the world is an avowedly racialist state—a state whose laws differentiate quite clearly and minutely between the rights of the white man and the man with a dark skin and where the implementation of such laws involves the conscious defence of the white man's political, social, and economic privileges. This state is the Republic of South Africa. A few words have already been said about the situation there in connexion with African nationalism (see pp. 65–66). It will be convenient here to expand on a few major points. Since 1948 the National Party, now under the leadership of Mr Vorster, has controlled the government with an increasingly powerful majority in the House of Assembly. The avowed policy of the National Party is to arrange for the segregation of Bantu and Coloured from the white people so that the two communities shall be able to develop separately (Apartheid). To this end, certain lands have been nominated "native areas" and these are being fostered as semi-autonomous Bantustans. The Transkei is the largest of these. What has been described so far is administrative policy: it scarcely adds up to an ideology. In practice, however, the policy presupposes discrimination. Non-whites form 80 per cent of the population; yet the Bantustans cover only 14 per cent of the area of the country. Bantus cannot be excluded from the industrial and mining centres since they are required as essential labour; and they are treated there as a proletariat. Mr Strijdom, prime minister in the 1950's, openly admitted the real nature of Apartheid:

> Call it paramountcy, *baasskap* or what you will, it is domination. . . . Either the white man dominates or the black man takes over. . . . The only way the European can maintain supremacy is by domination. . . . And the only way they can maintain domination is by withholding the vote from non-Europeans.[3]

Apartheid, then, is a policy based on belief in white superiority and a determination to maintain a dominant position despite the great disparity in numbers. What is more, non-whites have not just been excluded from voting. Since 1950 a veritable police-state has been established to forestall any attempt by the Bantus to challenge the régime. In 1957 a law was passed requiring all natives to carry pass books. In 1958 the black political party, the African National Congress, was banned. And in 1962 came the Sabotage Act, which enabled the death penalty to be imposed for a most generous range of offences. Afrikaner racialism is most thorough.

In South Africa the black people are the great majority, but are cowed at the moment into submission. In the U.S.A., on the other hand, the black people are a minority of 20 per cent, but are actively militant. At the moment we are looking at white racialism (the black back-lash will be treated separately later on), and it is clear that the feeling of white superiority has its foundation in the slave origins of the Negro people. White discrimination has been effected through segregation (separate schools and other facilities), exclusion from the right to vote, and active persecution. In the South, where prejudice is particularly deeply entrenched, there is a long tradition of lynching—extended in recent years to include white Civil Rights workers who have been campaigning on behalf of the Negroes. Active persecution has, in fact, been institutionalized in the Ku Klux Klan. As a racialist phenomenon the Klan has waxed and waned over the years, but whenever and wherever it has flourished it has been the focus of broadly racialist, not just colour, prejudice. It stands for the ideal of the U.S.A. as a WASP (White, Anglo-Saxon Protestant) nation. In the words of the Imperial Wizard in 1921 the K.K.K. "believes that never in the history of the world has a mongrel civilization endured."[4]

Let us finally in this section on white racialism look at the situation in Britain—the mother of the multi-racial Commonwealth and traditionally a tolerant country. The increased flow of coloured immigrants from the West Indies and the Indian sub-continent in the 1950's and the early 1960's placed a severe strain on this customary toleration. Although the 1966 census figures show that only about 2 per cent of the population is coloured, the distribution is, of course, uneven. Serious race riots broke out in 1958 in Nottingham and Notting Hill in London. Consequently, when a quite extraordinarily large influx of coloured immigrants entered Britain in 1960 and 1961, the Government felt impelled to act in order to preserve communal harmony. In 1962 the Commonwealth Immigration Act severely limited the immigration of coloured Commonwealth citizens by a voucher system. Fortunately, Britain has not suffered a recurrence of the 1958 violence. Nevertheless, racialism persists. In 1968 Mr Enoch Powell, M.P. for a Wolverhampton constituency where there is a dense concentration of coloured people, made the first of a series of speeches deploring the way in which he believes British racial harmony is being imperilled. In quite emotive language he has argued for the "repatriation" of British coloured citizens and has foretold serious bloodshed if his advice remains unheeded. Mr Powell's voice is clearly not crying in the wilderness, though the extent and commitment of his sympathizers is difficult to gauge.

White racialism is dominant in South Africa and it has led on occasions to negative responses like the restrictions placed upon coloured immigration into Britain; nonetheless, there has been considerable reaction by both U.S. and British governments. In the fields of social amenities and education integration has been imposed by the U.S. federal government against recalcitrant states; and similar forceful methods have secured voting rights for Negroes. Meanwhile, in Britain, Race Relations Acts have been passed and a Race Relations Board established to prevent discriminatory practices.

Nevertheless, despite these measures to provide justice for the coloured citizen, a radical back-lash movement has developed in the U.S.A. The colour racialism of the white man has provoked in its turn the self-conscious Black Power movement. At first the American Negro movement was peaceful and integrationist: black people co-operated with white liberals to achieve a harmonious society. Since the mid-1960's, however, the movement has become more violent and consciously self-sufficient. The reasons are complex, but fundamentally civil rights legislation has not alleviated the economic problem of the dreadful poverty of the Negroes, especially in the ghettoes of the northern cities. And, secondly, the Negro has the psychological need to assert his pride and to achieve an identity distinct from the white man's.

Violence has broken out during the "long hot summers" since 1963. Serious riots have occurred in scores of American cities, particularly severe in Watts, Newark, and Detroit. Immense damage has been done to property through acts of arson and lives lost in shooting incidents.

It was in 1966, however, that the movement to bring about a black revolution really got under way. The movement is inchoate, has a limited following, and many of the leaders have been killed (*e.g.*,

Malcolm X), imprisoned (*e.g.*, Huey Newton), or exiled (*e.g.*, Stokely Carmichael, Eldridge Cleaver). Nevertheless, the Black Panthers, who form the vanguard of this revolutionary movement, are resilient and dedicated. Taking their inspiration from the successful rebellions in Africa against colonial control, the Black Panthers demand "decolonization" in the U.S.A.—even the establishment of an independent black state inside the U.S.A. The mood has been expressed by Huey Newton, founder of the Black Panthers:

> The Black Panther Party, which is a revolutionary group of black people, realizes that we have to have an identity. We have to realize our black heritage in order to give us strength to move on and progress. . . . We believe that culture itself will not liberate us. We're going to need some stronger stuff.[5]

A number of observers foresee the whole world slipping into the abyss of a race war as coloured racialist tension is exacerbated by the widening economic gulf between the rich white nations and the underdeveloped coloured countries. It is a terrible vision. Insofar as the U.S.A. is a microcosm of a racially divided world, the achievement of racial harmony there is consequently of more than local interest—it is a universal concern.

The Main Events

Nationalism continues to be the most powerful political force in the world. Its expression outside Africa in recent years may be conveniently analysed in three categories. So much has happened in Africa that we shall need to discuss this continent separately.

Firstly, national pride and emphasis on national power are by no means obsolete even in Europe, where many hoped these attitudes were dying after a long life of over one and a half centuries. President de Gaulle was particularly insistent that the nation-state is still the only viable political unit, and strenuously asserted French independence of the U.S.A. by developing French nuclear weapons and withdrawing her forces from the integrated NATO command. Revival of national feeling in West Germany was highlighted by the success of the N.P.D. (National Democratic Party) in the Land elections in 1966. In eastern Europe too a similar feeling has been abroad: Rumania has been highly critical of Russian influence, while in 1968 Czechoslovakia gallantly, if unsuccessfully, tried to loosen Soviet control.

The second way that nationalism has been expressing itself is by irredentism—the claim by a nation-state to territory outside its frontiers. Minor incidents have occurred throughout the world. In 1961, for example, India shocked world opinion by using force to absorb the tiny Portuguese colony of Goa, while two years later Indonesia achieved a similar rounding-off of its territory by the acquisition of West Irian, which had been retained by the Dutch when they conceded independence to the rest of their East Indies possessions. In Europe disturbances have flared up intermittently since 1961 in the South Tirol, where a quarter of a million German-speaking inhabitants resent being governed from Rome; while farther west, Spain started a serious campaign in 1966 for the restoration of Gibraltar seized from her by Britain in 1704. But more serious clashes have occurred between major Powers. India particularly has been involved. She became engaged in a brief frontier war with China over the province of Ladakh in 1962. More prolonged has been her quarrel with Pakistan over the possession of Kashmir which burst forth into open war in 1965.

The third manifestation of nationalism has been its operation as a centrifugal force undermining newly created federations and leading to separatist demands by minority groups. The secession of Syria, Jamaica, and Singapore undermined respectively the United Arab Republic, the West Indies Federation, and Malaysia. More seriously, perhaps, the very existence of long-established states is being endangered by separatist movements of minorities; for, however sympathetic one may be towards their grievances, they are unstabilizing forces in a not very stable world. Language problems focus discontent in the French-speaking Quebec province and keep Walloons and Flemings mutually suspicious in Belgium. Luckily, little blood has been shed in these countries. This cannot unfortunately be said of the distressing war that has been waged for several years in North-east India between government forces and the Nagas, who claim independent statehood. The situation in Nagaland indeed epitomizes the bitter impossibility of nationalism: the Nagas have nothing in common with the Indians—race, language, or religion—yet the Indians dare not concede independence for fear of starting a chain reaction which could destroy India as a political unit.

Examples of nationalistic temper may be culled from almost any part of the world. But the area of greatest activity in recent years has been the continent of Africa. Movements for independence, encouraged in 1960 by Mr Macmillan's sympathetic reference to the "wind of change" sweeping through Africa and by the U.N. resolution condemning colonialism, have achieved remarkably rapid success. Seventeen former colonies, mainly French, obtained independence in 1960, and by 1966 only four major areas of white control remained—namely, the Portuguese and Spanish colonies, the Republic of South Africa, and Rhodesia.

So far there has been comparatively little violence. A gradual transition to self-government has been possible in most African states. Only where the colonial régime has been too rapidly withdrawn or where the existence of a large white minority has led to an attempt to maintain white control has there been large-scale bloodshed or does widespread violence threaten for the future. Events in the Congo following the surrender of control by Belgium in June 1960 provide a terrible warning against the handing over of authority without sufficient preparation. The quarrel between the President, Kasavubu, and the Premier, Lumumba, led to a state of civil war and anarchy, brutalized and complicated by inter-tribal feuds and the secession of the rich province of Katanga under the leadership of Mr Tshombe. Not until the beginning of 1963 was the situation adequately stabilized. If the Congo provides an object-lesson on the inadvisability of hasty withdrawal, Algeria supplies the parallel argument against a tenacious clinging to European supremacy. For seven years the Algerian problem had eluded the attempts at solution drawn up by a succession of French Governments. Fighting and terrorism rose to a crescendo as de Gaulle sought a formula that could be acceptable to or forced upon the Algerian F.L.N. and the settlers' O.A.S. (Secret Army Organization). It was one of his great achievements that the talks at Evian eventually led, in March 1963, to a ceasefire. To many the events in Algeria, and other parts of Africa too, prove conclusively the impossibility of maintaining European colonial control. Yet the Spaniards, and more particularly the Portuguese, refuse to draw these conclusions and continue to exercise authority over their ancient possessions, even after the serious uprising in Angola in 1961. A similar attitude is adopted by the Afrikaner Government in South Africa, which, despite its virtual expulsion from the Commonwealth and the frequent expressions of bitter hostility to it in U.N.O., continues to use severe police measures to push through its policy of Apartheid. And with the Unilateral Declaration of Independence by Mr Smith in November 1965, Rhodesia has been gradually aligning herself with the South African régime.

By 1961 most African states were either independent or, like the British East African possessions of Tanganyika, Uganda, and Kenya, could expect to achieve independence within a short time. The political momentum of the freedom movements, having achieved its immediate object, was therefore channelled into other causes—domestic organization and development, policies to be adopted towards the rest of the world, and assistance for the less fortunate African peoples still enduring colonial rule. The need for political, military, and economic strength to achieve these objects, together with the artificiality of the frontiers inherited from the colonial era, made many African politicians turn their attention to the possibility of regional or even continental federation. Some small states have achieved a successful fusion—for example, British and Italian Somaliland have formed the Republic of Somalia—but more ambitious unions like that between Ghana, Guinea, and Mali and plans for the federation of Tanganyika, Uganda, and Kenya have not materialized.

Yet even more grandiose schemes, for a Pan-African union of the continent, have been discussed. The movement owed much in its early stages to the initiative of Dr Nkrumah, the former Ghanaian leader, who saw in such a union the obvious way for Africa to exercise power in the world. But the difficulties have been immense. The five years between the African 'summit' meetings at Accra in 1958 and Addis Ababa in 1963 revealed the disagreements and rivalries through the creation of separate blocs. The Congo crisis particularly helped to crystallize latent hostilities. A group of states that had obvious interests and traditions in common were the former French colonies. All except Togo, Mali, and Guinea agreed to meet and formulate principles of co-operation, and, from their most important meeting-place, came to be called the Brazzaville Group. They have since taken the title of the Union of African States and Madagascar. One of the aims of the Brazzaville Group was the maintenance of firm links with France. Consequently those states wishing for a more rigid policy of non-alignment arranged a rival conference at Casablanca in January 1961; this was attended by delegates from Morocco, Egypt, Ghana, Guinea, Mali and the

Algerian rebel Government. A further meeting was arranged in May by the Liberian President in his capital, Monrovia, in an attempt to reconcile the two groups; however, since the Casablanca Group refused to attend, but six other states did join the Brazzaville states, it merely resulted in the strengthening of the anti-Casablanca bloc. The division was an ideological one, the Monrovia Powers standing for moderation, a slow experimental approach to continental union, and co-operation with the West, in opposition to the more radical programme of their rivals. Although Ethiopia and Somalia attended the Monrovia conference, the bulk of the countries involved in the groupings that have just been outlined are in the northern and western parts of the continent. But in the meantime an organization originally designed for promoting regional unity in East Africa was extending its activities, and, under the impressive title of the Pan-African Freedom Movement of East, Central, and South Africa, is pledged to work for the co-ordination of the peoples of the area, in particular to achieve the liberation of Central and Southern Africa from white control.

In May 1963 the most impressive expression of African unity to date was achieved at a meeting held in Addis Ababa. All but one of the thirty-two independent African states were invited and attended. (Togo was not invited because of internal problems.) The approach to the question of unity that was agreed upon was, despite Nkrumah's vigorous propaganda, the policy of gradualness, and an Organization of African Unity was set up to give effect to this plan. The question of 'decolonization' was also discussed, and complete agreement reached on the need to assist movements of liberation. The bickerings of the Casablanca–Monrovia rift seemed to be overshadowed in this new sense of unity achieved in 1963.

The momentum of the African independence movements carried the continent in 1963 to a high tide of confidence, stability, and collaboration, which has slowly ebbed away since, so that at the abortive O.A.U. meeting in November 1966 President Nyerere could be moved to say, "Africa is in a mess. There is a devil somewhere in Africa."[6] But not only had the movement for African unity lost its driving force: the several governments were facing internal instability. The precariousness of political power in Africa was highlighted in February 1966 by the downfall of Dr Nkrumah, though the coup in Ghana was only one of many that shook the continent in 1965–66. As John Hatch wrote in July 1966: "During the past thirteen months there have been revolutions in Algeria, Sudan, Congo (ex-Belgian), Dahomey, Central African Republic, Upper Volta, Nigeria, Ghana, Uganda. These states comprise a quarter of Africa's independent nations. In them eight Presidents and one Prime Minister, together with their régimes, have been deposed. In all but two military forces have been responsible for the revolutions."[7] It is not, indeed, surprising that the Army should exercise such influence in Africa: it is frequently the only source of discipline and power in countries where tribal suspicions are intense, education and administrative efficiency are only embryonic, and corruption so easily tempts the politicians.

The most serious collapse of authority in Africa in recent years has occurred in Nigeria. Its population of 55 millions makes it the most populous country in Africa and a potential leader; its success in self-government is therefore of more than local interest. The size of Nigeria has, however, been the main source of difficulty, since the country is a quite artificial agglomeration of mutually antipathetic tribes—Hausa in the north, Ibo in the south-east, and Yoruba in the south-west. Widespread ballot-rigging and intimidation in the Western Region elections in October 1965 brought into focus growing fears about political corruption and the dangers of domination by the very numerous Hausas. The government was overthrown by a mainly Ibo-inspired military revolt in January 1966 in which hundreds were massacred, including the Federal Prime Minister and the Prime Ministers of the Northern and Western Regions. By the summer of 1967 civil war had broken out with the secession of the eastern province, renamed Biafra. A terrible war of attrition was waged between the federal government and Biafra until all Biafran resistance collapsed early in 1970. The toll in human lives and suffering had been dreadful. The war had also been a classic case of the futility of nationalism. Nigeria is an artificial conglomeration of peoples, yet its disintegration into a number of states would be short-sighted in the extreme. On the other hand, once inter-tribal tempers had been inflamed, the Ibos feared their utter annihilation in a federal policy of genocide. A live-and-let-live policy is the only humane attitude in such a complex situation.

During the past decade a whole continent has been struggling to gain independence, to establish cohesion on a national and even on a supra-national level, and to achieve economic modernization. The speed has been vertiginous; collapse under the strain, such as has occurred in the Congo and Nigeria, should cause distress but not surprise.

While the states of Africa are striving towards closer integration, the Communist nations, which appeared in the post-War Stalinist era to be a monolithic bloc, are losing much of their former cohesion. Adherence to Marxist ideology and ultimate aims remains a co-ordinating formula, but the Kremlin is no longer the Vatican of the Communist faith. Instead, each party can adjust its policy to suit the local circumstances in a system dubbed by the late Italian Communist leader Togliatti 'polycentrism.' The limitations on polycentrism were, however, dramatically revealed by events in Czechoslovakia in 1968. A liberal government came into power under the leadership of Mr Dubcek with the popularly supported programme of establishing a régime of "Socialism with a human face". In a situation of mounting tension reminiscent of Hungary in 1956 (though without the extensive bloodshed) the Russian government asserted its control and enforced the re-establishment of a more conventional, authoritarian Communist government. Mr Brezhnev, General-Secretary of the C.P.S.U., justified this interference in the internal affairs of a supposedly sovereign state by proclaiming that a threat to one Communist régime represents a threat to all—the so-called Brezhnev Doctrine. The 1960's, however, witnessed a mounting quarrel within the Communist camp of potentially gigantic proportions. This was the quarrel between Russia and China, starting surreptitiously but developing to quite serious frontier fighting by 1969.

There has never, in fact, been complete identity of interests between the two countries, though it was only after about 1958 that a serious clash clearly developed. It will be convenient first of all to plot the main stages in the quarrel before collecting together the various issues over which opposing attitudes have been taken. As early as 1956, at the Twentieth Congress of the C.P.S.U., Khrushchev denied the Marxist-Leninist doctrine that war with the capitalists was inevitable, denounced the Stalinist personality cult, and declared that there were "several roads to Socialism." One of the results of this relaxation was the revolutionary movement that swept through Eastern Europe. The Chinese made it very clear that they considered a firm reassertion of authority was required. A strict adherence to Marxist dogma became the Chinese attitude in discussions about the freer interpretations of Moscow. But a great effort was made to camouflage the severity of the rift: Albania and Yugoslavia became cover names for China and Russia respectively; thus would Khrushchev denounce the dogmatism of Hoxha and Mao Tse-tung the revisionism of Tito. Not until the winter of 1962–63 did the principals openly identify each other as the true objects of their mutual abuse.

In June 1960 a meeting of Communist party delegates was held in Bucharest in an attempt to reach a settlement, but without any success. A similar meeting in Moscow in November was also a failure. In October 1961 the Twenty-second Congress of the C.P.S.U. was convened in Moscow. Khrushchev made vicious attacks on "Albania," and the Chinese premier, Chou En-lai, left Russia in the middle of the Congress as a mark of protest. Exactly a year later two very practical crises arose to test Sino–Soviet relations—namely, the Cuba affair and the Chinese attack on India. Mutual disapproval of the other's action was made quite clear. Then in July 1963 *Pravda* gave full publicity to the quarrel by carrying official replies to each of the Chinese charges, while in September revelations were made concerning frontier incidents in Sinkiang.

In many ways the conflict is concerned with old-fashioned national power. The border incidents are merely one example. The Chinese also claim that the Russians have damaged their economic progress by withdrawing technicians and failing to honour trade agreements. And even the ideological debate, although couched in theoretical language, has very practical foundations. There are four main issues —nuclear war, revolution, the racial question, and the personality cult. The attitude towards nuclear war is central. The danger that it presents must force the Marxist, according to Khrushchev, to adjust his attitude towards the possibility of world class conflict. Mao thinks that Russia's fears have made them unnecessarily cautious in their relations with the West and has condemned the revelation of Russian "weakness" in the Cuba crisis and in the nuclear test-ban treaty of July 1963. The Chinese leader considers the Western powers mere "paper tigers"; Khrushchev reminded Mao that they have "nuclear teeth." This fear of nuclear war, in the opinion of the Chinese, has made the Russians over-cautious in encouraging revolutions; gradual transition to Communism, Khrushchev replied, is safer. The channelling of Russian economic aid to bourgeois nationalists, justified in Khrushchev's 'Fabian' policy, has therefore been resented by the Chinese, particularly when China herself is in need of so much assistance. In adopting a more positive policy towards potential African, Asian, and Latin American rebels the Chinese have on occasion presented the issue in racialist terms—as a struggle against white control, with the increasingly affluent and white-skinned Russians on the side of the enemy. The immense danger of encouraging this view-point has, of course, been pointed out by the Russian leaders. There is nevertheless much truth in the Chinese interpretation that Russia's economic advance is cooling her ardour for revolutionary leadership. The decline of vigorous Russian leadership was exemplified, in Mao's view, by the de-Stalinization campaign: it has led to the disintegration of the Communist Commonwealth. It is a mark of Russian maturity that such a totalitarian cult is now inconceivable. And so the debate continues. It is not just an esoteric scholastic disputation; it is a struggle for power and authority by two of the largest powers in the world.

The quarrel between the Russians and Chinese was high-lighted in a dramatic way in the autumn of 1966, when Soviet protests over hostile demonstrations at their Peking embassy were ignored by the Chinese Government. The disturbances were part of the remarkable "Great Proletarian Cultural Revolution" movement which swept through China at that time. The movement had as its ostensible objects the purging from China of the last traces of bourgeois culture and habits and the boosting of the momentum of the revolution. In the words of the *People's Daily*, "The proletarian cultural revolution is aimed not only at demolishing all the old ideology and culture and all the old customs and habits which, fostered by the exploiting classes, have poisoned the minds of the people for thousands of years, but also at creating and fostering among the masses an entirely new ideology and culture and entirely new customs and habits."[8] To implement this revolution thousands of young people were recruited into the "Red Guards," a kind of political youth movement which was responsible in the autumn of 1966 for many demonstrations and some violence. Although the movement was rooted in the ideal of living according to the precepts of Mao, it inevitably had its seamier side. 'Revisionists' among the intellectuals, party cadres, and army units were purged, and behind the scenes there occurred a shuffling of party leaders for recognition as the ageing Mao's successor. President Liu Shao-chi was disgraced. To outside observers, however, the situation appeared very confused, and by the summer of 1967 break-down of central authority and even civil war seemed possible, though calm has since been restored.

If Communism as an ideological movement has forged ahead in China, elsewhere in Asia there has been little progress. The Vietnamese have been struggling bitterly against increasing U.S. military commitment since 1964, and there is little sign of the deadlock being resolved. In another state of South-east Asia, however, Communism has suffered a disastrous setback. In September 1965 a coup in Indonesia deposed President Sukarno from supreme power, and he was formally stripped of power at the People's Congress in March 1967. His régime had been based on the concept of 'Nassakom,' the conciliation of all political interests; his deposition set in motion a fearful slaughter of the Communists. In the most terrible civil blood-letting since 1945 probably some half a million people were massacred.

During the 1960's Communism in Europe has undergone a measure of liberalization. This process has been indecisive in the Soviet Union itself; indeed, the history of that country since the fall of Khrushchev in October 1964 has been unobtrusive. The most significant reforms have occurred in the economic sphere. Following the recommendations of Professor Liberman, Mr Kosygin, the Prime Minister, began in the autumn of 1965 a programme of reforms which reintroduced the profit motive into the Soviet economy in order to stimulate individual incentive. But by far the most interesting developments have occurred in Yugoslavia. During 1966 President Tito started a process which could have widespread consequences: it could transform an authoritarian Communist state into a new kind of democratic socialist state. In July Tito dramatically dismissed Party Secretary Alexander Rankovic and announced that the political police system he had operated would be dismantled. Plans have also been launched to loosen up the whole of Yugoslav society. The grip of the Communist Party is gradually being loosened, debate within the party is being officially encouraged, and widespread decentralization of administration is under way. Decentralization has probably been forced on Tito by Croat opposition to the dominance of the Serbs in the federation. However, the relaxation policy has led to the radical theory of 'self-management.' This is a technique for ensuring real control by ordinary people at every level of management and administration—representatives are freely elected and refreshed by rapid rotation. The logical conclusion of this process is the Marxist society—classless and stateless. This is why the fate of Tito's experiment is of such vital interest.

For the radical youth of the world, especially among the vociferous student populations in the U.S.A., France, and West Germany, the European Communists have been effectively outflanked on the Left by the colourful heroes of the underdeveloped world: Mao Tse-tung, Ho Chi Minh, Fidel Castro, and especially Che Guevara. Che Guevara has been particularly important in developing a theory of guerrilla warfare and revolutionary tactics more suitable for the underdeveloped countries than conventional Marxist-Leninism. Che became a hero in his lifetime because of his revolutionary activities in Latin America; he has been virtually canonized since his death in Bolivia in 1967.

No such doctrinal conflicts have disturbed the Western democratic world in recent years, largely because there is no doctrine to interpret. At the same time there has been an increasing realization of the artificiality of the Marxist–Capitalist confrontation and a serious questioning, if not of the theory of democracy, at least of its machinery. The shape of every society of the northern hemisphere is becoming more and more formed by the impact of modern industrialization. Thus the problems of policy-making and administration being presented to the Soviet and United States Governments are basically similar. The need throughout contemporary society is the provision of expert advice and the reconciliation of the power which the expert wields by virtue of his knowledge with the necessity for overall political control. The problem presents itself as a question of party authority in Russia, for example, and of parliamentary control in Britain. Machinery for adequate economic planning and the provision of authoritative advice upon which policy decisions may be made has been achieved, many critics believe, in a more effective way on the continent, notably in France, than in Britain. A reform of the civil service and its relation to Parliament seems imperative to ensure an efficient evolution of the Western democratic form of government. The year 1966, however, saw in Britain two interesting developments. The sphere of individual rights was invaded by the Labour Government's control of prices and incomes. At the same time, plans were evolved for the appointment of a Parliamentary Commissioner to protect the rights of the citizen (in a way similar to the Scandinavian ombudsman).

In recent years a very serious potential weakness has appeared in the process of representative democracy. This danger is the transference into the field of politics of the techniques of mass manipulation now being perfected by advertisers. Since the spread of television and the perfection of persuasive advertising are most advanced in the U.S.A., it is not surprising that the subtle undermining of the citizen's free choice in this way is to be seen most clearly in that country. Large sums of money were spent by the Republican Party in the 1956 presidential election (when these methods were used seriously for the first time) to project the 'image' of Eisenhower. His unsuccessful opponent, Adlai Stevenson, was bitter: "The idea that you can merchandise candidates for high office like breakfast cereal," he commented, "is the ultimate indignity to the democratic process."[9]

The U.S.A. has also been the centre of a wave of popular dissatisfaction and disillusionment with the democratic system that has swept a number of countries. This mood has expressed itself in disturbances in such disparate places as the U.S.A., Northern Ireland, France, West Germany, and India. There are two main elements to the movement and at times they barely seem connected. Firstly, there is the demand for participation, that is, for the individual to have a more direct and powerful voice in the government of his society. The most vociferous demands have often been made by students with extreme left-wing views about political matters. The numerous demonstrations on American university campuses against the war in Vietnam and the French revolt of May 1968 have been the most dramatic expressions of this attitude. In England things have been more peaceful; but schemes, like the Maud Report, for the greater decentralization of government to the regions is an aspect of the same movement. The other element in the demand for the greater democratization of government is the demand for full Civil Rights by minority groups. The most important example is the Negro Civil Rights movement in the U.S.A. The 1960's was a highly productive period. Both Presidents Kennedy and Johnson passed important legislation to clear away the tangle of regulations that prevented the Negro from exercising his right to vote; while a most dignified non-violent Civil Rights movement was mobilized by the late Dr Martin Luther King to ensure peaceful progress in this field. His assassination in 1968 may indeed have opened the way to the widespread use of less restrained methods (see p. 193). If the

Negroes are the oppressed minority of the U.S.A., the Roman Catholics are the oppressed minority of Northern Ireland. The Civil Rights movement in Ulster led, by the summer of 1969, to serious clashes between Catholics and Protestants; and some semblance of order has been re-established only by the infusion of British troops. The problems of democracy have thus become inextricably bound up with Communism (the radical students look to Mao, Ho, and Che as their heroes), with racialism (the Negro Civil Rights movement in the U.S.A. is struggling against entrenched white supremacy and discrimination), and with religion (the Ulster problem is a clash of religious sects).

Papal thinking on many social and political questions was revolutionized by the amazing vigour and fertility of Pope John XXIII's mind. His achievement was all the more remarkable because of his advanced years (he was 76 when he was elected) and the short duration (five years) of his pontificate. He had a single formula—that of reconciliation through the exercise of charity—which he tried to adapt to the various expressions of tension with which the Church was faced throughout the world—namely, the social and economic structure of modern society, the fragmentation of the Christian community among its numerous Churches, and the Communist–Capitalist conflict.

Social questions John tackled in a most enlightened way in his encyclical *Mater et Magistra* (July 1961). While maintaining the supreme importance of the individual and the subsidiary importance of material welfare, the encyclical firmly urges the need for corporate action in order to improve economic conditions. On the national level 'welfare state' policies are approved; on an international plane unconditional aid to underdeveloped countries is seen as a Christian duty. Without introducing revolutionary proposals, Pope John infused a refreshingly liberal attitude into papal thinking on economic and social problems. Three months after the publication of *Mater et Magistra* there assembled in Rome the delegates to the Second Ecumenical Vatican Council, the largest such gathering in the Church's history. The general aim of the Council was to foster moral advance to keep pace with man's technological progress. A vast range of subjects appeared on the agenda, but the subject which claimed most attention was the one that seemed fundamental to man's moral predicament—namely, the need for co-operative understanding. Mutual understanding among the Christian Churches is an obvious starting-point and was given some prominence in the Council's deliberations. Beyond the need for understanding among Christian peoples is the ultimate political question of universal human understanding. To this massive problem Pope John turned his attention in his second great encyclical, *Pacem in Terris*, which was issued shortly before his death in 1963. Its subject was the fundamental theme of war, peace, and coexistence. In this letter, which was addressed to the whole human race, John adopted a position of greater independence from the West than the Papacy had formerly taken up in the Communist–Capitalist conflict. Friendlier relations between the Vatican and the Kremlin were important for the Pope's aims of closer ties with the Orthodox Church and the easing of conditions for the Catholic Church in Eastern Europe. The encyclical expressed the need for Catholics to co-operate with non-Catholics and even non-Christians, so that by a diffusion of goodwill throughout the world complete international harmony may be achieved and the spectre of nuclear war be exorcized. This plea is based not on the impractical dissolution of ideological differences but rather on the common-sense recognition that ideological hatred must wither before the universal desire for human survival.

Conclusions

The nation-state and the concept of national sovereignty are becoming increasingly anachronistic as the twentieth century progresses. There are two main reasons for this—economic and military. The cost and complexity of modern industry and economic development generally need larger economic and trading units than most nation-states can provide—hence, for example, the development of E.E.C. and Britain's negotiations for membership. In the second place, the production of nuclear weapons has rendered inter-state conflict between the great powers on the traditional pattern virtually suicidal. Co-operation across national frontiers is therefore imperative and has led to both the creation of institutions as the means of co-operation and the evolution of a supra-national mentality among certain men. New institutions and a new mental outlook are both needed, but, as was argued above (see p. 186), it is the latter that is of really prime importance. The vital question is, therefore: are the new supra-national attitudes of mind the best ones? New political attitudes and their institutional expression are emerging at two different levels—namely, regional and universal. The great regional co-operative ventures are O.A.S. (the Organization of American States), E.E.C. (the European Common Market), Comecon (the organization for the economic integration of Russia and Eastern Europe), and the Pan-African movement (see pp. 191–193). Progress is slow and hesitant, yet a sense of community is developing in Europe, so that in Brussels or Luxembourg one may find officials who truly think of themselves as Europeans rather than Frenchmen or Belgians. On the higher plane of universal collaboration men have turned their attention to the problem of mutual understanding in many contexts in recent years. John XXIII's appeal in *Pacem in Terris* we have already noticed; one may also mention the eventual conclusion of a nuclear test-ban treaty between the U.S.A. and U.S.S.R. in July 1963, and, perhaps most significant of all, the selfless devotion of the late Dag Hammarskjöld to the ideal of world co-operation through the United Nations.

The difficulty, and indeed danger, is that these two parallel developments at different levels are not necessarily complementary. It is possible, of course, that regional federation may lead on, through co-operation among the continental blocs, to the evolution of an effective world authority. In an age when nuclear weapons have already spread to France and China, one would like to take this optimistic view. Unfortunately, however, the opposite tendency is becoming evident. In order to overcome national thinking and to consolidate the new regional institutions the political and cultural unity of the areas are being emphasized. There is a danger, therefore, of the new federations becoming ideologically selfconscious in the same way that nationalism developed in the past century and a half. The Communist states are already established as a group committed to Marxism; de Gaulle wished to see Western Europe evolve as a political unit independent of the U.S.A. and as a third force between the U.S.A. and the U.S.S.R.; while the Pan-African movement is tending to identify itself with black racialism against the last vestiges of white colonialism.

A world comprised of selfconscious, self-centred continental Federations would be a world disastrously divided in a way glimpsed at in Orwell's *1984*. Every effort must therefore be made to emphasize the *functional* purposes of the emerging regional organizations and to minimize their political and cultural significance. At the same time, those who are capable of thinking on a supra-national level must be encouraged to think in a world rather than a regional context. The second half of the twentieth century can still therefore be an age of hope, even if our immature political thinking renders complacency still dangerously inappropriate.

Much discussion has taken place in recent years on the state of political thinking. The present book has been criticized for its pessimism in this respect, and it has been thought necessary to clarify the position adopted here. Perhaps the best way to achieve this is to appeal to Sir Isaiah Berlin, who has written:

> It is a strange paradox that political theory should seem to lead so shadowy an existence at a time when, for the first time in history, literally the whole of mankind is violently divided by issues the reality of which is, and has always been, the sole *raison d'être* of this branch of study. But this, we may be sure, is not the end of the story. Neo-Marxism, neo-Thomism, nationalism, historicism, existentialism, anti-essentialist liberalism and socialism, transposition of doctrines of natural rights and natural law into empirical terms, discoveries made by skilful application of models derived from economic and related techniques to political behaviour, and the collisions, combinations and consequences in action of these ideas, indicate not the death of a great tradition, but, if anything, new and unpredictable developments.[10]

If this book was ever thought to contain a message it was that these "new and unpredictable developments" are urgently awaited.

APPENDIX A

REFERENCES

CHAPTER 1

1. Marx and Engels, *The Communist Manifesto* (ed. H. J. Laski), p. 168.
2. Crane Brinton, *The Shaping of the Modern Mind*, p. 16.
3. Walter Lippmann, *The Public Philosophy*, p. 85.
4. J. B. Bury, *A History of Freedom of Thought*, Epilogue by H. J. Blackham, p. 227.
5. Alfred Cobban, *The Crisis of Civilization*, p. 271.
6. F. M. Cornford, *The Republic of Plato*, p. 100.
7. George H. Sabine, *A History of Political Theory*, p. 147.
8. The phrase is Professor Renier's. Cf. *The Criterion of Dutch Nationhood*, pp. 16–17.
9. Machiavelli, *The Prince*, chapter xv.
10. Hobbes, *The Leviathan*, Part I, chapter 13.
11. C. E. Vaughan, quoted by C. L. Wayper, *Teach Yourself Political Thought*, pp. 137–138.
12. Hegel, quoted by Wayper, *ibid.*, p. 163.

CHAPTER 2

1. Crane Brinton, *Ideas and Men*, p. 500.
2. Alfred Cobban, *National Self-Determination*, p. 25.
3. G. J. Renier, *The Criterion of Dutch Nationhood*, p. 16.
4. John Bowle, *The Nationalist Idea*, p. 7.
5. Shakespeare, *Richard II*, Act II, Scene 1, line 50.
6. Renier, *op. cit.*, p. 11.
7. Frederick Hertz, *Nationality in History and Politics*, p. 411.
8. A. F. Pollard, *Factors in Modern History*, p. 19.
9. Bowle, *op. cit.*, p. 23.
10. Ernest Barker, *National Character*, p. 123.
11. Lord Acton, "Nationality," in *The History of Freedom and Other Essays*, pp. 273–275.
12. Royal Institute of International Affairs Report on *Nationalism*, p. 27.
13. Sieyes, *Qu'est-ce que le Tiers État?*, quoted by Alfred Cobban, *A History of Modern France*, vol. i, p. 161.
14. Georges Lefebvre, *Napoléon*, p. 508.

REFERENCES

15. Hegel, quoted by Bowle, *op. cit.*, pp. 36–37.
16. Cobban, *op. cit.*, p. 6.
17. Mazzini, *Faith and the Future*, quoted by Cobban, *ibid.*, pp. 58–59.
18. Mazzini, *The Duties of Man*, quoted by R.I.I.A., *op. cit.*, p. 89.
19. Treitschke, *Politics*, vol. i, p. 21.
20. Bowle, *op. cit.*, p. 40.
21. Mussolini, quoted by George H. Sabine, *A History of Political Theory*, p. 709.
22. Mussolini, "Fascism, Doctrine and Institutions," quoted by Sabine, *ibid.*, p. 728.
23. R. H. S. Crossman, *Government and the Governed*, p. 277.
24. Hitler, *Mein Kampf*, pp. 371–372.
25. Tacitus, *Germania* (trans. H. Mattingly), p. 101.
26. T. Hodgkin, *Nationalism in Colonial Africa*, p. 17.
27. D. W. Brogan, *The Price of Revolution*, p. 139.
28. *Daily Success*, quoted by John Gunther, *Inside Africa*, p. 736.
29. Brogan, *op. cit.*, p. 143.
30. Cobban, *op. cit.*, p. ix (American edition).
31. Rabindranath Tagore, *Nationalism*, quoted by Cobban, *ibid.*, pp. 125–126.
32. Bowle, *op. cit.*, p. 49.
33. *Ibid.*, p. 51.
34. N. A. Smirnov, *Esssays on the Study of Islam in the U.S.S.R.*, quoted by C. W. Hostler, *Turkism and the Soviets*, p. 195.
35. Bowle, *op. cit.*, p. 54.
36. Stanley Mayes, "Forces and Pressures in South-East Asia," in *The Listener*, April 30, 1959.
37. W. Z. Laqueur, *Communism and Nationalism in the Middle East*, p. 8.
38. The Balfour Declaration, quoted in the *Penguin Dictionary of Politics*, p. 231.
39. C. W. Hostler, *Turkism and the Soviets*, p. 110.
40. Gunther, *op. cit.*, p. 154.
41. "Profile of Abdul Nasser," in *The Observer*, August 12, 1956.
42. Abdul Nasser, *Philosophy of Revolution*, quoted by Gunther, *op. cit.*, p. 215.
43. William Clark, "The Needs of Nationalism," in *The Listener*, April 18, 1957.
44. J. S. Mill, *Considerations on Representative Government*, p. 298.
45. C. A. Macartney, *National States and National Minorities*, p. 501.
46. Brogan, *op. cit.*, p. 109.
47. Hertz, *op. cit.*, p. vi (Preface to the third impression).
48. R.I.I.A., *op. cit.*, p. 232.

CHAPTER 3

1. Plato, *The Republic*, III, 416 (trans. F. M. Cornford, p. 106).
2. Rule of St Benedict, Section XXXIII. *Cf.* Henry Bettenson (ed.), *Documents of the Christian Church*, p. 167.
3. C. L. Wayper, *Teach Yourself Political Thought*, p. 196.
4. Marx, *Theses on Feuerbach*, quoted by H. J. Laski in his Introduction to *Communist Manifesto: A Socialist Landmark*, p. 15.
5. Engels, quoted by R. N. Carew Hunt, *The Theory and Practice of Communism*, p. 37.
6. Marx, quoted *ibid.*, p. 11.
7. H. J. Laski, *op. cit.*, p. 31.
8. Marx, *Critique of Political Economy*, quoted by John Plamenatz, *German Marxism and Russian Communism*, p. 20.
9. Marx, quoted by George H. Sabine, *A History of Political Theory*, p. 693.
10. Isaiah Berlin, "The Father of Russian Marxism," in *The Listener*, December 27, 1956.
11. Stalin, quoted by Carew Hunt, *op. cit.*, p. 135.
12. Lenin, *What is to be Done?*, quoted by Plamenatz, *op. cit.*, p. 224.
13. Sabine, *op. cit.*, p. 693.
14. Lenin, quoted by Carew Hunt, *op. cit.*, p. 148.
15. Lenin, quoted by Isaac Deutscher, "The Moral Dilemmas of Lenin," in *The Listener*, February 5, 1959.
16. Quoted by Suzanne Labin, *Stalin's Russia*, p. 71.
17. Ryazanov, quoted by Wayper, *op. cit.*, p. 231.
18. Carew Hunt, *op. cit.*, p. 180.
19. Stalin, quoted by Edward Crankshaw, *Russia without Stalin*, p. 166.
20. Stalin, quoted by Carew Hunt, *op. cit.*, p. 182.
21. Labin, *op. cit.*, p. 372.
22. *Izvestia*, quoted *ibid.*, p. 65.
23. Crankshaw, *op. cit.*, p. 203.
24. Crankshaw, "Khrushchev's Oration," in *The Observer*, June 17, 1956.
25. Crankshaw, *Russia without Stalin*, pp. 219–220.
26. *Ibid.*, p. 218.
27. Khrushchev, Speech at the Twentieth Congress of the C.P.S.U. *Cf.* T. E. Utley and J. S. Maclure, *Documents of Modern Political Thought*, p. 170.
28. L. Trotsky, *The History of the Russian Revolution*, quoted by C. Wright Mills, *The Marxists*, p. 266.
29. Quoted *ibid.*, p. 451.
30. Mao Tse-tung, *Strategy in China's Revolutionary War*, quoted by S. Schram, *Mao Tse-tung*, p. 157.

31. Radio Moscow, quoted by Harry Welton, *The Third World War*, p. 197.
32. Khrushchev, quoted by Eddie Gilmore, *Me and My Russian Wife*, p. 255.
33. Lenin, quoted by M. Kennedy, *A Short History of Communism in Asia*, p. 123.
34. Mao Tse-tung. "On the Correct Handling of Contradictions among the People," quoted by C. Wright Mills, *The Marxists*, p. 386.
35. *Peking Review*, February 3, 1959, in R.I.I.A. Documents, 1959, p. 569.
36. Lu Ting-yi, speech at Thirtieth Anniversary of the Founding of the Party, June 25, 1951, quoted by C. P. Fitzgerald, *The Birth of Communist China*, p. 164.
37. *People's Daily*, quoted by *The Guardian*, April 24, 1965.
38. Djilas, *The New Class*, p. 125.
39. E. Durkheim, *Socialism and Saint-Simon*, p. 7, quoted by W. G. Runciman, *Social Science and Political Theory*, p. 47.
40. Djilas, *op. cit.*, p. 190.
41. R. N. Carew Hunt, *The Theory and Practice of Communism* (Penguin ed.), p. 9.

CHAPTER 4

1. T. D. Weldon, *The Vocabulary of Politics*, p. 87.
2. Aristotle, *Politics*, 1253a.9 (trans. E. Barker, p. 5).
3. Thucydides, *The Peloponnesian War*, II, 35–46 (trans. Rex Warner, pp. 117 and 119).
4. Plato, *The Republic*, 473d (trans. F. M. Cornford, p. 174).
5. A. W. Gomme, "The Working of the Athenian Democracy," in *History*, February and June 1951, p. 28.
6. Alfred Cobban, *A History of Modern France*, vol. i, p. 119.
7. The Clarke Papers, vol. i, p. 301.
8. Second paragraph of "A Declaration by the Representatives of the United States of America in General Congress Assembled."
9. Rousseau, *Du Contrat Social*, chapter 1.
10. Article 2 of the "Declaration of the Rights of Man and the Citizen" prefaced to the Constitution of 1791.
11. J. S. Mill, *On Liberty*, quoted by Lord Radcliffe, *The Problem of Power*, p. 93.
12. *Cf.* C. N. Parkinson, *The Evolution of Political Thought*, chapter 18.
13. A. F. Pollard, *The Evolution of Parliament. Cf.* T. E. Utley and J. S. Maclure, *Documents of Modern Political Thought*, pp. 68–69.
14. Lord Hailsham, *The Case for Conservatism*, quoted by Utley and Maclure, *ibid.*, pp. 74–75.

15. Lady Wootton, *Freedom under Planning*, quoted by Utley and Maclure, *ibid.*, p. 69.
16. H. J. Laski, *A Grammar of Politics*, p. 152.
17. Speech at the time of the Suez Crisis.
18. Edmund Burke, Address to the Electors of Bristol at the Conclusion of the Poll, *Works* (Beaconsfield Edition), vol. ii, pp. 95–96.
19. *The Observer*, November 4, 1956.
20. M. Salvadori, *Liberal Democracy*, p. 126.
21. F. A. Hayek, "Freedom and the Rule of Law," in *The Listener*, December 27, 1956.
22. Blackstone, quoted by Hayek, *ibid.*, December 13, 1956.
23. André Gide, *Journals*, vol. iii, quoted by Walter Lippmann, *The Public Philosophy*, p. 101.
24. Rousseau, *Du Contrat Social*, Book I, chapter 7.
25. Mme Roland. Cf. *The Oxford Dictionary of Quotations*.
26. Milton, *Areopagitica*, quoted by George H. Sabine, *A History of Political Theory*, p. 431.
27. J. S. Mill, *On Liberty*, quoted by Lord Radcliffe, *op. cit.*, p. 95.
28. J. L. Talmon, *The Origins of Totalitarian Democracy*, p. 249.
29. *Ibid.*, pp. 1–2.
30. Tocqueville, *Democracy in America*, quoted by David Thomson, *The Democratic Ideal in England and France*, p. 134.
31. Robert Lowe. Cf. *The Oxford Dictionary of Quotations*.
32. Montesquieu, quoted by Salvadori, *op. cit.*, p. 130.
33. Lippmann, *op. cit.*, p. 56.
34. Salvadori, *op. cit.*, p. 70.
35. Lippmann, *op. cit.*, p. 31.
36. Matthew Arnold, *Culture and Anarchy*, p. 114.
37. G. B. Shaw, *The Apple Cart*, Act I.
38. Lippmann, *op. cit.*, p. 21.
39. Lord Acton, quoted by A. L. Rowse, *The Use of History*, p. 150.

CHAPTER 5

1. Bishop Berkeley, *Siris*, 350, quoted by R. H. Tawney, *Religion and the Rise of Capitalism*, p. iv (Penguin edition).
2. St Matthew xxii, 21.
3. Leo XIII, *Immortale Dei*, quoted by T. E. Utley and J. S. Maclure, *Documents of Modern Political Thought*, p. 192.
4. Leo XIII, *ibid.*, quoted by Walter Lippmann, *The Public Philosophy*, p. 119.
5. D. W. Brogan, *The Price of Revolution*, p. 160.
6. President Eisenhower and Sir Anthony Eden, "The Declaration of Washington," February 1, 1956.

REFERENCES

7. William Temple, *Christianity and the Social Order*, p. 100.
8. A. Victor Murray, *The State and the Church in a Free Society*, p. 29.
9. G. C. Field, *Political Theory*, p. 234.
10. Paul Blanshard, *Freedom and Catholic Power*, p. 46.
11. J. A. Spender, *The Government of Mankind*, p. 330.
12. C. N. Parkinson, *The Evolution of Political Thought*, p. 151.
13. Pius XI, Encyclical Letter, *Divini Redemptoris*, quoted by Utley and Maclure, *op. cit.*, p. 223.
14. Lambeth Conference of 1948, quoted by Cyril Garbett, *In an Age of Revolution*, p. 231.
15. D. W. Brogan, *op. cit.*, p. 181.
16. Count Coudenhove-Kalergi, *Crusade for Pan-Europe*, quoted by Blanshard, *op. cit.*, p. 236.
17. Murray, *op. cit.*, p. ix.
18. M. P. Fogarty, *Christian Democracy in Western Europe*, pp. 7-8.
19. The Belgian P.S.C., quoted by Fogarty, *op. cit.*, p. 28.
20. Jacques Maritain, *Man and the State*, quoted by Utley and Maclure, *op. cit.*, p. 185.
21. Pius XI, *Quadragesimo Anno*, quoted by Utley and Maclure, *ibid.*, p. 213.
22. Leo XIII, *op. cit.*, quoted by Utley and Maclure, *ibid.*, p. 190.

CHAPTER 6

1. *Cf.* Alfred Cobban, *Ambassadors and Secret Agents*, p. 17.
2. Bertrand de Jouvenal, *Sovereignty*, p. 170.
3. *Ibid.*, p. 198.
4. Article 3 of the "Declaration of the Rights of Man and the Citizen" prefaced to the Constitution of 1791.
5. Walter Lippmann, *The Public Philosophy*, pp. 157-158.
6. Crane Brinton, *The Shaping of the Modern Mind*, p. 17.
7. Lord Radcliffe, *The Problem of Power*, p. 4.
8. Milovan Djilas, *The New Class*, pp. 145-146.
9. John Bowle, *Adapt or Perish*, p. 6.
10. *Ibid.*, pp. 14-15.

CHAPTER 7

1. Nuremberg Law of 15th September, 1935, quoted in L. Snyder, *The Idea of Racialism*, p. 164.
2. UNESCO, *The Race Concept: Results of an Inquiry*, quoted *ibid.*, p. 173.

3. J. G. Strijdom, quoted in J. L. Henderson (ed.), *World Questions: A Study Guide*, p. 133.
4. Quoted in J. Barzun, *Race: A Study in Superstition*, p. 185.
5. H. Newton in "Huey Newton Talks to *The Movement*," quoted in R. P. Young (ed.), *Roots of Rebellion: The Evolution of Black Politics and Protest since World War II*, p. 371.
6. Julius Nyerere, quoted by John Hatch, "Devils in Addis Ababa," in *New Statesman*, November 18, 1966.
7. John Hatch, "Power Politics in Africa," in *New Statesman*, July 22, 1966.
8. *People's Daily*, quoted by Roderick MacFarquhar, "Mao's Grand Design," in *New Statesman*, August 12, 1966.
9. Adlai Stevenson, quoted by Vance Packard, *The Hidden Persuaders*, p. 164.
10. I. Berlin, "Does Political Theory Still Exist?" in P. Laslett and W. G. Runciman (ed.), *Philosophy, Politics and Society (Second Series)*, p. 33.

APPENDIX B

SELECTED BOOK LIST

No attempt has been made to produce an exhaustive bibliography. Titles available in paperbacks are marked (p); more difficult works are marked thus *.

GENERAL

BARRACLOUGH, G.: *An Introduction to Contemporary History* (Watts, 1964).
BROGAN, D., AND VERNEY, D.: *Political Patterns in Today's World* (Hamish Hamilton, 1963).
*COBBAN, A.: *In Search of Humanity* (Cape, 1960).
(p)CORBETT, P.: *Ideologies* (Hutchinson, 1965).
(p)*CRICK, B.: *In Defence of Politics* (Penguin, 1964).
(p)FRIEDMANN, W.: *An Introduction to World Politics* (Macmillan, 1966).
*SABINE, G. H.: *A History of Political Theory* (Harrap, 1963).
SETON-WATSON, H.: *Neither War Nor Peace* (Methuen, 1960).
*STANKIEWICZ, W. J. (ed.): *Political Thought since World War II* (Collier-Macmillan, 1964).
UTLEY, T. E., AND MACLURE, J. S.: *Documents of Modern Political Thought* (C.U.P., 1957).
(p)WATKINS, F. M.: *The Age of Ideology* (Prentice-Hall, 1964).
WAYPER, C. L.: *Teach Yourself Political Thought* (E.U.P., 1954).

NATIONALISM

(p)DAVIDSON, B.: *Which Way Africa?* (Penguin, 1964).
HATCH, J.: *A History of Post-war Africa* (Deutsch, 1965).
(p)*KEDOURIE, E.: *Nationalism* (Hutchinson, 1961).
(p)KOHN, H.: *Nationalism: Its Meaning and History* (Van Nostrand, 1955).
(p)KOHN, H., AND SOKOLSKY, W.: *African Nationalism in the Twentieth Century* (Van Nostrand, 1965).
(p)MANSFIELD, P.: *Nasser's Egypt* (Penguin, 1965).
*R.I.I.A.: *Nationalism* (O.U.P., 1939; Cass ed., 1963).
(p)RENSBURG, P. VAN: *Guilty Land* (Penguin, 1962).
THOMSON, I.: *The Rise of Modern Asia* (Murray, 1957).

Communism

Berlin, I.: *Karl Marx: his Life and Environment* (O.U.P., 1963).
(p)Carew Hunt, R. N.: *The Theory and Practice of Communism* (Penguin, 1963).
(p)Crankshaw, E.: *The New Cold War: Moscow v. Pekin* (Penguin, 1963).
(p)Fitzgerald, C. P.: *The Birth of Communist China* (Penguin, 1964).
(p)Frankland, M.: *Khrushchev* (Penguin, 1966).
Pelling, H.: *The British Communist Party* (Black, 1958).
Seton-Watson, H.: *The Pattern of Communist Revolution* (Methuen, 1960).
(p)*Wilson, E.: *To the Finland Station* (Fontana, 1966).
(p)Wright Mills, C.: *The Marxists* (Penguin, 1963).

Democracy

(p)*Berlin, I.: *The Two Concepts of Liberty* (O.U.P., 1958).
(p)Cahn, E.: *Common Sense about Democracy* (Gollancz, 1962).
(p)Field, G. C.: *Political Theory* (Methuen, 1956).
(p)Lippmann, W.: *The Public Philosophy* (Mentor, 1959).
(p)Mackenzie, N.: *Socialism* (Hutchinson, 1966).
Magee, B.: *The Democratic Revolution* (Bodley Head, 1964).
(p)*Talmon, J. L.: *The Origins of Totalitarian Democracy* (Mercury, 1961).
(p)*Tawney, R. H.: *Equality* (Allen and Unwin, 1965).

Religion

(p)D'Arcy, M.: *Communism and Christianity* (Penguin, 1956).
*Fogarty, M. P.: *Christian Democracy in Western Europe* (Routledge, 1957).
Murray, A. V.: *The State and the Church in a Free Society* (C.U.P., 1959).
Proctor, J. H. (ed.): *Islam and International Relations* (Pall Mall, 1965).
(p)Temple, W.: *Christianity and the Social Order* (Penguin, 1956).

Racialism

(p)Baldwin, J.: *The Fire Next Time* (Penguin, 1964).
(p)*Barzun, J.: *Race: A Study in Superstition* (Harper, 1965).
(p)Deakin, N.: *Colour, Citizenship and British Society* (Panther, 1970).
(p)Segal, R.: *The Race War* (Penguin, 1967).
(p)Snyder, L.: *The Idea of Racialism* (Van Nostrand, 1962).

APPENDIX C

CHRONOLOGICAL TABLE

B.C.

429	Pericles' Funeral Oration.
427–347	Plato.
384–322	Aristotle.
338	Battle of Chæronea.
106–43	Cicero.
5	Birth of Seneca.

A.D.

65	Death of Seneca.
413–426	*De Civitate Dei* written (Augustine).
1215	Magna Carta.
1227–74	Aquinas.
1265–1321	Dante.
1513	*The Prince* (Machiavelli).
1516	*Utopia* (More).
1483–1546	Luther.
1576	*Republic* (Bodin).
1598	Edict of Nantes.
1644	*Areopagitica* (Milton).
1647	"Agreement of the People."
1649	The Diggers at Cobham.
1651	*The Leviathan* (Hobbes).
1679	Habeas Corpus Act.
	On Civil Government (Locke).*
1689	*First Letter on Toleration* (Locke).
	Revolution Settlement.
1748	*L'Esprit des Lois* (Montesquieu).
1751	First volume of the *Encyclopédie*.
1762	*Du Contrat Social* (Rousseau).
1770	*Thoughts on the Present Discontents* (Burke).
1772	First Partition of Poland.
1774	Burke's "Address to the Electors at Bristol."
1776	*Fragment on Government* (Bentham).
	American Declaration of Independence.

* Written in 1679–80.

1789	*Introduction to the Principles of Morals and Legislation* (Bentham).
	Qu'est-ce que le Tiers État? (Sieyes).
	French Declaration of Rights drawn up.
1790	*Reflections on the French Revolution* (Burke).
1791	*Rights of Man* (Paine).
1796	Babeuf's Conspiracy.
1805–72	Mazzini.
1807–8	*Addresses to the German Nation* (Fichte).
1821	*Philosophy of Right* (Hegel).
1832	First Reform Act.
1835	*Democracy in America* (Tocqueville).
1838	The People's Charter.
1848	Revolutions in Europe.
	The Communist Manifesto (Marx and Engels).
1849	Marx to England.
1834–96	Treitschke.
1859	*On Liberty* (J. S. Mill).
1861	*On Representative Government* (J. S. Mill).
1864–71	Wars of German Unification.
1864–77	First International.
1871	The Paris Commune.
1877	*Anti-Dühring* (Engels).
1884	Virtual manhood suffrage in Britain.
1885	Indian Congress established.
1893	Independent Labour Party established.
1894–95	Sino-Japanese War.
1895	Lenin to Geneva.
	Establishment of Kuomintang Party by Sun Yat-sen.
1900	Boxer Rebellion.
1901–14	Second International.
1903	Bolshevik and Menshevik Parties established.
1904–5	Russo-Japanese War.
1906	Moslem League established.
1909	*Materialism and Empirio-Criticism* (Lenin).
1911	Kuomintang Government established.
1912	*Pravda* established.
1916	*Imperialism: The highest stage of Capitalism* (Lenin).
1917	Russian Revolutions.
	Balfour Declaration.
1918	Socialism adopted by the British Labour Party.
	Partial female suffrage in Britain.
1919	Versailles peace settlement.
1921	Lenin's N.E.P.

1922	Stalin General Secretary of the C.P.S.U.
	Mussolini's March on Rome.
	Egypt given partial independence.
1923	Treaty of Lausanne.
1924	Death of Lenin.
	Foundations of Leninism (Stalin).
1923–27	*Mein Kampf* written (Hitler).
1928	First Five-year Plan.
	Exile of Trotsky.
	Adult suffrage in Britain.
1929	Stalin supreme in Russia.
	Kuomintang recognized by Stalin.
1932	Iraq granted independence.
1933	Second Five-year Plan.
1934–35	The Long March.
1935	Resignation of Sir Samuel Hoare.
1936–39	Arab revolt in Palestine.
1938	Third Five-year Plan.
1939	Molotov-Ribbentrop Pact.
1941	Independence of Syria and the Lebanon.
1942	Peak of the membership of the Communist Party in Britain.
1943	Dissolution of the Comintern.
1946	Fourth Five-year Plan.
1947	Cominform established.
	Independence granted to India, Pakistan, and Ceylon.
1948	Independence granted to Burma.
	Expulsion of Yugoslavia from the Cominform.
	Coup d'état in Czechoslovakia.
1949	Victory for Communism in China.
1950	Start of the Korean War.
	Tripartite agreement on Israel.
1951	Fifth Five-year Plan.
1952	"Black Saturday" in Egypt.
1953	Death of Stalin.
	Khrushchev First Secretary of the C.P.S.U.
1954	Nasser Prime Minister of Egypt.
1956	Independence granted to Tunisia and Morocco.
	Twentieth Congress of the C.P.S.U.
	Nationalist uprisings in Eastern Europe.
	Sixth Five-year Plan.
1957	Mao Tse-tung's "Hundred Flowers Speech."
	Khrushchev Prime Minister.
	Independence granted to Ghana.
1958	People's communes established in China

	Guinea independent.
	United Arab Republic established.
	Conference held at Accra.
1959	Invasion of Tibet.
	Disturbances in Central African Federation and the Belgian Congo.
1960	"Wind of change" speech by Mr Macmillan.
	Apartheid disturbances in South Africa—Sharpeville shootings.
	Independence granted to seventeen African states.
	Anarchy in the Congo following independence.
	Sino-Soviet quarrel at Bucharest and Moscow meetings.
1961	Casablanca and Monrovia conferences of African states.
	Uprising in Angola.
	Twenty-second Congress of the C.P.S.U.
	Papal encyclical *Mater et Magistra*.
	Britain's application for membership of E.E.C.
1962	Algerian independence.
	Cuba crisis.
	Second Vatican Ecumenical Council called.
1963	Addis Ababa conference of African states.
	Creation of Malaysia.
	Papal encyclical *Pacem in Terris*.
	Partial nuclear test-ban agreement.
	Dissolution of the Central African Federation.
1964	Kenya and Zambia became independent republics.
	Deaths of Communist leaders Togliatti and Thorez.
	Downfall of Khrushchev.
1965	Civil Rights disturbances in the U.S.A.
	Full U.S. commitment to Vietnam fighting.
	Unilateral Declaration of Independence by Mr Smith for Rhodesia.
1966	Communal riots in Nigeria.
	Fall of Nkrumah.
	Indonesian Communist Party outlawed.
	"Cultural revolution" in China.
	Government reforms in Yugoslavia.
	Appointment of British Parliamentary Commissioner.
1967	Secession of Biafra.
	The Six-Day War.
	Serious Disorders in China.
	Death of Che Guevara.
	Renewed application by Britain to join the E.E.C.
1968	Dubcek in power in Czechoslovakia; Soviet repression.
	Assassination of Martin Luther King.

1969   Commonwealth Immigration Act.
        The Brezhnev Doctrine.
        Fighting between Russia and China.
        The Maud Report.
        Start of serious riots in Northern Ireland.

APPENDIX D

ESSAY QUESTIONS

1. How much do we owe the Greeks in the sphere of political thought?
2. Examine the interaction of religion and politics in the sixteenth century.
3. Assess the importance of the concept of the Social Contract.
4. Must nationalism inevitably become violent in its expression?
5. How has nationalism differed in its operation in the twentieth century compared with the nineteenth?
6. Assess the validity of the materialist interpretation of history.
7. What was new in Marx's Communism?
8. Show how Marxism became adjusted by events up to the outbreak of the Second World War.
9. What changes have been made in Communist doctrine since the death of Stalin in 1953?
10. How far is Communism as a world-wide political movement still controlled by Russia?
11. Examine the validity of the statement that man is born free.
12. Show how liberty and equality can run counter to each other. Which is more important?
13. Consider the view that democracy is an ideal form of government that can never be perfectly attained.
14. Argue the cases for and against representative democracy as a political system.
15. Is the term 'People's Democracy' a misnomer as applied to Communist states?
16. Is a conflict between Church and State inevitable?
17. How far has politics replaced religion as the dominant emotional force in the world?
18. Compare the similarities and differences between Marxism and religion.
19. Consider the view that Christianity can be the only effective force to prevent Communism from spreading throughout the world.
20. Is dictatorship always an undesirable form of government?
21. Examine the need for effective international co-operation in the world to-day.
22. What justification is there for the study of political ideas?

INDEX

Accra, 64, 197
Addis Ababa, 197–198
Addresses to the German Nation, 37
Aden, 47
Adenauer, Dr Konrad, 174
Africa, 32, 42, 44–46, 51–52, 67, 69, 70, 99, 102, 103, 148, 152, 164, 194, 196–200, 202
Afrikaners, 63, 65, 66, 192
Agreement of the People, 122
Albania, 42, 101, 201
Alexander II, Tsar, 82
Alexander the Great, 21, 119
Algeria, 47, 54, 56, 58, 62, 63, 196, 198–199
Allenby, Field-Marshal Viscount, 55–56
Alsace, 68
America (U.S.A.), 25, 51, 53–54, 96, 99, 102, 103, 107, 111, 117, 121, 124–127, 130, 132, 148, 172, 188, 189–194, 204–206, 208
Angola, 63, 66, 196
Anti-Dühring, 78, 81
Anti-Semitism 43–44
Apartheid, 46, 65, 66, 173, 191, 197
Aquinas, St Thomas, 22, 160
Arab Legion, 59
Arab nationalism, 54–61, 161–162, 164, 170
Arif, Colonel Abdul Salam, 59
Aristotle, 11, 19–20, 22
Arnold, Matthew, 157–158
Aryan race, 42–43, 189
Asia, 32, 42, 44–54, 57, 69, 70, 99, 101, 102, 109, 111, 112, 148, 152, 164, 165, 202–203
Athens, 18, 116–120
Augsburg, Peace of, 23
Augustine, St, 22, 160
Auschwitz, 16, 44
Austria, 14, 35, 36, 39, 40, 43, 44, 67, 84, 105, 173. *See also* Habsburg monarchy
Avignon, 35
Ayub, General, 149
Azikiwe, Dr Nnamdi, 62, 64

Babeuf, Gracchus, 74, 129, 146
Baghdad Pact, 59
Bakunin, M. A., 81
Balfour Declaration, 55, 57
Banda, Dr Hastings, 62, 65
Bandaranaike, Solomon, 49
Bantus, 63, 66, 191
Belgium, 38, 65, 71, 77, 173, 174, 195–196
Benedict, St, 73
Bentham, Jeremy, 26, 127–129, 180, 183
Beria, L. P., 93, 182
Berkeley, Bishop, 159
Bernstein, E., 81

Biafra, 62, 199
Bidault, Georges, 174
Bill of Rights, 123
Bismarck, Prince Otto von, 28, 31, 33, 38–39
Black Power, 193–194
Blackstone, Sir William, 141
Blanc, Louis, 130
Blanqui, L. A., 74
"Bloodless Revolution," the, 121–123
Bodin, Jean, 24
Bolsheviks, 81, 83–84
Bourbons, 33, 35
Bourguiba, Habib, 58
Boxer Rebellion, the, 52
Brave New World, 181
Brazzaville Conference (Union of African States), 197–198
Brazzaville proposals, 62
Brest-Litovsk, Treaty of, 84
Brezhnev, Leonid I., 166, 169, 200
Bucharest Congress, 94, 201
Buddhists, 49, 165
Bukharin, N., 89
Bulganin, N. A., 92–93
Bulgaria, 100, 101
Burke, Edmund, 26, 126–127, 138
Burma, 48, 53, 148, 152
Byron, George Gordon, Lord, 37

Calvin, Jean, 166, 171–172
Cape Coloureds, 63, 66
Capitalism, 73, 78–80, 89–91, 93–94, 96, 98, 111, 112, 183, 188, 204
Casablanca Conference, 197–198
Castro, Dr Fidel, 98, 102, 204
Catholicism, Roman, 12, 30–31, 123, 144, 160–161, 163–166, 168–173, 175–178, 206–207
Caucasus, 40, 51
Central African Federation, 65
Ceylon, 48–49, 148
Chamberlain, H. S., 41, 43–44
Charles I, King of Great Britain and Ireland, 121–122
Chartists, 128
Chiang Kai-shek, 106, 107
China, 44, 48, 50–53, 70, 98, 101–110, 145, 165, 170, 176, 195, 200–203, 208
Chou En-lai, 103, 106, 108, 201
Christian Democracy, 155, 162, 173–175
Christian Socialism, 174
Christianity, 21–23, 30, 59, 73–74, 80, 122, 134, 160–168, 170–175, 206–207
Church of England, 162
Cicero, 21
City of God, 22
City-state (*polis*), 19–21, 26, 34, 117–120

Civil Rights Movement, 188, 192, 205–206
Civil Service, 118, 128, 157, 204
Civil War in France, The, 78
Civil Wars, English, 24, 73, 121–122
Class Struggle in France, The, 78
Cold War, 50, 70, 96, 102, 145, 188
Cole, G. D. H., 131
Comecon, 70, 101, 208
Cominform, 91, 97, 100, 101, 103, 106
Comintern, 91, 95, 100
Commonwealth of Nations, 49, 103, 192
Commune of Paris, 81
Communist Manifesto, The, 78
Communist Party of Great Britain, 101
Communist Party of the Soviet Union, 87–89, 92–93, 168, 200
Competitive (peaceful) co-existence, 94, 100, 108
Concert of Europe, 17, 69
Condorcet, Marquis de, 75
Confucianism, 99, 170
Congo, 62, 65, 196–197, 199–200
Conservatism, 26, 132–133, 139, 152
Contrat Social, 17, 26–27
Cosmopolitanism, 21–22, 33–34, 37, 69, 185–186, 207–209
Council of Europe, 71
Crimea, 51, 84
Critique of the Gotha Programme, 78, 81
Critique of Political Economy, 78–79
Cuba, 98, 102, 103, 104, 201
Cultural Revolution, 202
Cynics, 21
Cyprus, 67, 69, 164
Czechoslovakia, 40, 43, 44, 68, 100, 194, 200

D'Annunzio, Gabriele, 42
Danquah, Dr J. B., 62
Dante Alighieri, 22
Danton, Georges Jacques, 14, 36
Danube, 40, 68
Darwin, Charles, 76, 189
Das Kapital, 17, 77–78, 117
Declaration of Independence, the, 124–125, 136
Declaration of the Rights of Man, 126, 136, 181
De Jure Belli ac Pacis, 186
De Monarchia, 22
De-Stalinization, 92–93, 95, 103, 202
Dialectic, the, 28, 78–79, 85–87, 112, 166, 168, 180
Dialectical and Historical Materialism, 90
"Dictatorship of the proletariat," 86, 88, 95, 112
Diderot, Dennis, 75
"Different roads to Socialism," 93, 95, 104, 200
"Diggers," the, 73–74, 123, 129
Divine Right of Kings, 23, 163
Divini Redemptoris, 176
'Double-talk,' 16, 90, 145–146
Dr Zhivago, 113
Dubcek, Alexander, 200
Dudintsev, Vladimir, 113
Dutch Reformed Church, 65, 173

Education, 14, 20, 46–47, 69, 87, 92, 129, 132, 150–151, 153, 160, 169, 175, 182, 193
Egypt, 54–60, 103, 161, 165, 197
Eighteenth Brumaire of Louis Napoleon, The, 78
Eisenhower, Dwight D., 135, 162, 205
Elizabeth I, Queen, 24, 121–122, 166
Encyclopedists, 26, 34
Engels, Friedrich, 76–79, 81, 86, 90, 112, 166
Eoka, 70
Epicureans, 21
Esprit des Lois, L', 124
Essay concerning Human Understanding, 124
Estonia, 40, 84
Ethiopia (Abyssinia), 42, 62, 64, 137, 198
European Common Market, 70, 71, 207–208

Fabians, 131
Fanaticism, 16, 150–151
Fascism, 28, 32, 41–42, 156, 171, 174, 179
Female suffrage, 128–129, 136
Feudalism, 19, 22, 121, 134, 142, 162
Fichte, J. G., 37
Fifth Republic of France, 101, 155
Finland, 40, 84
Fiume, 42
Five-year plans, 91
Formosa, 52, 107
Foundations of Leninism, The, 90
Foundations of the Nineteenth Century, The, 44
Fourier, François, 74
Fourth Republic of France, 58, 101, 155
France, 14, 23, 25–26, 30, 32–33, 35–36, 38–39, 44, 53–54, 55–59, 62–64, 68, 70–71, 73–75, 77–78, 81, 98, 100, 101, 125–127, 130, 136, 140–141, 144, 146, 155, 163, 172–174, 176–177, 194, 196–197, 204–205, 208
Franco, General Francisco, 148–149
French Community of Nations, 63
French Revolution, 12, 14, 16, 26, 32, 34–35, 45, 73–74, 97, 111, 114, 121, 125, 127, 129, 143–144, 146, 171–172, 185
French wars of religion, 23–24
'Front' organizations, 99

Gandhi, Mahatma, 48, 69
Garibaldi, Giuseppe, 38
Gasperi, Alcide de, 174
Gaulle, President Charles de, 58, 62, 64, 70, 194, 196, 208
Gaza, 57
General Will, 27–28, 34–35, 37, 126, 143, 146
Geneva, 26, 82, 121
Gentile, Giovanni, 41
George III, King, 124, 126
German Ideology, The, 78
Germany, 28, 31–32, 34 36–44, 67, 68, 75, 77, 81, 83–84, 87, 89, 96, 113, 130, 144, 148, 173, 176, 181, 185, 189; Federal German Republic, 71, 174, 194, 204–205; German Democratic Republic, 97, 101, 104, 105, 116, 145

INDEX

Gerö, Ernö, 105
Gestapo, 12, 182
Ghana, (Gold Coast), 62, 63, 152, 153, 197, 199
Gibraltar, 195
Glubb Pasha, 59
Goa, 195
Gobineau, Comte de, 43
Godwin, William, 127, 136
Goebbels, Dr Joseph, 14
Gomulka, Wladislaw, 101, 104, 105, 106, 169
"Grand Design," the, 186
Great Britain (England), 11, 23–24, 28, 30–33, 47–48, 53–56, 59–60, 62–70, 73, 75–77, 83–84, 87, 101–102, 113, 116, 120–131, 133, 136–137, 139, 141, 145, 152, 154, 163, 172, 181, 189, 192–193, 195, 197, 204, 207
"Great Leap Forward," 108
Greece, ancient (Greeks), 19–21, 34, 117–120
Greece, modern (Greeks), 56, 101, 103, 164
Green, T. H., 28
Grimm brothers, 69
Grotius, Hugo, 186
Guevara, Che, 204, 206
Guild Socialism, 131
Guinea, 62–64, 197–198
Guizot François, 74
Guyana (British Guiana), 152

HABEAS CORPUS, 145
Habsburg monarchy, 32–33, 35, 37–40, 43, 81
Hammarskjöld, Dag, 208
Hardie, J. Keir, 131
Hegel, G. W. F., 27, 37, 41, 75, 78–79
Henry IV, King of France, 144, 186
Herder, J. G. von, 36, 67
Hindus, 48–49, 164
Hitler, Adolf, 13, 31, 37, 42–44, 69, 148, 171–172, 179–180, 182
Hoare, Sir Samuel (Viscount Templewood), 137
Hobbes, Thomas, 24–25, 33, 160, 180–181
Ho Chi Minh, 98, 204, 206
Holy Roman Empire (Emperor), 19, 22–23, 32–33
Houphouet-Boigny, Félix, 62
Hoxha, Enver, 101, 201
"Hundred Flowers Campaign," 108, 110
Hungarian revolution, 13, 70, 95, 102, 105, 132, 186
Hungary, 38, 40, 68, 70, 99, 100, 101, 102, 104, 105, 169, 200
Huxley, Aldous, 181

Immortale Dei, 176
Imperialism (colonialism), 12, 45–46, 50–53, 57, 59, 86–87, 94, 102, 149, 152, 190, 196–197, 208
Imperialism: The Highest Stage of Capitalism, 85
India, 31, 45, 48, 50, 52, 68, 70, 100, 103, 153, 164, 165, 192, 195, 201, 205

Indian National Congress, 48
Indochina, 48, 53
Indonesia (Dutch East Indies), 46, 48, 52, 53, 96, 103, 148, 152, 165, 195, 203
Industrial Revolution, 31, 69, 76, 133, 163, 177, 183
Inevitability of war theory, 51, 87, 93, 94, 183, 200
Inquisition, 12, 167
International, Socialist, 81
International Court of Justice, 71
Iraq, 54, 55, 57, 59
Ireland, 164, 205, 206
'Iron Curtain', 169
Iskra, 82
Islam, 49, 56, 144, 162, 164–165
Israel, 31, 54, 57, 59
Istiqlal, 56, 58
Italy, 24, 32, 37, 38, 41–43, 55, 71, 96, 100, 101, 132, 137, 148, 172–173
Izvestia, 92

JACOBINS, 12, 35, 125, 143, 146
James II, King, 25, 123, 125
Japan, 46, 48, 52–53, 107, 148
Jefferson, Thomas, 125, 142
Jews, 31, 44, 55, 57, 77, 164, 189
John Birch Society, 102
John XXIII, Pope, 169, 177, 206–208
Johnson, L. B., 205
Jordan (Transjordan), 54–55, 57, 59
Justice (law), 19, 22, 121–123, 140–141, 145, 148

KADAR, JANOS, 105
Kaganovitch, L. M., 92–93
Kamenev, L. V., 89
Kant, Immanuel, 75, 186
Kasavubu, Joseph, 196
Kashmir, 195
Kassem, General Abdul Karem, 51, 59
Katanga, 196
Kautsky, Karl, 81
Kazakhs, 50–51, 92
Kemal, Mustafa (Atatürk), 56–57
Kennedy, J. F., 205
Kenya, 47, 62, 64, 152, 197
Kenyatta, Jomo, 64
Kerensky, Alexander, 84, 97
Khrushchev, N. S., 15, 92–95, 98, 103, 104, 166, 200–201, 203
King, Dr Martin Luther, 205
Komsomol, 170
Korea, 53, 96, 99, 101, 103
Kostov, Taicho, 101
Kosygin, A., 203
Ku Klux Klan, 192
Kulaks, 89
Kun, Bela, 81
Kuomintang, 52, 98, 106, 107

LABOUR PARTY, 102, 129, 131–132, 139, 204
Ladakh, 100, 195
Laissez-faire, 111, 128, 130, 183, 188
Lassalle, Ferdinand, 81, 130
Latin America, 70, 98, 102, 165, 167, 172, 202, 204

Latvia, 40, 84
Lausanne, Treaty of, 56
Lawrence, T. E., 55
Laws, The, 20
League of Nations, 17, 40-41, 56
Lebanon, 54-55, 57, 59
Left-wing Communism: An Infantile Disorder, 86
Lenin, V. I., 16, 51, 82-88, 90-91, 94-95, 97, 102, 109, 111, 166
Leo XIII, Pope, 160, 176-178
Letter concerning Toleration, 139
Levellers, 122-133
Leviathan, The, 17, 24-25
Liberalism, 28, 129, 131, 139, 142
Liberia, 198
Liberman, Y., 203
Libya, 54, 155
Lilburne, John, 122
Lithuania, 40, 84
Liu Shao-chi, 202
Locke, John, 25-26, 110, 123-124, 127, 139
Logical positivism, 18, 28, 183
"Long March, The," 107
Louis XIV, King of France, 33
Lowe, Robert, 151
Ludwig, Feuerbach, 78
Lumumba, Patrice, 65, 196
Luther, Martin, 23-24, 134, 160, 172
Luthuli, Chief Albert, 66
Luxemburg, Rosa, 81

MABLY, ABBÉ, 74, 146
McCarthy, Joseph, 102, 155
Machiavelli, Niccolo, 24, 160
Macmillan, Right Hon. Harold, 63, 196
Maghreb, 55-56
Magna Carta, 22, 120-122
Makarios, Archbishop, 164
Malaya, 48, 52-53
Malaysia, 195
Malenkov, G. M., 92-93
Mali (Soudan), 62, 197
Malvern, first Viscount (Sir Roy Welensky), 65
Manchuria, 52-53
Mao Tse-tung, 96, 98, 106-110, 113, 166, 201-202, 204, 206
Maquis, 13
Maritain, Jacques, 163, 176
Marx, Karl, 12, 28, 74-82, 86-87, 95, 97, 110-114, 130, 166, 169, 180, 183
Marxism and the Nationalities, 90
Masaryk, Jan, 100
Mater et Magistra, 206
Materialism and Empirio-Criticism, 85
Mau Mau, 64
Maud Report, 205
Mazzini, Giuseppe, 37-38, 41, 69, 183
Mechanistic theory, 18
Mein Kampf, 42, 117
Mendès-France, Pierre, 58
Mensheviks, 83-84, 86
Middle East, 32, 45, 47, 54-61, 70, 148, 164-165, 170, 185
Mikoyan, A. I., 92-93
Mill, J. S., 26, 66, 68, 129, 136, 142-143, 145, 158

Milton, John, 143, 162
Mindszenty, Cardinal, 169
Minorities, 40, 47, 67, 138, 149
Molotov, V. M., 89, 92-93
Monarchy, 19-20, 22-23, 25, 33, 118, 120-123, 126, 128
Mongolia, 52, 96
Monrovia Conference, 198
Montesquieu, Baron de, 25, 124, 153
More, Sir Thomas, 73
Morocco, 54, 56, 58, 197
Moscow Radio, 14, 98
Moslem Brotherhood, 60
Moslem League, All-India, 48, 164
Moslems, 48-49, 59-60, 170. *See also* Islam
Mozambique, 63, 66
Mukden, battle of, 46
Munich Agreement, 68
Mussolini, Benito, 28, 41-42, 56, 69, 148-149, 172
Myth of the Twentieth Century, The, 43

NAGALAND, 195
Nagy, Imre, 105
Napoleon I, 31, 36, 126, 172, 182
Nasser, G. A., 51, 54, 59-61, 70, 102
Nation-state, 19, 23, 28-29, 32-35, 37-38, 40, 43, 45, 52, 120, 166, 185, 207
National Communism, 103-106, 200
NATO, 71, 194
Natural law, 21, 25, 28, 176-178, 185
Natural rights, 25-26, 123, 126-127, 185
Nazism, 12-13, 16, 32, 41-44, 55, 117, 140, 181, 189-190
Négritude, 61
Neguib, General Mohammed, 60
Nehru, Jawaharlal, 50, 58, 102
Nenni, Pietro, 132
Néo-Destour Party, 56, 58
N.E.P., 84
Netherlands (Holland), 32, 38, 44, 46, 53, 71, 121, 172-173
New Democracy, 99
Newton, H., 194
Newton, Sir Isaac, 110, 124, 184
Nicholas II, Tsar, 83
Niebuhr, Rheinhold, 163
Nigeria, 62, 199-200
1984, 181, 208
Nkrumah, Dr Kwame, 63-64, 69, 102, 197-198
Nordic race, 43-44
Not by Bread Alone, 113
Nuclear test ban treaty, 201, 208
Nuremberg Laws, 189
Nuri es-Said, 55, 59
Nyasaland (Malawi), 65, 152
Nyerere, Julius, 62, 64, 198

ODER-NEISSE TERRITORY, 68
Ogpu, 12
Ombudsman, 141, 204
On Liberty, 117, 129, 142, 145
On Representative Government, 66, 129
On the Correct Handling of Contradictions among the People, 110
On the People's Democratic Dictatorship, 109

INDEX

On the Subjection of Women, 129
Organic theory, 18, 26–28
Organization of African Unity, 198
Origin of the Family, Private Property and the State, The, 78
Orthodox Churches, 23, 164, 166, 170, 207
Orwell, George, 208
Ottoman Empire, 37–38, 54
Owen, Robert, 74, 130

Pacem in Terris, 207–208
P.A.F.M.E.C.S.A., 198
Paine, Thomas, 127
Pakistan, 48–49, 68, 148, 152, 164, 165, 195
Palestine, 55, 164
Pan-Africanism, 62, 64, 197, 208
Pan-Arabism, 51, 59–60, 164
Pan-Germanism, 39, 41, 43
Pan-Slavism, 39
Pan-Turkism, 51
Parliament (Westminster), 117, 121–123, 126–128, 131, 137–138, 141–142, 144, 153–154, 204
Parliamentary Commissioner, 141, 204
Pasternak, Boris, 113
Patriotism, 31, 36, 81, 89
Paul VI, Pope, 169
People's communes, 100, 108, 110
People's Daily, 103, 202
Pericles, 18, 118–120
Persia, 50, 165
Persian Gulf, 47, 60, 165
Petition of Right, 121
Pflimlin, Pierre, 174
Philip of Macedon, 21, 119
Philippines, 48, 53
Philosophy of History, 28
Philosophy of Revolution, 60–61
Philosophy of Right, 28
Pius VII, Pope, 172
Pius XI, Pope, 168, 172, 176–177
Pius XII, Pope, 176–177
Plato, 19–20, 28, 72–73, 119, 156
Plebiscites, 30–31, 41, 68, 136, 137
Plekhanov, G. V., 82–83
Plural society, 175, 177
Poland, 33–34, 38–40, 43–44, 68, 84, 96, 97, 100–101, 104–106, 169, 180
Political Justice, 127
Pope (Papacy), 22, 24, 35, 121, 166, 168–169, 171–172, 175–178, 188, 206–207
'Popular Front', 99, 131
Populists, 82
Portugal, 63, 148, 196
Poverty of Philosophy, The, 77
Powell, E., 193
Pravda, 83, 201
Press (newspapers), 14, 39, 62, 82, 83, 92, 137, 145, 147, 151, 157, 158
Prince, The, 24
Problems of Leninism, 90
Project of Perpetual Peace, 186
Propaganda, 14, 15, 59, 62, 99, 103, 145, 146, 151, 156, 170
Proportional representation, 139
Protestantism, 23, 30–31, 77, 144, 163–164, 169, 171–173, 175, 206

Proudhon, Pierre-Joseph, 74, 77, 130
Prussia, 14, 35–37, 173
Puritans, 121–122, 172

Quadragesimo Anno, 176
Quebec, 195
Qu'est-ce que le Tiers État?, 35

RACIALISM, 31, 42–44, 46, 65–66, 173, 189–194, 202, 205–206, 208
Rajk, Laszlo, 101
Rakosi, Matyas, 101
Rashid Ali, 55
Red army, 84, 98, 100, 103
Reflections on the Revolution in France, 26
Reform Bills, 128–129, 151
Reformation, 23–24, 31, 121, 163, 172
Renaissance, 24, 160, 162
Republic (Bodin), 24
Republic (Plato), 19–20, 72–73
Rerum Novarum, 176–177
Restoration (1660), 123
Revolution Betrayed, The, 88
Rhodesia, 63, 65, 66, 196–197
Ribbentrop, Joachim von, 89
Ricardo, David, 75
Richelieu, Cardinal, 33
Rights of Man, 127
Risorgimento, 38, 172
Robespierre, Maximilien, 16, 35, 146
Romanovs (dynasty), 38–40, 81, 83
Romanticism, 36–37
Rome (Roman Empire), 18, 21–22, 42, 69, 184, 186
Rosenberg, Alfred, 43–44
Rousseau, Jean-Jacques, 16, 26–28, 34–37, 74, 120, 126, 137–138, 143, 146
Rule of law, 134, 138, 140–141, 148–149, 186
Rumania, 40, 68, 97, 100, 106, 169, 194
Russia (U.S.S.R.), 13, 28, 36, 38–40, 46, 48, 50–52, 60, 70, 81–86, 88–98, 100–110, 112, 114, 115, 131, 135, 145, 148, 161, 165, 167–170, 181, 194, 200–204, 208
Russian Revolution, 40, 51, 83–86, 88–90, 95, 97, 167, 170

SAINT-PIERRE, ABBÉ DE, 75
Saint-Simon, Comte de, 74, 130
Salazar, Dr Antonio, 148
Saragat, Giuseppe, 132
'Satellites', Communist, 13, 95–96, 100–101, 103, 105, 148, 169
Satyagraha, 48
Saudi Arabia, 165
Sceptics, 21
Schuman, Robert, 174
Secret ballot, 128
Sékou Touré, 64, 102
Seneca, 21, 162
Senegal, 62
Senghor, Léopold-Sédar, 62
Separation (balance) of powers, 25, 125, 153–154
Serov, General I., 93
Sharpeville, 66
Shepilov, D. T., 93

Sieyes, Abbé, 35
Singapore, 48, 52–53, 195
Sinkiang, 52, 201
Sino-Soviet conflict, 104
Slavery, 20, 46, 110, 120, 190, 192
Smith, Adam, 75
Smith, Ian, 197
Social contract, 25–26, 28, 123–124, 127
Socialism (Social Democrats), 63, 78, 81, 84, 86–87, 112, 114, 130–133, 155
Socialism and the Political Struggle, 82
"Socialism in One Country," 90–91
Socrates, 19, 90
Somalia (Somaliland), 62, 64, 197–198
Sorel, Georges, 131
South Africa, 45, 63, 65, 173, 186, 189, 191–193, 196–197
Sovereignty, 12, 19, 24–25, 33, 40, 118, 126–127, 134, 136, 147, 154, 157–158, 160, 166, 180–181
Soviets, 84, 85, 97, 104
Spain, 32–33, 36, 144, 148, 195–196
Sparta, 20, 73
Spartacists, 81
Stalin, J. V., 15, 39, 85, 88–92, 98–109, 113–114, 200
State and Revolution, 85
Stoics, 21–22, 165
Stolypin, P. A., 83
Stridjom, J. G., 191
Student demonstrations, 204–206
Sudan, 45, 54–56, 62, 199
Suez (Canal Zone), 47, 56–57, 60
Sukarno, Dr Ahmed, 53, 103, 149, 203
Summa Theologica, 22
Sun Yat-sen, 52
Surplus Value, theory of, 75, 78, 80
Switzerland, 30, 34, 120, 173
Syndicalism, 131
Syria, 54–55, 57, 59, 195

TACITUS, 44
Tanzania (Tanganyika), 64, 65, 197
Taoism, 169
Terror, the, 12, 16, 146
Thailand (Siam), 52–53
Theses on Feuerbach, 75
Third Republic of France, 81
Thorez, Maurice, 111
Thucydides, 118–119
Tibet, 52, 70, 96, 99, 165, 186
Tilak, B. G., 48
Tirol, 195
Tito, Marshal, 98, 103, 104, 201, 203
Togliatti, Palmiro, 101, 106, 200
Togo, 197–198
Toleration, 15, 138–140, 144, 149, 156
Totalitarianism, 12, 14–15, 32, 37, 41–44, 91–92, 115, 145, 172, 181, 202
Trade unions, 81, 85, 100, 102, 130, 131, 157, 177
Transylvania, 68

Treatise of Civil Government, 25, 117, 123
Treitschke, Heinrich von, 39, 41
Trotsky, Leon, 82, 84, 88–91, 97
Tshombe, Moise, 196
Tunisia, 54, 56, 58
Turks (Turkey), 50–51, 56, 103, 164. *See also* Ottoman Empire
Twentieth Congress of the C.P.S.U., 92–93, 200
Twenty-second Congress of the C.P.S.U., 201

UGANDA, 64, 197, 199
Ukraine, 40, 50, 92
Ulbricht, Walter, 101
Unilateral Declaration of Independence, 197
United Arab Republic, 59, 195
University of the Toilers of the East, 51
U.N.O. 17, 30, 57, 71, 135, 140, 185–186, 196, 208
Utilitarianism, 26, 127–129, 131
Utopia, 73

VATICAN COUNCIL, Second Ecumenical, 206–207
Versailles, Treaty of, 68
Verwoerd, Dr H. F., 66
Vichy France, 55
Vienna, Congress of, 37–38
Vietnam, 48, 53, 96, 98, 101, 103, 186, 203, 205
Voltaire, F. M. Arouet de, 26, 34, 140
Vorster, J. B., 191

WAFD PARTY, 56
Warsaw Pact, 101, 169
West Indies, 192, 195
West New Guinea (Irian), 53, 195
W.F.T.U., 100
What is to be Done?, 85
'White' Army (Russian Revolution), 84
W.H.O., 71
Wilkes, John, 127
Wilson, Thomas Woodrow, 39–40
"Wind of change," 63, 196
Winstanley, Gerard, 73, 123
Worker-priests, 177
Workers' Programme, The, 130
World Bank, 71
World War, First, 39, 42–43, 53–55, 81, 83, 136, 148
World War, Second, 52–53, 55–56, 92, 95, 96, 101, 104, 148, 153, 173, 179
Wyszinsky, Cardinal 105, 169–170

YUGOSLAVIA, 40, 97–98, 100, 103–104, 115, 169, 201, 203

ZHDANOV, A. A., 89, 102, 113
Zhukov, Marshal G. K., 93
Zinoviev, G. E., 89